ENDORSEMENTS

I have committed a great deal of my life to the field of museums, learning to compete for attention in our modern society by becoming experts in storytelling through design, technology, interactivity and precious artefacts.

When I met Paul in the Bourke Tourist Centre in the mid-90's, I came to know a very gifted storyteller who had two great passions in life - the people of indomitable spirit who make outback Australia their home and his love of Jesus Christ whose life is woven through all aspects of the Australian story. We agreed that never has it been more important to recognise and counter the aggressive attempts being made to remove the Christian roots of the Australian story. Together we've been dreaming of creative ways we could show our fellow countrymen their immense significance.

As Paul has so eloquently presented in his book, it's time for all Australian Christians and even secular historians, to correct the ledger and acknowledge the significant role that Jesus has had and still has in shaping this Nation.

Brad Baker
Museum Exhibition Consultant
Head of Exhibitions and Events, Museum of
Australian Democracy 2015-2018
Head of Exhibition Development and Design,
Powerhouse Museum Sydney 1983-2013

This is a rich feast of stories told by one for whom storytelling is in his blood. Paul's life experience in his early years and in the outback are interwoven in the fabric of the book as he opens our eyes to the stories of Australian heroes and quiet achievers who followed Jesus and embodied His selfless life and actions in the history of our nation. The journey through its pages can connect a new generation to the way God worked through His people in the past to build a better world and heal injustices. What a valuable resource for classrooms to inspire and equip others to follow the Master storyteller and be purposeful storytellers for the Kingdom of God.

Helen Blanch
Christian Education Executive
The Excellence Centre, Pacific Hills Schools

It seems inevitable that Paul should write a book like this. On two cotton farms west of Bourke he co-founded a Christian community where many hundreds of Australian youth learned to follow the most remarkable person in history, Jesus Christ. His passion for history continued as he listened to the men and women who had pioneered the Outback. At this time, our greatest need is to learn that the good life of our civilisation depends on the values embedded in our society by countless followers of Jesus whose personal details have faded, but whose accomplishments remain. Their stories deserve to be told and Paul is a man whose destiny it is to tell them.

Laurie McIntosh
Civil Engineer and Anthropologist
Visionary and Co-Founder, Cornerstone Community

Paul Roe is certainly a master of storytelling and, from his account, it's in his blood. I was enthralled by the natural way he painted a visual picture of each person and place he introduces us to and I found the page-turning was effortless. He tells 'rousing faith stories' from Australia's forgotten past and from today. Each one strengthens our faith, warms our heart and makes us proud. As Paul says in this book, 'Who will hunt these stories out and let them shine?' Paul Roe will! And he is painting them afresh (or for the first time) for a new generation. Thank you Paul!

Jane Faase
Producer, Faith Runs Deep
Creative Director, Olive Tree Media

'Tell Me Another' is written in Paul Roe's easygoing 'Let me tell you a yarn' style but it contains a lot of information that will interest and educate many. It raises questions about who we are as a people, where we come from and where we're headed. It's a book that needed to be written about Australia and Paul Roe, with his broad appreciation of Australian history and particularly of the Christian context of such, has always been the man to write it. I'm glad to call him a friend of mine and I would recommend the book to anyone who desires to hold a mirror up to themselves and this place called Australia. I think it's in the sharing of our stories that we will gain a greater understanding of who we are and hopefully in the process learn a bit more of who we should be and where we are meant to be going.

Riverbank Frank Doolan
Wiradjuri elder and Poet,
Community Worker

Having had the pleasure of walking a few tracks and sharing a few yarns with Paul, I am delighted to reassure that the laconic, ironic, humorous and insightful storyteller is just as adept and engaging on the written page. Within beautifully crafted paragraphs there's a premise to this book that is bold and central, but there is a sub-text too, embedded in the structure. Because this is overwhelmingly a collection of stories, observations and experiences retold and refined, the work asks us, above all else, to listen. Paul shows us how to pay attention, to delight in the everyday, to scratch at the surface, and to always stay connected to that great hearth of humanity, our stories.

Andrew Hull
'The Bard of Bourke'
Poet, Artist, Videographer

In the world of documentary film, to be given on-camera the personal story of an interviewee is a sacred trust. You're granted access to formative events and their emotional impact on a person's life, sometimes unveiled for the first time. Paul Roe has been granted a treasure of such stories by rural Australians for more than forty years and he weaves them together in an effort to repair the fabric of our neglected spiritual heritage. 'Tell me Another' does that for us as he shares his love of story and the journey of listening to an amazing diversity of people. He crafts from their stories outback history that tells us better who we are.

Christopher Gilbert
Associate Lecturer in Christian Formation, Excelsior College
Producer/Director Lamp Post Media

In Tell Me Another, Paul has brought together his three loves. First, his interest in people's stories and his love of story-telling. Next, his love of Jesus the Master Story-teller and his passion to bring to life the stories of those who have been changed by Jesus. Finally, his love of history and his compulsion to bring to light the overarching narrative of modern Australia and the Christians of astounding faith whose contribution has been so significant. For any who share these three loves, I commend this book as essential. For those even remotely interested, I implore you to read, learn and apply it.

Jenine Varady-Szabo
Social Welfare Worker
School Chaplain and Camp Director

It is over 20 years ago since I first met Paul Roe in Bourke, encountering, a most engaging storyteller with perspectives that had distinctive and great intellectual finesse. My twin passions relate to small town reinvention and the pivotal role our Christian heritage should play in renewal. After 50 years of wanderlust around the world's rural landscapes, I am convinced, that the starting point for effective rural reinvention is conversation and sharing stories. This creates the necessary mindset, passion and direction to initiate positive change. In this timely publication, Paul has given community builders help in the mission of renewal. This is a brilliant demonstration of effective storytelling and an amazing collection of inspirational stories. I know it has certainly changed my own world view for the better. We are in your debt Paul for your reminder that storytelling remains the most powerful way to both challenge status quo thinking and put ideas into action. For people of faith, it should be a personal challenge to no longer be ignorant or bashful of Christian contributions to national and local community building, but to have the courage to tell those stories vividly and boldly.

Peter Kenyon O.A.M.
Director, Bank of I.D.E.A.S.

Great read Paul and a timely prompt to know and tell the stories that have gone before us, stories of people with a 'love your neighbour as yourself' character. This book lifts up the role of storytellers in re-weaving the fabric of our increasingly diverse communities. Strong stories build stronger communities.

Rosita Vincent
CEO, Neighbourhood Collective Australia
Regional Lead, Ethnic Communities Council of Victoria

As you read Paul Roe's book you feel the red dirt in your nostrils, the black earth beneath your feet; you see the wide-open plains and the over-arching skies. His journey to rediscover the power of the story of Christian faith to reshape our understanding of our heritage is compelling. In his testimony we realise that in the expanse and harshness of outback Australia the Almighty Creator has left footprints of Redeeming Love along pathways trodden by his messengers. In my years as a bishop criss-crossing the areas about which Paul writes, and having sat with Paul in conversation with some of the characters he talks about, I get what he says about the forgotten story of Jesus in the lives of men and women who have shaped our nation. Paul is one of those who is leading the way in reclaiming these stories of grace for all Australians.

The Rt Rev'd Ian Palmer,
10th Anglican Bishop of Bathurst

TELL ME ANOTHER

A STORYTELLER'S SEARCH FOR AUSTRALIA'S LOST FAITH

PAUL ROE

Ark House Press
arkhousepress.com

Cataloguing in Publication Data:
Title: Tell Me Another
ISBN: 978-0-6454117-7-5 (pbk)
Subjects: Biography; Australiana;
Other Authors/Contributors: Roe, Robyn

Cover photography courtesy of Ian Cole
Design by initiateagency.com

CONTENTS

Foreword.. xi

Acknowledgements..xv

Preface...xix

Introduction..xxiii

1. Plastic Souls... 1

2. Bourke To Beersheeba.. 13

3. At The Back O' Bourke....................................... 25

4. From Little Things, Big Things Grow 35

5. Looking Forward, Looking Back.......................... 46

6. Voices From The Wilderness 59

7. Shared Song-Lines 71

8. Forgetting To Remember 84

9. Muscular Faith.. 97

10. A Compass, A Map And A Harbour 110

11. Root Stock Stories 121

12. On The Road To Find Out.. 133

13. The Interpreter's House 147

14. Bringing The Stories Home 160

15. Telling Another Story 174

Endnotes 191

FOREWORD

It's 3 November 2021. Australia is happy – a rare experience these days! Cleo Smith, aged 4, abducted 18 days ago, has been rescued alive and well and reunited with her parents, ending their worst nightmare. I am reminded of the story in the great Australian classic, *Such is Life*, of the little girl gone missing. She is identified as 'Dan O'Connell's little girl – five or six years old' and the Indigenous trackers call her 'piccaninny', but she is otherwise unnamed. I read the story once to a high school class of riotously noisy adolescents. That hushed them.

It is the stories which quell the riot and hush the noise that we need to hear. We need to hear them so that we can think about the things which matter instead of always looking to anaesthetics to dull the pain. Paul Roe's passion is for telling the stories which matter. Equally his heart is in finding the lost, especially lost young Australians, cut adrift from any hope of navigating their way to a safe harbour by the appalling irresponsibility of denying them any knowledge of the foundations of faith. How happy we are at the news of Cleo's homecoming. Why do we fail to hear the rejoicing in heaven when every lost child finds the way which is truth and life?

Paul Roe and I have much in common. Both of us are Sydneysiders who studied history at University. Both of us taught for a while. Both of us have lived significant periods of our life outside of Sydney: Paul in Bourke ('to know Bourke is to know Australia'); me in the Riverina where Joseph Furphy acquired the wisdom to write *Such is Life*. Both of us are followers of Jesus of Nazareth and have visited his homeland, awed by the Sea of Galilee and touched by the sight of the eucalypts which link that land with ours. I shared with him in his research which led to the writing of this book, delighted as I am that it is even more readable than the wonderful PhD thesis on which it is based. Both of us share his unfinished dream to have built in the national capital, where the spiritual vacuum echoes the hollow heart of lost Aussies, a worthy exemplification of Australia's rich but unknown Christian heritage. Both of us were stunned by the vision of the great civic architect, Eric Kuhne, designer of the Titanic Museum in Belfast and a trustee of the Washington Cathedral, for the construction of the 'Southern Cross Sanctuary' in the heart of Canberra. And, when challenged by opposition to this dream, both of us were galvanised by Eric's insistence that 'great ideas never die'.

What a heart-warming, enriching, ennobling, cleansing, inspiring read this is. We are privileged to join Paul on his journey of faith as he and Robyn visit significant sacred sites in acquisition of the insights which crowd these pages. His global pilgrimage feels providential, consisting of lightning tours through scores of museums in the United States, the awe-inspiring Bible Lands Museum in Jerusalem, and the life-changing Sydney Jewish Museum. We learn here of the progressive acquisition of the knowledge and sensitivity which empowered him to envision the transformative Back of Bourke Museum and the planning of the Southern Cross Sanctuary. Crowding these pages, too, are the best insights of the twentieth-century's greatest minds on the civic power of the Christian heritage, from Churchill, C.S. Lewis and G.K. Chesterton in Britain to Mary McKillop, Charles Bean, Henry Lawson, and Fred Hollows in Bourke, where they are joined by a score of Indigenous voices to whom Paul has listened attentively, including Pastor Bill Reid, George Mungindi, Billy Williams, Aunty Pat Doolan, and Peter 'Chicka' Gibbs.

Miraculously, by telling all their stories, this book navigates matters which are normally contested and divisive in Australian history in a manner which educates, entertains, and reconciles all at once. Paul Roe embodies a Christian faith which is comfortable in multicultural Australia, profoundly aware of the legacy of Empire and War on our nation, and empathetic with Indigenous Australians. Apparently, these matters, critical to the future of our nation, are better understood through the stories of participants than by the abstractions of professional historians. It helps that this passionate advocate of the art of storytelling knows how to tell a story. When you get to the end, you will exclaim, 'Paul, tell us another one', and he will reply, 'No, it's your turn to tell stories now.'

Associate Professor Stuart Piggin,
Director, Centre for the History of Christian Thought and Experience,
Macquarie University. (retired)

ACKNOWLEDGEMENTS

I want to tip my hat to some of those who have been my fellow travellers. Australia's ace Christian historian Professor Stuart Piggin challenged me to do the hard yards to turn my raw experiences with story into a doctoral thesis. I thank him for his patience in walking this bush boy through it. Writing coach Jo Kadlecek advised me to transform that research into the more readable form of a memoir. Her wise counsel made the exercise both a reflection and a joy.

That freed me to name many pilgrims who have fallen in to step along the way, gifting me their time and wisdom. In particular, I want to acknowledge the brothers and sisters with whom I have shared the adventure in Cornerstone Community. You'll find just a few of them dotted through the pages of the book and I'm personally richer for their input. The lengthy process of deliberation reinforced to me that I'm indebted to a host of good people. Thanks to you all.

I appreciate friends who have proof-read and discussed the content and those who have written kind commendations. Special thanks goes to my wife Robyn - my friend and life partner, for listening, correcting, advising and checking. She smiled patiently through most of it. She had long-held an ambition for me to write a book.

Well, here it is!

I'm dedicating the book to my 14 grandchildren who I hope will represent a new generation of Australian storytellers.

PREFACE

I come from a long line of storytellers. Frozen on my screensaver is the image of my grandfather, hands dramatically outstretched, holding the attention of a bunch of coal miner's kids in a park somewhere in the Hunter Valley of NSW. It's a daily reminder that storytelling is in my DNA. I was the boy lying on his bed in the afternoon sun with a book, roaming away in his imagination with the heroes who had waited patiently for me on my shelf. So I learned to love reading Australian stories – the ones that spoke my heart-language.

I still get animated telling home-grown stories that stir the blood, fire the imagination, or make us weep and laugh together. They speak to us of who we are and whisper to us of where we belong. The Condamine horse bell propping up books in my library has faintly etched words in the patinated, copper surface that tell me that once-upon-a-time, in outback Bourke, I was a yarn-spinning champion. It's about the only trophy I ever won, hopefully my grandfather would be proud.

So, it will come as no surprise to hear that I became a historian – a proud member of the ancient clan who were the custodians of the tribal memory from the dawn of history. I was delighted when I discovered that the 'histor' was multi-skilled in ancient Greece as the storyteller, soothsayer, sage or wisdom man. I like that cluster, and I dare to think I've grown to become a little of all of those. True historians hunger to search out the accounts that shape the spirit and then burn to relay their meaning. This book is a sort of travelogue – an expedition tracking my own adventure with stories. If you join me, you'll see the path has many twists and turns that have delivered me to some unexpected places and, in the process, helped me to understand my craft.

I want to introduce you to the many gifted storytellers I've met along the path as a way of stirring each of you to use your particular gift. You'll find yourself rubbing shoulders with an assortment of bush poets, artists, songwriters, Sunday School teachers, historians, curators, yarn spinners, writers, filmmakers, and a host of others. My hope is you'll join them in rejuvenating our Australian faith story at this critical time when it is fading from the national memory.

One of the privileges of my life has been working with three amazing teams devoted to researching, rethinking and retelling stories. I linked up with my friend and mentor Laurie McIntosh to build a band of teachers who set themselves to unravel the ancient biblical saga while living and working in communities located in raw, rural environments across three States.

For over forty years, Cornerstone Community has provoked generations of students from all over the globe to think out what it means to follow Jesus for themselves. Many have become skilled storytellers in their own right. These gifted friends helped me see the urgency of introducing present generations of Australians to the Jesus they think they know but don't.

Then, serving as a local councillor in the isolated outback town of Bourke, I found myself part of an innovative group who set themselves to uncover the town's unique narrative and make it accessible with creative story-telling. It was my grass-roots apprenticeship as a historian. The displays we developed in the Back O' Bourke Exhibition Centre now draw thousands of pilgrims into lost chapters of our national history. Untold stories of people of faith emerged in the process and I observed their great appeal to travellers.

These first-hand experiences in a remote setting convinced me there was a nationwide task ahead. What if we could recover this lost trove and broadcast them on a grand scale? Step by step, a skilled team of specialists comprised of historians, a museum curator, a businessman, an events coordinator, a social researcher and an architect launched into an extended effort to make these invisible stories visible. We shared the dream of building an iconic structure, in Canberra, to gather and articulate Australia's Christian story on a national platform for the first time. This Heritage Foundation was determined to create a world-class showcase for a world-class story. While that vision has made substantial progress, it is presently circling like a plane in a holding pattern.[1]

This book is my attempt to help land it on the tarmac.

Working alongside these passionate storytellers made the far-fetched idea of jogging our failing corporate memory a real possibility. They shared the urgency I felt to retrace the spiritual journey of our ancestors because the path they had trodden was the one that has brought us to the present and continues to influence our future direction.

It's probably fanciful, but I like to think there's a mystical edge to my calling as a historian related to my Celtic ancestry. My mother belonged to the Baird clan – traditionally, they were the bards who wandered the bare hills and heather of Scotland reciting the stories of their kinsfolk, reminding them of people and events in their lineage that had shaped them. They played a critical role in maintaining the spiritual heartbeat of the clan.

Their secret was simple. "Storytelling is eye to eye, mind to mind and heart to heart."

That saying sings to me. It directs me to be honest in my approach, reasoned in my research, and compassionate in my delivery. It chimes with a vital lesson I learned in fifty years as a storyteller–separating the spiritual from the temporal robs the music of its melody. It convinced me that storytelling is vital in linking the sanctuary to the street. A bright window of faith stories held up before fellow Australians would give fresh glimpses of forgotten things.

Mapping our spiritual genome could generate enormous social capital for Australia's multicultural future. Modern Australia needs to hear authentic stories of the innovative Christian faith that has shaped us as a counterbalance to the dominant narrative of failure currently broadcast about the church. Shameful deeds should indeed come into the light, and church communities repent of the bitter animosity that has divided them in the past. I visualise a space where visitors embark on an expedition to learn the bigger picture of what has shaped Australia's soul.

My journey has taken me to many corners of Australia, and everywhere I've been, I've observed the same set of footprints. They tell a most remarkable story – one that belongs to everyone who calls Australia home. But I'm grieved that in my lifetime, I have watched these distinctive footmarks scuffed over by people careless of their significance or removed by vandals determined to blot them from our memory. It puzzles and angers me because they belong to the man who is widely rated the most influential leader in human history - Jesus of Nazareth.

Whether we know it or not, whether we like it or not, Jesus has left an indelible mark on this country. Many Australians I meet are 'psychological Christians' vaguely aware of some distant religious roots but quite oblivious to the historical journey that has given them their society. I have detected an unrealised longing in people for the kind of redemptive story that lifts us above the ordinary.

I believe the chronicle of deeds done in our own country as genuine responses to Jesus can do just that. It's time to blow the dust off the archives, open the bunkers and give this story the exposure it deserves. I dream of equipping a band of storytellers who will boldly remind Australia of its spiritual heritage. They won't rant or try to force religion on people. I visualise them as both conversationalists and presenters, skilled in using every means to engage their neighbours with a hopeful narrative at a time when many feel rootless and lost.

In the purest of Australian phrases, to call them to give it a fair go!

INTRODUCTION

As far as I know, I'm one of the few people in Australia paid to tell stories in a grave-yard. It's a cemetery set among coolabah trees in the town of Bourke on the edge of the Outback, crammed with interesting characters, most of whom have remained silent for well over a century. My job is to bring them to life, to help them step briefly from their graves into the bright sunlight to tell their stories.[2] Their tales unfold to the shriek of cockatoos in the gums, and the rumble of road-trains headed south down the Kidman Way to Cobar. Twigs and dried grass crunch underfoot as the small crowd weaves through the headstones behind me.

Unseen all around us, enchantment is happening – researchers who study the brain call it 'neural entrainment'.[3] I call it simply, 'the mystery of storytelling'. Curiously, these scientists have discovered that while our brainwaves operate independently from those of another person, there's one notable exception. Once I start telling a story among the tombstones, something astounding happens as the listeners tune in. Their brainwaves fall into sync with mine – we are literally on the same wave-length! Because of this, the experts say that if you want to shift your ideas to others, stories are the absolute prime method. A well-told yarn releases chemicals in the grey matter of the hearer that will make them empathise and get busy with a whole palette of emotions, each painting their own picture. Old memories are triggered, fresh ideas spring to life on their inner canvas. Stories can actually make our human communities thrive.

Someone summed it up, "Humans not only crave stories, we **need** to hear them!"

When I learned about this mental hard wiring, I realised why speaking for the dead energises me. I was doing more than just telling ghost stories. As I walk in the cemetery gate, waiting unseen in the wings is a cast with great tales to tell, and in front of me, an audience hungry to hear them. I see eyes soften as we pause beside one weathered gravestone of an eccentric bush bard and help him reminisce about working the riverboat *P.S. Nile* around the sweeping bends of the Darling River with his brothers. I conjure up images of shearers listening raptly to his poems about poor 'Barefoot Harry' and a swagman perishing on a lonely track or the doings of a notorious local cop called 'Sudden Death'.

Nearby I help a German-Jewish civilian to rise up from beneath his slab and tell how he was shipped from Singapore and confined in a POW camp in Bourke in 1915, supposedly to stop him being a threat to the British Empire! And there next to him lies a young ANZAC, Donald Fraser from Bourke, captured on the Western Front. I hold up his photograph, which shows him working the salt mines in Germany as a POW in 1917. The visitors are touched by the irony of these two men lying side by side in the backcountry of Australia and I wonder if maybe they're reflecting on the futility of war. Again, I feel the power of story at work.

The past speaks loudly to the present as I give some buried fringe-dwellers a voice. A small group of Afghan cameleers huddles together near the tiny tin mosque as I recount the story told to me by Myrtle Perooz, a part-Jewish girl sold to one of their number. It's a strange tale of worlds apart – a child bride living her life inside a closed Muslim community in a remote outback town.

I lead my guests to a burial site away from the rest where a sign says 'ASIATICS'. They were a long way from home too. The Chinese tell of their life on the margins, strangers toiling in vegetable gardens and smoking opium in their joss house. I explain that they and their kind were the targets of the exclusion policy built into the Australian Constitution in 1901 to keep Australia 'white'. The assortment of faces I see looking back at me as I say this tells me I'm now part of a multi-cultured society.

A century later, we're writing a new story together.

I see consciences stabbed awake as I spell out other chapters from the long struggle with racial prejudice. Here lies Francis Williams, a member of the local Ngemba tribe, who survived a massacre at nearby Mt Gundabooka by being hidden by his grandmother. He tells of being raised by a station family, awarded the King's Imperial Service Medal for his services as a police 'black-tracker', yet being forbidden to speak his native language and denied citizen's rights. Further on, faces sober as they hear the story of the three indigenous brothers who fought on the Western Front for 'King and Country'. One died there, two came home only to be told Aboriginals weren't welcome in the local Returned Soldiers Club.

A chorus of others jostles around me, seeking their turn to speak. Then they lie down again quietly, side by side, waiting for another opportunity. Guiding people through the silent marble markers of forgotten lives like this has taught me how first-hand stories drawn from our native soil can trigger chemistry that causes us to recalibrate our thinking.

It quietly assured me that I'd become a grassroots historian.

It's been a long trek for a boy raised in suburban Sydney to become a narrator in an iconic Western town. Each stage taught me something new about the craft of storytelling – but not all of it was in the graveyard! I think I was as surprised as anyone else to discover that, almost by accident, I'd transformed into a kind of bush-troubadour singing the heart-music of Bourke. More astonishing still was the revelation that, hidden inside this remote micro-world were unfolding episodes of a saga stretched on a continent-wide frame.

Out of the shadows stepped wandering poets like Henry Lawson, Will Ogilvie, and Harry 'The Breaker' Morant, who had gained coast-to-coast attention with tales of mateship and the full-bodied doings of shearers, drovers and pastoralists. Journalist Charles Bean followed the men he met west of Bourke to the battlefronts in Gallipoli and France and returned to write the ANZAC story into the nation's heart. And here I was, a city bloke, gifted with the privilege of leading these invisible stories back onto the stage and watching them impact locals and travellers alike.

It was an unexpected honour.

As I ventured wider and began tracing their fading tracks across the western plains, connecting forgotten events and places, I discovered the enchantment of old words when we spoke them on location. As people of all ages, from all walks of life, came through Bourke and fell into step with me, a curious thing happened. For a fleeting moment, we were pilgrims together, sharing our passage. Instead of them being nomadic tourists taking selfies and me being a guide, we became a band of travellers seeking meaning. Storytelling was more than entertainment. It not only allowed people to reach out and touch the past, it spoke to the life-questions that they carried deep inside and helped them better understand their own journeys.

We tested the claim I heard in The Scottish Storytelling Centre in Edinburgh that stories are always the shortest distance to the truth.

Of all places, it was in remote Bourke that this university-trained historian learned some wisdom that Aboriginal peoples had understood for aeons. As they walked across their country they created song-lines that contained their cultural history, mythology, hunting patterns and their relationship to the Creator-spirit. These were connected to the mountains, rivers, rocks and trees that composed the landscape.

Through the drama of campfire corroborees, they taught their wide-eyed children their place in the broad scheme of things and how to play a vital part in maintaining the creation. They said this story telling was critical – a matter of life and death. Their deeply held belief was, 'If you don't know your song-line, you don't exist.' [4]

This belief resonated with the ancient wisdom that I had learned as a boy from my own tribe. My parents and elders had repeated the solemn words of the prophet Moses, speaking across 3000 years, as he laid out a blueprint for his nomadic people on the edge of the Sinai desert:

Write these commandments that I've given you today on your hearts. Get them inside of you and then get them inside your children. Talk about them wherever you are, sitting at home, or walking in the street; talk about them from the time you get up in the morning to when you fall into bed at night. [5]

Along with their law went their folklore. Moses' strong advice was, 'Don't forget to embed our defining narrative in your children!' I grew up in the middle of an adult community that took this charge seriously, and the powerful stories of the Bible sculptured my inner landscape like a steady wind blowing across its surface. Solid, craggy characters like Abraham and Aaron, Moses and Miriam, Ruth and Rahab, David and Daniel, Elijah and Elisha, Mary of Nazareth and Mary of Magdala, Peter and Paul loomed large and have cast long shadows in my life.

Though I didn't realise it at the time, missing from my childhood world were stories of champions from among my own people. The red ochre deserts, sapphire blue seas, olive greens of the gum trees, and dusty brown plains of Australia were rarely the backdrops for the stories of faith I learned as a boy. No sharp-eyed tracker pointed out the footprints of Jesus in every corner of my native country. I was ignorant of the epic story that lay all around me. Heroes wasted away unsung – a host of ghostly figures stood mute, waiting for people to help them sing their song-line.

Eventually, that music would connect me to both my distant and immediate past.

All of us grow up in a narrative world. Perhaps the most astonishing discovery in recent years has been that the intricate encryption in every cell in our bodies contains a library that, to some extent, shapes our destiny. The 3 billion DNA base pairs in every cell with a nucleus, have persuaded even hardened sceptics to concede that only an unseen Author could have written such a complex script.

One that stood out to me was philosopher Anthony Flew who had built a highly acclaimed academic career publicly debunking the existence of God. Eventually, in the face of mounting evidence, he concluded that, 'The only satisfactory explanation for such 'end-directed and self-replicating life' as we see on earth is an infinitely intelligent Mind.'[6] If this is true, each of us begins with a tiny spark of genius, which grows into a story that we can co-author as our years unfold.

In other words, the vast genetic wall of human history is like the tomb of a Pharaoh – hieroglyphed with a saga.

So, all life springs from a code already in place. Each of us has been gifted a set of tools and the intelligence to write a unique story. Years of listening to all manner of tales have taught me that we are always shaping our communities with the snatches of stories, reports, myths, dramas, hear-say, fables, predictions and poetry that we repeat to each other. I've found overwhelming evidence that backed researcher Michael Novak's conclusion, '… the human being alone of the creatures on earth is a storytelling animal: sees the present arising out of the past, heading into the future: perceives reality in a narrative form.'[7]

I've found it is one thing to recite a story, but the real skill is to *detect the meaning* – to interpret our stories in a way that helps us map our journey to the present. History contains narrative threads that dare us to believe that our small individual accounts were woven into a purposeful cosmic story.

The first-century historian Luke is one of my heroes, and he recorded a significant moment that illustrates this. A couple of Jesus' disciples were walking home from Jerusalem, shattered by his brutal crucifixion. A stranger fell into step and retold their native narrative in such a way that it snapped their eyes open to realise they were players in a vast, unfolding drama. Over a meal, their mysterious interpreter suddenly dissolved into focus and then disappeared. Luke says they set off at a run with their hearts on fire to tell of their encounter with the risen Jesus to the other disciples hiding in Jerusalem. [8]

The rest, I'm proud to say, is history.

In a nutshell, that is precisely my purpose in writing this book. As you walk with me on my journey I hope that you will develop an appreciation for the remarkable people of faith who left footprints that criss-cross the whole of Australia. It could be an eye opening experience to see Jesus as a vital part of our shared history. Then, like those two astonished disciples, you might set off in an excited, breathless run to share this news with others.

I kick-start my cemetery tour with a sharp observation from Sydney Morning Herald journalist Charles Bean, commissioned to paint a word-picture of the wool industry around Bourke in 1907. His candid observations brought a smile of recognition to my face when I first read them. He said the experience taught him, 'The West is a place where the bad men are very bad, the good men are magnificent, but all men are interesting!'[9] That's exactly the kind of reporting I'd like to foster in a new wave of storytellers – recounting the stories of Christian men and women in Australia with honesty and courage.

A friend of mine, who was called in to clear deceased estates, told me she's appalled by the number of families who have no interest in caring for their family inheritance. They junk the lot without bothering even to examine what their ancestor had considered precious. My travels and research have shown me a rich store of narrative that was either left to gather dust by careless custodians or buried quietly at midnight by antagonists who want to edit them out of the script of our Australian Story. I'm certain we would be guilty of criminal neglect if we carelessly dump our spiritual history.

But who cares? Does it really matter?

I've done this long enough now to know how powerful well-told stories are in buttressing faith and inspiring vision for the future. I've watched firsthand as my grandchildren's pliable souls were being formed by impactful biographies, just as mine were in my boyhood. As a teacher, I'm weary of hearing the pious platitude from parents – I'm not going to tell my children what to believe – I'm just going to leave them to work that out for themselves.' It sounds noble but more often than not, ends up being neglect. That equates to 'Just let them loose on the smorgasbord.' The trouble with that approach is that there are poisonous options among the healthy.

Wise adults will watch over their soul food.

See if Storyteller Susan Katherine Klassen's job description for her vocation wins you over to the task.

> Once upon a time, not so very long ago, stories were counted among the most precious possessions in our homes. To have known the stories of a family, of a people, was to have the key to the very heart of being. To have spoken these stories in wise and timely ways was to have fulfilled a calling esteemed by both paupers and kings. And to have heard those stories, to have really listened to them with heart and mind, was to have participated in the oldest and perhaps most intimate of human arts – storytelling.[10]

1

PLASTIC SOULS

… our only goal is to awaken, nurture and strengthen in the responsive soul of a child, this invaluable ability to feel compassion… Without this, a man is inhuman.[11]

Kornei Chukovsky

I first met the Jungle Doctor in a tight corner of the kitchen in the house my Dad built with his own hands in Epping – then a semi-rural suburb of Sydney. It was around 1957, and every Sunday afternoon, I would hunch down in front of the valve radio in its ornamented brown case and turn the dial to 2CH. As I put my head down onto arms folded on the red and white-flecked Formica table, Dr Paul White's voice made the sounds and smells of an African jungle rise all around me. I found myself sitting in a circle of dark-skinned people in a village half a world away, riveted as the tribal storyteller told of a little leopard adopted by an innocent family of villagers. Their great chief warned them over and over, "Little leopards grow into big leopards, and big leopards kill." I tensed as the story climaxed and winced as his words eventually came to pass. The children were rescued by the heroic intervention of the chief, who was wounded in a fight to the death with the grown beast. The storyteller soberly warned the circle of faces lit by the flickering campfire, "Small sins can grow to big sins, and big sins can kill."

How strange that the truth contained in a story drawn from Paul White's experience in distant Tanganyika should touch the heart of a young boy an ocean away in Australia and prompt him to reach out to God – praying alone at night in bed. I distinctly remember my heart singing gladly in the darkness. The Jungle Doctor's passion to tell good stories and tell them well on mass media changed the course of my life. He understood that children's souls are soft and plastic – responsive enough to be shaped. In his sure hands, these stories not only gripped my imagination, they sliced like a scalpel deep into my heart.

Like me, I discovered that Paul White was once the kind of kid whose mind vibrated to well-told stories and rebelled at drabness. 'I felt indignant when our minister read the Bible in a dull voice, each word falling with the monotony of a dripping tap. Why should he make a great story and a wonderful happening sound so uninteresting?'[12] He set himself to change that.

So, it was natural that when he was serving in Africa, the Western-trained medic would seize on the skills native to his Tanganyikan friends when they gathered around the evening campfire in the village. Instinct had taught their wise men to weave history and morality into the imaginings of the younger generations with tales, fables and myths. Paul White set about absorbing the colour and vigour of centuries-old African stories and mused on ways to transfer them. Returning to Australia he developed a persona as *The Jungle Doctor* and animated a generation of eager young minds with wondrous tales of lions, vultures, monkeys, hippos and snakes.

Now that's a story about great storytelling!

There was a whimsical storyteller like this in my own family. Old-timers have told me repeatedly that my grandfather, James Roe, would be found telling stories to kids anytime, anywhere. He was inventive, they recollected, and never afraid to stretch the sketch. I noticed their faces creased into laugh lines when reminiscing his rollicking recitals of Bible stories. In fact, I can still hear my Dad chuckling as he recalled his father leading them to church. He was resplendent in a cream silk suit topped by a white cork pith helmet, looking for all the world like Dr David Livingstone, the pioneer missionary to Africa, immune to the mirth it provoked.

Why wouldn't children at Sunday School love to listen to a character like that? No boredom there! Sadly, I never met him, but I feel I know him well. That energetic Yorkshireman's passion for laughter, relaying the stories of the Bible and yarn spinning is alive and well in me.

Later in life, I began to wonder just where his urge for cheerful storytelling had come from. It would be easy enough to write Jim Roe off with a tolerant smile as a harmless eccentric or just another religious nut. However, patient research by my cousin Helen pieced together the fragments of my grandfather's life, and found he had walked a path marked by suffering. Before leaving the coal mining town of Barnsley in the north of England for a new beginning in Australia in 1887, his two younger sisters and a brother died as infants. Then, only a month after the *Port Victor* docked in Newcastle, his mother Emily died of typhoid fever, leaving nine-year-old James and his sister Harriet with just their father David to care for them in their adopted country.

At 13, he began coal mining alongside his Dad under Newcastle Harbour, sometimes waist-deep in water – so rheumatics and silicosis became his life-long companions. In 1896, when monoxide gas tragically claimed the lives of 11 of their fellow-miners in the Stockton Colliery, the family packed up and headed 2000 km north to the booming goldfields near Charters Towers in Queensland. Calamity struck again when he took his wife Bertha and their young son Erick to Hillgrove, a gold-mining town in the high-country near Armidale. The autumn of 1906 turned bleak as a diphtheria epidemic claimed the life of their cherished two-year-old boy. Heartbroken, they buried him in the bush cemetery on the edge of town.

The pain of that loss became part of the family folklore and furnished another clue as to why my grandfather was so passionate about enchanting children with stories. In his memoir, my father Allan recalled, 'The deep grief of Erick's death made them seek spiritual help. Dad and Mum wanted to know how they could be sure of going to Heaven, where their little son was. They were told, "Attend your church, say your prayers and you'll be alright."' But the assurance they longed for came through a fresh telling of the story of Jesus by an unknown Salvation Army lassie. It ignited a warm personal faith that never left them.

Grandfather capped the chapter in his own inimitable style by recalling he was baptised in the creek where they drowned the unwanted cats and dogs! In the years that followed, people recalled the old miner singing with great feeling the words of a hymn, *Oh yes, my friend there's something more, there's something more than gold, to know your sins are all forgiven is something more than gold!*

A century later, that anecdote took me on a pilgrimage to Hillgrove because in my bones I knew it was a sacred site in my family's spiritual journey. Fires passing through the beautiful bush cemetery had removed any trace of my Uncle Erick's wooden cross. Still, in the fusty local museum, I caught some echoes of my grandparent's spiritual odyssey. The swarms of rugged miners had long since gone, the shafts were closed, and the town had shrunk, but among the yellowing photographs on the wall were the faces of others who, like them, could tell enduring stories of faith. Of course, they were just fragile fragments, but there was every chance my grandparents knew them.

It was like finding some bright gold nuggets when sifting through an old mullock heap.

Sitting arms crossed, moustache resplendent, with the clear gaze of a man of calibre, was mining foreman Charlie Nicholson. His son had tapped out on an old typewriter the details of the dramatic day his father was crushed by the boiler his team of men was dragging up a steep incline. They reported how, just before the rope snapped, Charlie had been assuring them of the eternal security he had found in his Christian faith. When he was snatched from that hillside a few minutes later, crushed by the runaway load, a number of his mates told how they returned home shaken and set about seeking that same certainty.

On a wall nearby was the serene face of 'Nanna' Annie Gamble - deserted by her husband and left with seven children. In the days before social welfare, she set about training as a midwife – travelling backwards and forwards to Sydney. She served the women giving birth in that lonely mining town for decades. When her sister died, Annie took in her two children. The lasting impression she left was of a cheerful disposition and strong faith. Her favourite saying was, "The Lord will provide."

In the museum that day, I felt James and Bertha looking over the shoulders of these characters, eyes bright and nodding in agreement. My grandparents were always poor in material terms but rich in faith. Stories of their generosity and kindness became local legends. No matter what their background, homeless swagmen were never turned from their door in Maitland during the lean days of the Great Depression.

These seemingly slight stories spoke of the larger narrative they felt part of.

I left the deserted gold mines of Hillgrove wealthier than I came. It was a sacred site indeed. I felt I understood the root system that fed my grandfather's compulsion to gather children around him to tell stories. He had turned the ache of loss into a burn to communicate the ancient story that had healed the hearts of he and my grandmother Bertha. The powerful biblical narrative was a cure that had been faithfully passed by storytellers from generation to generation for nearly forty centuries. Tucked away in that same forgotten corner of the country, Charlie Nicholson and Nanna Gamble had told their chapter of Australia's faith history. It stirred me to imagine a phantom host lingering in neglected locations across Australia, a life-changing story on their lips.

Who will hunt these stories out and let them shine?

I think James Roe clued out that children are far more likely to say, "Tell me a story" rather than "Teach me some facts." The natural tendency is to deflect messages blatantly directed at us and feel less threatened when the story is about someone else. If I'm honest, I know that I tend to tolerate lectures but readily absorb stories. I've even heard it declared the world has been changed more by "Once upon a time…" than by "Thou shalt not…" Jesus did commend cultivating childlike simplicity when it came to entering his kingdom. Soren Kierkegaard noted that Jesus' storytelling strategy meant the truth he was delivering was more overheard than heard.[13] It was a kind of ambush where you are surprised in discovering, "Hey, that's my story!"

My grandparents Robert and Jane Baird had also relayed Bible stories to my mother and her siblings, though in a sober Scots fashion that contrasted with grandfather Roe's hilarious recitals. My elders knew instinctively what experts are now saying, that children's souls are hungry for stories with meaning – that infants are hardwired to believe in God and that atheism has to be learned.[14] My experience, both as a teacher and a parent, has reinforced the conviction that my grandparents were more than quaint relics – they understood the need to sow images into children that produce a vigorous faith in later life. The plastic souls of the young need careful nurturing if they are to play an influential role later in life.

It underlined what I had heard from Tim Costello speaking out of his experience as CEO of World Vision Australia. He wrote, 'Family is the greatest driving force in history.'[15]

James Roe's lively renditions infected both my father and uncle with enthusiasm for capturing young imaginations with ripping yarns. I breathed in countless stories at home – the air was thick with them. My Dad's epic stick figure battle scenes drawn on butchers paper brought Old Testament stories alive for us at Sunday School. His training as a metallurgist gave him a fascination for the endless curiosities in the world and he used theatrical props like magnets, dry ice and chemicals to awaken wonder in us.

Mealtimes at our Orchard St home in the 50's were seasoned with adventures of guests from exotic places like Thailand, China, India, Nepal, New Guinea, Fiji,

New Zealand, and the USA. Along with hearing family folklore, linguists, teachers, doctors, nurses, pilots, and athletes transported us to places we'd never been. We were never a wealthy family, but my parents supplied a rich store of narratives, and nothing is as enticing as a good story well presented. Their magic drew us in, set our imaginations to work, and quietly taught us valuable life-lessons.

Curiously, native-born narrators rarely came to visit my story world so I never really got to know them. Foreign figures with louder voices elbowed their way into the life of my generation, pushing our Australian cousins into the background. My childhood storybooks were filled with talking animals that inhabited very English hedgerows and forests and rosy-cheeked children living in quaint thatch-roofed cottages with adventures in fields bordered by stonewalls. I waited expectantly for *Boys Own* magazines to arrive in the mail from half a world away.

In the aftermath of World War Two, fiction books in the library provided me with square-jawed RAF heroes who soared into the grey skies over London to fight the Battle of Britain while I was lying in the bright Sydney sunlight that slanted through my bedroom window. My boyhood horizons were bounded by the English Channel and the Irish Sea. I grew up with few champions who squinted through the heat haze of an Australian summer.

Meanwhile, in our 1930's vintage dark-brick school building, I scratched away with nib and ink on projects about brave Englishmen in the King's uniform staggering across our desolate inland and navigating Australia's endless coastline. We saw nothing odd about marching in our Primary school playground arranged into flocks named for native birds – Rosellas, Kookaburras, Currawongs, and Kingfishers, while we saluted the flag of England. There we sang a ragged version of *God Save The Queen* accompanied by a deafening orchestra of cicadas because, it seemed, Australia didn't deserve either a flag or an anthem. The incongruities didn't occur to us. We celebrated Empire Day, gleefully burning effigies of the British villain Guy Falkes on bonfires. It certainly gave us colonial kids a perfect excuse to demolish our neighbours' letterboxes with 'tuppenny bungers'!

So, I grew up in summery suburban Sydney, Southern Hemisphere on the outside, but with a decidedly wintery Northern Hemisphere landscape on the inside. Where were the heroes speaking with an Aussie accent, ranging across vast plains of the Inland, clambering over our rugged Blue Mountains or fighting the tempests of our Southern oceans? A feeling of embarrassment smuggled its way in about these family members. We caught occasional glimpses of them, but they remained distant, lurking like dingoes in the shadows on the edge of the bush. Tales from Mother England were 'The Real Thing'. Somehow, stories springing from our native soil seemed second-rate. The fact was that Britain was obviously 'Great' and Australia was by comparison – well, 'Average'. The Union Jack was firmly planted in the centre of my colonial imagination.

Then one Sunday afternoon, an unpretentious wandering bard stepped out of the bookshelves that lined our lounge room. An extended bout of bronchitis made me something of a recluse in early adolescence, housebound and absorbed in adventure stories. This swagman storyteller eased into my imaginative world with real life heroes from Australia's so-called 'Dead-Heart'. There was penniless Sidney Kidman, forging a cattle empire larger than the United Kingdom; the exploits of Red Kangaroo, the heroic chief of the Gunnedah tribe; the prospector Lasseter vanishing into the shimmering heat of the Outback seeking his fabulous gold-reef, and Flynn of the Inland weaving his fabled 'mantle of safety' with aeroplanes across the Inland. I lay wide-eyed and rigid late at night as Ion Idriess[16] told me blood-curdling tales of head hunters in the Torres Straits.

Vance Palmer, writing about colonial Australia's search for identity, said we can't really feel at home in any environment until we have transformed the natural shapes around us by colouring them with myth.[17] I didn't know it at the time, but Ion Idriess was conjuring a mythological Australia for me – a more authentic one that spoke my native language. This rough-cut yarn spinner made the so-called 'Dead Heart' pulse with life – a vast space alive with intriguing people. That compelling sense of mystery has never left me.

Out of the blue, one of John Flynn's Australian Inland Mission padres appeared in my classroom at Epping Boys High. Long, lanky, bespectacled Reverend Scott McPheat enthralled a bunch of rowdy lads with his adventures and made us shout with laughter at his entertaining rehearsal of incidents from the Biblical epic. This Presbyterian preacher became something of a hero in the rough-and-tumble environment of a boys' school. His passion for following Jesus across the red plains at Australia's heart made it seem an adventure worth joining. The vibrancy and colour he generated helped cultivate faith in me in a way that many dismal two-dimensional RE lessons had failed to do. For an adolescent schoolboy, groping his way towards manhood, he ignited images of a noble Christian heritage and how a real Australian might look.

That entertaining padre didn't preach but instead wielded the story in such a way that connected to familiar parts of my native landscape. I was beginning to wrestle with more abstract questions, and there was something about the genuineness of his life that won me. His faith had been hammered out in harsh realities, and that gave realism to what he taught us. I am grateful to this RE teacher who etched an image of muscular Christianity into my life, and I owe him for that.

Down the track, I was delighted to discover *Flynn, A Vision of the Inland*, authored by none other than Scott McPheat. As I read, I realised that he had infected us with his champion's spirit through our RE lessons. It shone out of a letter that 21-year-old John Flynn had written to his father, wondering what cause he would give himself to as the 20th century dawned over a newly federated Australia.

> … the more I think, the more I see the beauty and grandeur of Christianity, and the hollowness of human life considered as complete in itself… If it is true that Jesus is God's son and that through him 'whosoever-will' may approach the Father, what more honourable calling can a man follow than getting his fellows to realise this fact and to act upon it.[18]

As a boy hungry for heroes, John Flynn attracted me because he was a man who refused to rust; he was dead-set determined to shine with use. His faith energised him to dream what others said were impossible dreams. Zigzagging in his old Dodge in the service of the people of the frontier for over 50 years, he slashed his favourite lines of poetry from Robert Browning in bold strokes in skies across the continent. 'A man's reach should exceed his grasp, or what's a Heaven for?'

As a high schooler, it never dawned on me that the founder of the Royal Flying Doctor Service had moved into my life to stay. Several years ago, I stood beside my daughter-in-law at the RFDS base in Dubbo, watching my infant grandson being transferred into a $13M Beechcraft, poised to fly him 500 km to Westmead Children's Hospital in Sydney. I was moved as I said to her, "We should thank God for John Flynn. Where else in the world would a child receive this level of care?"

I felt this pioneer had stepped out of story-land to raise his hands in benediction over my family. A few years earlier, I had stood in that exact spot watching the flying ambulance soar into storm clouds, carrying my wife Robyn to specialist medical care in Sydney. It was really something to have had Scott McPheat explain to me when I was young, that the fabric of the 'mantle of safety' John Flynn spread across Australia, had been woven from thread spun in Galilee, 2000 years ago. Yet, for most people, he remains the mute face on the $20 notes they spend daily in the shopping mall.

Stories quickly fade if they're not painted fresh for each new generation. Nearly a century ago, a Riverina priest, Father Patrick Hartigan, spoke of his sadness when he met young Australians growing up, as he put it, unable to sing in their native tongue. He heard no spontaneous hymn of praise welling up for their own country – they sang the songs of other places. He set himself to write local stories in colloquial dialect and became famous as the poet John O'Brien.[19]

I feel that challenge still remains in the 21st century.

I grew up like those children – but one by one, a rag-tag band of storytellers came alongside, determined to acquaint me with my own heart language. They brought me the scent of true mythology – tales of women and men who dared to venture into, what for me had been, the voiceless soul of Australia. A haunting native melody captured me. I began to hear the cadences of the familiar Bible stories vibrating in the lives of the people they talked about. These minstrels awakened, nurtured, and strengthened my soul. So, I am deeply indebted to my grandfather, my father, the Jungle Doctor, Scott Mc Pheat, Ion Idriess, and others, whose patience and skill set me on a journey to manhood. They awakened a hunger in me to discover the stories of Australia.

The necessity remains. In 2018, popular children's author Morris Gleitzman pleaded with the Australian Government to avoid what he called 'a tragedy beyond words.' He was provoked by trade policies he saw driving the work of local authors out of the market.

Echoing Father Hartigan he wrote, 'Australian stories are crucial and irreplaceable to Australian young people. Just as American stories are to American young people, Slovenian stories are to Slovenian young people.'[20] I'd go beyond that. I believe there's an urgent need for creative storytellers who will foster authentic belief in God in young minds using materials from our native soil.

My PhD mentor, Professor Stuart Piggin, delivered a challenge that has driven me for the past 20 years. His extensive research had convinced him that Australia's Christian story was in danger of disappearing altogether. 'It is not that we knew it once and have forgotten it. We never knew it. Nobody has ever told us. Our Christian heritage has never been identified as such and therefore is in danger of being totally lost before it has ever been found.'[21] I soon realised that it was no good looking over my shoulder to see if someone else would pick up the gauntlet he had thrown down.

Commuting on a crowded bus into the heart of Sydney last year, I had a warm conversation with a well-qualified man who shared his concern about his children being corralled into a ghetto defined by their Indian background. He wanted his family to become contributors to the broader culture of their adopted home. Then, one afternoon not long ago, at the Royal Flying Doctor Visitor Experience near my home in Dubbo, I saw Zimbabwean, Indian and Chinese families come alive with amazement as I led them through the John Flynn story. They left eager to learn more.

Now I ask myself who will sing native melodies into the malleable souls of new generations of Australians, many of them born in Asia, Africa, the Middle East, South America and the Pacific? What stories will fire their affection for the society that has blessed them with such opportunities? Where are the spaces for open dialogue where we might develop new stories together?

More crucially, who will relay the narratives that can open their eyes to see the watermark etched into the currency of our culture – the face of the carpenter from Nazareth?

2

BOURKE TO BEERSHEEBA

It is the first part of our journey, the journey of our ancestors. So, in retelling their life stories, we have a serious obligation to get their histories straight. We are not merely creating literature: we are retelling a personal story that really happened and that helped make us the people that we are.[22]

Thomas Cahill

Smithy was 95 when I interviewed him at Bogghi Bend on the Darling River near Bourke. An ANZAC cameleer who fought the Turks in the Sinai desert in World War One, he broke down and wept as he relived the three brutal bayonet charges that had plunged him into war. Harold was just seventeen years old at the time. Those gristly encounters were so terrifying that eighty years later, his voice choked and his body shook uncontrollably. As I sat listening to this weathered veteran, the depth of his anguish touched me, and I knew I was witnessing the extended power of old memories.

There were tears in Roy Dunk's eyes too, as he painted the picture of the Australian Light Horse hurling themselves over enemy trenches in a last-ditch effort to take the wells of ancient Beersheba. It was a critical battle in the effort by British and Australian troops to drive the Turks out of Palestine in October 1917. The details were still vivid, even though his voice was frail, as he led me from the day in 1914 his boss at Currawinya Station on the Queensland border had gifted him a horse to begin the 10,000-mile journey to Egypt.

As he talked, I rode with him on the jaunty first leg to Bourke, where he sold the horse to pay his fare on the riverboat to South Australia to join the hundreds of young volunteers from all over the bush, eager for an overseas adventure. I felt with him as their exotic dreams were shattered by scything shrapnel, the rattle of rifle fire, the long, thirsty marches in the Sinai desert, and the sight of mates falling bloodied and lifeless beside them. And I could only try to understand what it meant to those men having to shoot their beloved horses before heading back to Australia. I've seen the photos that captured that moment – brought home in the wallets of other Bourke veterans. I felt that I had been there before.

Through the breathless words of Trooper Ion Idriess' war diary, I had ridden side by side with the 4th Light Horse Brigade as they charged for the wells at Beersheba. It was a powerful picture that had stirred my boyish imagination.

> At a mile distant, their thousand hooves were stuttering thunder, coming at a rate that frightened a man – they were an inspiring sight, galloping through the red haze – knee to knee and horse to horse – the dying sun glinting on their bayonet points. Machine guns and rifles roared… We heard shouts among the thundering hooves, saw balls of flame among those hooves – horse after horse crashed… The last half mile was a berserk gallop with the squadrons in magnificent line, a heart-throbbing sight as they plunged up the slope - leaping the redoubt trenches…and to a triumphant roar of voices and hooves was galloping down into the town… Beersheba had fallen![23]

And now here I was in Bourke, sitting with some of the ANZACs scarred by that battle, touched by their emotions, capturing their eyewitness experiences. A few brief minutes of close attention had helped me glimpse what had scored the souls of my grandfather's generation and, to some extent, shaped mine. It was why I loved history! Here was the heart of the business – the honour of rescuing fragile memories and keeping them alive with the ancient art of storytelling.

In my bones, I knew this was authentic communion.

The start to my career wasn't nearly so romantic. As a student, I was jarred awake by a tough training sergeant at boot camp – Professor Frank Crowley, the Dean of the Arts Faculty at UNSW. He singled me out in his Honours class with a scornful, "Are you a Christian? I thought we worked that nonsense out of you blokes in First Year!" He took the blowtorch to my faith and over the following three semesters of his Philosophy of History course, I endured his acid comments in tutorials and his sarcastic red pen scrawling on my essays.

But he did me a power of good.

His stringent challenges worked sinews into my faith. He dragged me out of my sheltered Christian world and made me fight for what I believed. Desperation taught me to prepare my case well and to argue it vigorously. Mostly he outgunned me, and I'd often leave his class shell-shocked and discouraged. But I took heart when a redheaded fellow student came alongside me one day and said, "I really envy you having a point of view to argue. I have no idea what history means."

I didn't appreciate it at the time, but Professor Crowley's course was actually combat training in storytelling. If he taught me anything, it was that a 'professor' should do just that, boldly profess their belief, settle on a standpoint and be prepared to defend it spiritedly. In fact, this was 'professionalism' in the truest sense. I learned that to practice as a historian it was critical to have a world view sturdy enough to tackle the hard questions about the purpose of the whole human story. We were training as interpreters, and his hostility made me realise this was a deadly serious vocation.

A dairy farmer from Yackandandah in Victoria supplied the answers I needed, and believe me, this bloke was even more tough-minded than the Dean. Laurie McIntosh was raised an atheist in the rugged foothills around Mt Hotham as part of a farming clan where hard-headedness was a badge of honour. But, while working as a civil engineer in the Snowy Mountains, he grappled with intellectual proofs that, in time, convinced him the story of Jesus was believable.

In particular, he had set himself to master the historical evidence that underpinned the New Testament documents, which supplied the steel scaffolding I lacked. By becoming my mentor and demonstrating that the Christian faith was both defensible and intelligent, he added courage to my skillset as a budding historian. He introduced me to C.S. Lewis who opened my eyes to see that God probably created a dangerous world as a proving ground for our character. 'Courage is not simply *one* of the virtues, but the form of every virtue at the testing point, which means at the point of highest reality… Pilate was merciful until it became risky.'[24]

I saw that I was no longer just preparing for a career but being equipped for a calling.

Looking into the faces of Holocaust survivors living in Sydney, I read a story etched by unimaginable pain. These people had stared annihilation in the eye. At the time, I was immersed in the 1940's chapter of this 2500-year-old saga – the extermination camps, the bloody struggle between Zionists and Palestinians, and the wild threats by the Arab States, as they opposed the partition of Palestine on the floor of the fledgling United Nations organisation. I was walking across the quadrangle of the Arts Faculty with Dr Bill Hudson, a lecturer in Middle Eastern Studies, discussing my thesis on the part Australia had played in establishing modern Israel when he said something that stuck in my mind like a burr. "There's one group of people in history that defy logical explanation – the Jews! By rights, the State of Israel should not exist, given the centuries of systematic effort to wipe them off the face of the earth."

The people I interviewed in my research made this statement all too vivid. The Nazis had murdered most of Max Freilich's Polish family, and this atrocity fired his dream of a sanctuary for the Jews in Palestine. As the leader of the Zionists in post-war Sydney, he pursued Dr Evatt, a passionate advocate of justice and a founder of the United Nations. I was intrigued when Max told me that a sympathetic Dr Evatt promised them his utmost support 'when the time came.' That moment arrived on November 29th 1947, at the UN in New York when, as the member nations voted alphabetically, Chairman Evatt's 'Yes' came first and was met by an excited cheer. "That was Evatt's greatest speech," lobbyist Abram Landa told me when we spoke.[25] Both men agreed that Dr Evatt was admired for his astute legal mind and prodigious capacity for work. This was critical in persuading many undecided nations to vote for partition. His biographer Alan Dalziel said it well, 'The tiny Republic, which embodied the age-old dreams of a world Jewry and militant Zionism, was born in 1948 with Evatt as midwife.' [26]

It was a cathartic experience for a young historian to realise that ancient Israel – the home of the Bible stories I had learned in boyhood – had a living connection with my native country. Moreover, it strengthened the sense that my profession as a historian and my Christian worldview were tracking inexorably into conjunction.

Later, I realised that boys from the Australian bush like Smithy, Ion Idriess, and Roy Dunk had helped make this possible when they captured Beersheba in 1917. The dust of that battle in the Negev hadn't even settled when the British Parliament endorsed Lord Balfour's promise of 'a home for the Jews' in Palestine. The pall of the Second World War had hardly cleared when Evatt too, fought with great determination to see his ideal of justice for the Jews carried through in the newly formed United Nations.

As a young historian, what heartened me was the discovery that this passion for righteous judgement had been incubated in the strong Anglican setting where young Herbert Evatt developed an encyclopaedic knowledge of the Bible. Undoubtedly this bedrock narrative helped make him an ambitious champion of the United Nations in the aftermath of the War. So, while working on my university thesis, I saw first-hand that the biblical narrative was still active in shaping the world in which I lived.

Sydney's Rabbi Rudolph Brasch brought this home when he wrote that Jews everywhere were in Australia's debt because of Dr Evatt's lead on the crucial vote. 'Strange that one of the world's youngest nations played so vital a role in recreating one of its oldest nations,' he said.[27] Dr Evatt came under intense criticism at home for his drive to achieve the partition of Palestine. Though driven by personal ambition, his prime motive was to see the United Nations live out the biblical symbol cast in bronze outside its headquarters in New York – the image of a sword being beaten into a ploughshare as prophesied by Isaiah. It was moving to discover that the Australian Jewish community had honoured Dr Evatt by planting a forest in his name on the slopes of Mt Carmel overlooking Haifa. It was where the prophet Elijah had single-handedly defended Israel's faith nearly three millennia before. There, resilient Australian eucalyptus trees took root in the soil of the Promised Land.

I had an epiphany of sorts as I finally put the pieces of that story together. It was like the moment when you've been staring at a Magic Eye puzzle, and the mass of dots resolves to reveal a hidden 3D image. These stereograms were first used to study how our eyes see different images and our brains create a single cohesive one. In my case, I realised that I had been squinting at history alternately through a secular eye and a spiritual eye. It was the realisation that a two-eyed stance was not only possible, but also preferable if you wanted to see the picture in depth. Educationalist Parker Palmer has the right word for it – 'whole-sightedness', which he defines as 'a vision of the world in which the heart and mind unite – our seeing shapes our being. Only as we see whole can we and our world be whole.'[28]

It stood out that the solution to the riddle of Israel's survival was hidden in their sense of divine destiny. I realised that it was precisely the historicity of the faith my professor had derided that qualified it as an interpretive tool. I became confident that it was as valid as any objective technique he was offering. I saw my two worlds had resolved into one strong, coherent image.

Prominent Australian historian Manning Clark voiced something of what I experienced – the merging of mind and soul, which lifted me up to catch a glimpse of an expansive, hopeful horizon. 'The story of the past should have the same effect as all great stories. It should increase wisdom and understanding. It should make the reader aware of what he had seen "through a glass darkly". It should turn the mind of the reader towards the things that matter. It must bring the reader to the frontier where music takes over from words.'[29]

Here was a template for telling our Australian story.

But there was still the nagging thought; was this just wishful thinking or genuine historical method? I was reassured after limping into the University Chaplain's office, discouraged following another bruising round with my professor. Bruce Wilson loaned me *Christianity and History*, written by an experienced historian with the very British name of Herbert Butterfield. He lifted the spirits of this lowly undergraduate when he wrote,

> But for the fulness of our commentary on the drama of human life in our time, we… have to stand back and see the landscape as a whole – and for the sum of our ideas and beliefs about the march of the ages, we need the poet and the prophet, the philosopher and the theologian. Indeed, we decide our whole attitude to the whole of human history when we make our decision about religion – and it is the combination of history with religion or with something equivalent, which generates power and fills the story with significances.[30]

What a relief to have the Vice-Chancellor of Cambridge University in my corner! He voiced what I had been groping towards. I felt I had the makings of a worldview capable of integrating my faith story into a reasoned approach to history. Having tried my story out against those of others, I had emerged with a more vigorous one that was my own. Herbert Butterfield neatly encapsulated the gratifying experience of whole-sightedness. 'Nothing can exceed the feeling of satisfaction that many people have when they meet with some such system which helps them through the jungle of historical happenings and gives them an interpretation of the story seen as a whole.'[31]

I walked out of the cloistered University straight into the gritty reality of an Australian high school at Drummoyne in Sydney's inner western suburbs. Now I was the 'professor', and a classroom full of rowdy year 11 boys was as good a place to test a theory as any. So when I started the Modern History lesson with, "Your decision about what history means is the most important decision of your life", it was met with a wave of good-natured banter. But over the next two years, it opened up a stimulating debate that rescued history from being merely an examinable subject and spilled out beyond the red-brick buildings on Lyons Rd into the lives of the boys I was teaching. Those lads knocked the rough edges off me, and their robust questioning taught me much about making history real at the grassroots level. For some of them, it brought whole-sightedness. One fierce Macedonian boy eventually headed back to Greece to recast the New Testament narrative for his people on the Island of Crete.

I was discovering that history tackled this way refused to leave you comfortable. It was not a matter of fashioning a timid fable designed for safe harbours. Instead, according to the piratical Sir Francis Drake, it was embarking on adventures in the open sea that revealed the wider, deeper meaning.

Disturb us, Lord, when
We are too pleased with ourselves,
When our dreams have come true
Because we dreamed too little.
When we arrived safely
Because we sailed too close to the shore.
Disturb us Lord, to dare more boldly
To venture on wilder seas,
Where storms will show your mastery;
Where losing sight of land,
We shall find the stars.
Francis Drake[32]

At the start, it was probably the 'Down Under' factor that launched me 12000 km away, from high school teaching in suburban Sydney, across the Pacific to Vancouver. The idea that the tyranny of distance has shaped our Australian story, fed the urge in me to do more than take a ferry across Sydney Harbour to Manly. I think I wanted to reverse the tyranny – to find a distant vantage point from which to get a fresh perspective. And a deeper impulse ran alongside that. It was a hunger to venture outside the world that had shaped me and to test myself elsewhere. If I was going to take other people further, I needed to expand my vision and gain a greater depth of field in my understanding.

The adventure to Canada affected a permanent widening of our horizons. A far-sighted friend urged my wife Robyn and me to head to Regent College on the University of British Colombia campus. They were pioneering workplace theology. Its founder's vision was to create a place where post-graduates could forge a worldview that matched their profession. With our young son Chris in tow, we found ourselves immersed in a community of teachers willing to take risks and challenge the comfortable beliefs we had absorbed, largely untested in safe settings. The diverse student body came from across the globe – a mix of every denomination from Mennonite to Episcopalian and representatives of every profession, from engineers to actors.

Dangerous questions and vigorous debate were bread and butter at Regent in 1977.

At the same time, in our downtown flat, we were befriended by a lapsed hippy, a recovering alcoholic, a cosmic free spirit, and a medical student from the radical Berkeley campus in California, whose partner specialised in erotic paintings. This random assortment of neighbours challenged our story in different ways, making us work at testing it on a pretty raw edge of the world. Then, as we travelled the beautiful wilds of Canada and the majestic Rocky Mountains beyond the city to the east, we caught echoes of a narrative as old as time. It may not have been quite the buccaneering adventure that Francis Drake prayed for, but it was definitely a startling change from our monochrome religious and cultural background in Australia. There's nothing like sailing in unchartered waters to force changes in the way you navigate.

It was exhilarating to watch the fragments of the simple biblical picture taught to me in childhood resolve into a coherent panorama at college. It involved some severe demolition work and robust rebuilding but it transformed the Old Testament from a stilted collection of stories into an unfolding epic. Formerly two-dimensional characters loomed larger and more believable as I uncovered their earthiness and their audacity in actually wrestling with God. Israel became a grounded place with grainy topography and real scars. The Jews became pilgrims struggling on a long and arduous journey towards a unique destiny. Historian John Bright gave me an 'Aha!' moment with his description of the crisis caused by Babylonian battering rams as they breached the walls of Jerusalem. Israel's faith was on trial for its life – their God seemed powerless to protect them.

> When one considers the magnitude of the calamity that overtook her, one marvels Israel was not sucked down into the vortex of history – to lose forever her identity as a people. And if one asks why she was not, the answer surely lies in her faith: the faith that had called her into being in the first place proved sufficient for even this.[33]

Bright more than answered my tutor Dr Hudson's curiosity about Israel's capacity for survival. He gave me a sharp insight about the tenacity of Israel's story that totally reshaped my thinking. He showed me how suffering welded them into the most story-formed people on earth.

A phenomenon emerged from the furnace into which the Jews had fallen in Babylon – a unique teaching unit they called the synagogue. The displaced children of Abraham were so convinced that their narrative was still travelling towards a destiny that scholars among them dedicated themselves to gathering its scattered splinters and shaping them into a cohesive collection. It survives to this day, and you can find it in hotel rooms across the world –the Old Testament in the Gideons' Bible.

These localised schools sprouted up across the Ancient world, patiently teaching their children to memorise the Law and the Prophets. The chronicle of Yahweh's dealing with them became a favourite topic for discussion at home and work. I could visualise them poring over their scrolls, teaching it, singing it together, rehearsing it around the meal table, celebrating it at feasts, and all the time dreaming of restoration. They had no country, no integrating system or government. Only their singular anthology of memories held them intact.

A Melbourne Rabbi reminded me recently that over the past 2500 years, his people had endured onslaught after onslaught, sustained by this defining narrative. I now understood more fully the part their story played in helping them survive the Holocaust and resurrecting the State of Israel in 1948. This unique narrative was the powerful sub-current that guided Dr Evatt's thinking as he steered the United Nations to vote 'Yes' and grant the Jews a home.

More than that, I saw that when connected to the story of Jesus, it had spun into a new orbit. Anyone who made a serious claim to being God visiting the planet demanded absolute attention. In time, it became the most defining story on earth, and somewhere all stories have had to measure themselves against it. Even the cynical Professor Crowley had to pick a fight with it!

As a historian and a Christian, I was ashamed of my total ignorance of the past 2000 years of my own story. My instructors made the narrative arches of intervening Church history emerge from the mist to create a bridge between the climactic events in Jesus' life and the place where I stood in the 20th century. Again, I was experiencing Butterfield's 'deep satisfaction' at seeing an integration of faith and history. Skilful teachers at Regent College had helped me construct a meta-narrative that made the most sense of all the rival interpretations in the human archive. It was a whole-sightedness, which matched the rigorous world of reason to the warmer world of heart-belief.

I departed Canada feeling more prepared, not only to steer others through the biblical narrative, but also to re-examine its connection to the story of my native country. I remember being a bit disconcerted when a bemused American student had asked me why the Aussies he had met were generally friendly but very reluctant to talk about spiritual things.

Good question – and one I am still working on an answer for.

As the Canadian Rockies faded in the rear-view mirror, the broad plains around Bourke filled the windscreen, and a whole other world beckoned. The unforgiving Australian outback was to be the laboratory in which I tried my newfound skills – not an altogether improbable place to put the ancient history of the Bible to the test.

Robyn and I joked as we drove the 800 km North West of our comfort zone in Sydney that Bourke was indeed located at the uttermost part of the earth from Israel where Jesus had walked. There, I was to meet ANZAC veterans Harold Smith and Roy Dunk, who had left the imprint of their Army-issue boots in the sand of Palestine, around Beersheba, where Abraham had left his indelible footprint almost four thousand years before. But intriguingly, all these figures began to connect as players in a much larger story. It was becoming clear to me that not only had Australia helped form modern Israel, but also in a far more profound way, ancient Israel had played a significant part in shaping modern Australia. But how many of us realise that?

The task of helping to surface that invisible storyline out of the soil of my native land eventually became my calling.

3

AT THE BACK O' BOURKE

Beyond the outer rim of the comforts and safety of close settlement, the Outback is the pulse-point of the national folk-nerve.[34]

Patsy Adam Smith

There is no map of the Australian Outback. It has no known boundaries. Historian Patsy Adam Smith described it as 'an elusive acreage of the mind.' That was certainly true for me. For the early part of my life, like most Australians, I had clung like an oyster to the well-watered coastal fringe. I was one of those that journalist Charles Bean wrote of a century ago, who knew little about the 'second Australia… the core of Australia, the real, red Australia of the ages.'[35] Patsy Adam Smith has argued that most Australians feel a combination of 'fear, love, admiration and curiosity' about the Outback. [36]

That described precisely how Robyn and I felt as we drove from Sydney on the last, long, straight stretch of the Mitchell Highway to Bourke. For us, it was a journey of faith into an unknown region. We felt a bit like Israel's patriarch Abraham stepping out into the void, 'not knowing where he went.' But how else do you prove the story you claim to live by? With only a spiritual compass to guide them, Abraham and Sarah stirred a storm of great stories by voting with their feet. We weren't quite their calibre, or their age, for that matter, but in a strange way we did feel that our journey was genuinely connected to theirs.

The 'Silent Heart' of our vast continent has become a sounding board for the national story, in the same way 'The West' has for Americans. I felt it was telling that, at the 2000 Olympics in Sydney, the symbols we chose to showcase the culture of our island home mostly came from the bush. The longer I lived in the Outback, the more I came to understand that we, too, have peopled the core of the continent with fabled heroes. With chains and sextants, surveyor/explorers like Sturt and Mitchell painstakingly sketched new lines over the top of ancient song-lines of Aboriginal tribes. The settlers who followed filled the heart of Australia with tales of a different kind.

Bourke itself was a metaphor – the custodian of a national myth much bigger than itself. For coastal dwellers, the expression *Back O' Bourke* morphed into the definition of a place balanced precariously on the edge of nowhere – 'at the end of the line', 'on the lip of the far horizon', 'out-to-blazes' at the entrance to the 'Never-Never'. For a century and a half, it has sat alone on the wide Darling River flood plain under an infinite dome of pale blue, with stories rolling through its streets like tumbleweeds.

Important ones, I was to discover.

Two of those mythical figures materialised out of the heat-haze when we first arrived in March 1978. They were not bushie-Australians, but adventurous Americans who in the 1960's had answered the fabled call of the frontier, 'Go West, young man!' From their homes on the Californian coast, the next place West was Australia, and if you were fair dinkum about going West – well, you went to the other side of Bourke!

Owen Boone and Jack Buster were strong ex-Marines with big visions and hearts to match, working side by side with their wives on Fort Bourke Station. These cotton farmers impetuously volunteered to host the kibbutz-style teaching community that we and our friends Laurie and Elvira McIntosh had dreamed up a year or two before. This radical experiment in socialisation-education was hatched sitting in the simple farmhouse kitchen at McIntosh's *Lodebar Dairy*, on the Cunnamulla road north of Bourke.

Futurist author Tom Sine described the adventures that drove the Biblical narrative as 'the conspiracy of the insignificant'. That's exactly how I felt as the ideas flowed around the rustic kitchen table when we visited Lodebar back in 1976. It seemed like we were drawn back into the world of the New Testament. Instead of being on the outside of the narrative, we were on the inside. Like Jesus' first followers, our resources were minimal, and our dream was outsized. It seemed we were joining a conversation that had begun long ago in Jerusalem. Father William Bausch traced this story telling habit to the early Christians,

> … they sat around the table and asked the original witnesses to tell them once more the stories and deeds of Jesus. And in the telling, as in all good stories, they sensed his presence again. The spirit of Jesus was rekindled – that's how the faith got started – in storytelling. And that's what was recorded in the gospels. The development of an intellectual and creedal approach to faith later overshadowed this pristine story form, radically altering its essential character for future generations.[37]

Sparks flew as we talked. Stories from every era melded into a plan for training the present generation of young Australians. We freely borrowed various strategies from the past. The brilliant way Jesus had discipled a team of storytellers, the apostle Paul's skilful deployment of mobile mission bands across the Roman Empire, and the far-flung communities created by the Celtic monks that reshaped Europe in the fifth and sixth centuries.

Then in the eighteenth and nineteenth centuries, there was the worldwide spread of Count von Zinzendorf's Moravian missionaries. Springing from this, the ingenious cell group strategy of John Wesley's Methodists. More recently, the defiant count-er-Nazi teaching hubs of Dietrich Bonhoeffer and the teams of Frank Buchman's Moral Re-armament movement brought hope in the post-war era.

We were fired by these heroic ideals and proud of our lineage. Laurie and Elvira brought fresh insights from their immediate experience working with Bill Bright's Campus Crusade teams on the University of Sussex in England. Together we dreamed of a self-supporting community away from the metropolis in a rural set-ting, where we would work, unpack the biblical narrative in the classroom and then reconstruct it together while living in close quarters. It was to be a crucible – a daily testing ground for the Christian story. But, more than anything, we wanted the students who came to work out a really grounded faith of their own.

These animated discussions led Robyn and I to realise that we needed to be better equipped and so in 1977 we left for the year of study at Regent College. As that year rolled by, the idea of Cornerstone took a more definite shape. Laurie sat at the kitchen table in Bourke, sketching it out on blue airmail paper, and a week later we pored over it in our downtown Vancouver flat. He gave the dream contours: 'I can't get away from the thought that it is as romantic a thing as I've ever heard of… Purpose: to hammer out a useful Christian lifestyle relating to our 20th century civil-isation with a perspective that sees everything (church, job, art, family, politics) from God's point of view and which is based on an articulate understanding of our faith.'

He was dead right about the ideal – a teaching community in the Outback seemed fine when studying in a rarefied atmosphere, with a head full of fresh insights in a beautiful city on the other side of the world. But then romance met reality. For two city-bred school-teachers, it hit us like shock therapy. We found ourselves in an arid landscape of saltbush, mulga scrub, and gidgee stretched across a vast canvas of red soil. Kangaroos and emus ceased being national symbols and became active companions on our daily walks. Our home, first in a caravan and then in shear-ers' quarters, was often shrouded in dust from road trains, juddering past on the Wanaaring road, carrying stock from stations far to the West.

In the next door paddock, mobs of sheep were mustered, shorn, and slaughtered, accompanied by their stink and clouds of flies. Our kids rolled in red mud after rain and came crying with cats-head thorns in their feet. Daily we swung the axe on the iron-tough gidgee wood to feed the 'donkey' that heated our hot water. Life in the community took on a rhythm of droughts and floods, ploughing and sowing, irrigation and harvest, hard work and exhaustion. Everything took effort and patience. Together we learned to wait, accept crop failures, cope with extreme heat, drive long distances and do without. There was nowhere to hide. It was a tough school that rubbed us raw at times, but it was scribing new stories deep into our lives, and we learned to love it.

The bush had a voice of its own. We learned to hear God's quiet whisper in the silences, stand in awe under wide-flung sunsets, worship under a night-time dome of galaxies, marvel at the carpet of wildflowers after rain, and appreciate the morning chorus of birds. Even the raucous cockatoos had their own hymn! Again and again, we saw the narrative being written daily in the natural world, quietly healing bruised and broken spirits jaded by the turmoil of modern life.

Then there were the people living their lives out against that backdrop. We were part of a resourceful community of men and women who bent their backs for long hours and whose hard hands spoke volumes. The Boones and Busters brought agricultural skills, generosity, and a 'can-do' attitude. They were the kind of Christians who preached their sermons best in overalls and through their hospitality. Pancake breakfasts and leaping bonfires under a canopy of stars became legendary among the students. Their more conservative approach to religion was challenged again and again by the young people who arrived on their doorstep from every conceivable background. They came from countries all across the world, with assorted personal baggage and unrighteous behaviour. But these 'sunburnt-saints' were big-hearted enough to accommodate them, teach them to farm and to love them.

Our remote community was a matrix where amazing stories unfolded one after the other for the next twenty-seven years. For example, the young bloke who walked two kilometres late one night to Jack Buster's sprawling, mud brick home to apologise for his brashness at work. Sitting in bed, the weary farmer listened to his tale of an absent father and numerous foster homes. After asking forgiveness for his attitude, Jack startled him by saying, "John, you need a father – I'll be that father." True to his promise, he not only put him through medical training, he eventually helped restore the broken relationship by persuading John's Dad to come to Bourke to captain the riverboat.

Hundreds of stories like this were added year after year. Everyone was faced with their shortcomings and given opportunities to change. The tenacity of the New Testament story proved itself by flourishing twenty centuries later and half a world away in Bourke.

The McIntosh family, with their Celtic / Aztec mix and unique blend of experiences, stimulated breadth of vision. In the revolutionary Sixties, they had plunged in among hippy university students in Brighton, England, and later on campus in Mexico City and witnessed first-hand the transformative effect of the Christian gospel. Laurie was a practical, farm-bred man through and through. With his studies in sociology and anthropology and his experience as a linguist in Mexico, he was well equipped to conjure up Cornerstone's socialisation education model. Elvira's love of music, dance, and fiesta, plus her passion for teaching children, added colour and joy that made the community crackle with energy and ideas. They figured that the rawness of the outback environment and the daily rubbing against one another living in community would test the reality of Jesus' life and teachings even further. They had a thirst to take the story of Jesus' life deep so that it would last life-long.

I soon found it was no good me climbing into a pulpit to speak down to the students as if I was six feet above contradiction. On the contrary, there were constant incongruities that rubbed my nose in my limited capacities. A no-nonsense workshop like this made a profound difference to the texture and feel of the Bible stories as we taught them.

There was nothing manicured or predictable about life at Bourke. Instead, it had the kind of randomness and surprise that characterised the environment in which

Jesus trained his disciples. There's nothing like sorting out a fistfight over an untidy bedroom, facing a hefty man spitting blasphemies, or a Muslim man fresh from the war in Lebanon asking why God chose Isaac and not Ishmael to bring reality to what you teach. Jesus had taught his disciples in response to things that cropped up as they walked the country, and we found ourselves doing much the same. It was quite a ride, and it forced us to see that if our faith was going to survive, we had to make our spiritual lives more natural, and our natural lives more spiritual.

The bush is a great leveller. Living among Outback people who have learned to survive in unforgiving country, I saw that they had developed thick skin, but underneath their sensitive hearts had thin walls. From weathered faces they watched you carefully and measured you more by what you did than what you said. Under the shadow of a broad-brimmed hat, their eyes were inquiring, "Do you take us seriously? Do you value our story?" For some, the tough times had shrivelled any religious faith they may have inherited, and a scepticism nourished by drought, lay just beneath the surface in many Western landholders.

And the indigenous people we worked alongside, entertained, met in the street, played sport with, and worshipped beside challenged our comfortable perceptions of what was genuine about our storytelling. Dislocation and disillusionment had been their daily bread for a century or more. So how could we share a common story about Australia?

Put bluntly, Bourke had a sharp nose for 'bull-....' and a deaf ear for Bible-bashers. Any religious talk that was going to cut it in this end-of-the-line township, had to be real and grounded. My eager efforts at broadcasting the 'Good-News' on the fledgling public access radio station 2WEB, contained good solid stuff that might have gone down well with a university audience. The pity was, the nearest Uni was 500 km away!

I was rescued by two secrets about being authentic that I learned reading John Flynn's biography. First, he gained acceptance in the Outback by listening. There's a classic photo of the bespectacled preacher, complete in tie and vest, hunched atop a stockyard fence, yarning easily to a drover in dungarees. It still speaks volumes to me as an echo of a thirsty Jesus seated on an ancient well, in conversation with a woman jaded by hard experiences.

Secondly, like Jesus, Flynn had an acute interest in the people he met. He was avid in gathering their stories and set them to work, shocking city audiences with the desperate situations faced by isolated bush people. He doubled the impact of his story by relaying the pathos of their lives through his camera lens. He advised his travelling padres, "If you want to commend your gospel to men, first of all, do something for them that they understand."[38] These lessons, from one of Australia's most effective storytellers, have never left me. It stood out like a windmill on a claypan that I was still a novice communicator in this country.

The station manager of 2WEB was candid. He looked me in the eye and said, "Paul, I think you've earned far more credibility doing the *Bourke and Beyond* oral history programme, than when you were just doing a religious broadcast." It took me back at first. He had invited me to record the stories of old-timers in the district. After a while I gained a reputation as 'The Grim-Interviewer' – senior citizens would go pale when they saw me approaching with a microphone, thinking it signalled their time was up! It trained me to ask good questions and to listen. Instead of just preaching, I was honouring them and their extraordinary experiences. I had to unlearn the irritating habit of assuming they only needed to sit and listen to my message.

Instead, I learned to serve them first, recording, editing, and broadcasting their stories across a local region as large as Denmark. People began to approach me in the main street or at the local show to share further reminiscences. I felt I was helping Bourke listen to its own voice and perhaps, for the first time, understand its own journey and hear the music of its own heart. More important, as an outsider, I was learning to love them and their story. I think my manager-friend sensed that once that was in place, the locals would be more prepared to listen to mine. Years later, a grazier/historian friend from Tilpa looked me squarely in the eye at the bar of the Hungerford Hotel and said, "Y' know Roey, when you first came to Bourke, you were talking **at** us; now you're talking **with** us!"

The nomadic Aboriginal tribes considered the storyteller their richest man. Time had taught them that real wealth lay in the wisdom contained in their stories. I don't think I understood, as I sat listening to Captain Bill Drage over the roar of the water pouring down the Bourke weir, that he was depositing useable currency into my account.[39] Bill was the last of the riverboat skippers to negotiate the meandering 1400 kilometres of the Darling from Wentworth to Bourke. He transported me into a world I knew nothing about. He painted images of barges loaded with a thousand bales of wool, negotiating shoals in low rivers, an engineer blown clean out of the boat by an exploding boiler. He described paddle wheelers trapped for years by a falling river, navigating by river-charts drawn on canvas scrolls like ancient Egyptian hieroglyphs. A strange nostalgia came over me as the stories flowed out of this courteous gentleman with his skipper's cap perched at a jaunty angle. It was like the echo of a tune I had lost without knowing it.

I felt I was receiving a rare gift – a passport into a fast receding past that was part of my story as an Australian.

A hundred others made deposits into my reserve of narratives – patient as I plied them with questions to help them revive half-forgotten moments. I felt privileged to listen to aviatrix Nancy Bird Walton recall landing in Bourke as a 19-year-old woman pilot in 1935. The Rev Stanley Drummond had challenged her to fly his Far West Children's Scheme nurses to remote stations and villages. At nearly eighty-years-old, her observant eyes spoke of someone who had spent a lifetime making shrewd judgements. She entranced me into a world of adventurous Australian aviators who were making history in the 1930's. As a slip of a girl, she had braved vast, waterless distances with no more than a road map. I watched as her adventures lit a fire in a group of young girls at our small Pera Bore School. She wrote warmly of the mettle of the women she met when she landed on lonely stations.

> The heroism of some of the outback women was inspirational. Their courage was sustained year after year in terrible conditions. They had no help, conveniences, proper diet, or holidays. Many

of them took great pride in their homes, trying to keep them spotlessly clean despite the eternal, blowing sand.[40]

I felt myself flying with her and sharing her admiration of the visionary Christian minister who had given such a timely gift to the isolated families out west. As Nancy told story after story, it seemed to me Drummond and his team had left the footprints of Jesus all across the backcountry – but they were steadily being blown away. Then, just before she died, she told me her one regret was not building more on the faith she had received as a child in the timber town of Kendall near Port Macquarie.

Bourke's modest narrators took me back to school. By simply laying out the story of their lives, they taught me a great deal about myself. They opened the eyes of a city-trained historian to a powerful story, hidden beyond the Great Dividing Range that separates the east coast of Australia from the Inland. They showed me that I was naïve to neglect the narratives of the outback because they were a vital ingredient in our national mythology. "Don't undervalue unheralded history, unlikely localities, and unknown individuals," they seemed to say. And as they handed me their stories with work-worn hands, I felt they charged me with the task of making fragile fragments of that crumbling story more permanent – more meaningful.

I felt like an oarsman propelling the skiff forward, while looking steadily behind.

4

FROM LITTLE THINGS, BIG THINGS GROW

The writing of a national history is a good thing, but other histories are necessary first. We must have the lesser histories, histories of towns, districts, schools, churches, even families. This study is the foundation upon which national and international histories rest.[41]

J.J. Alderson

You could say I became the interpreter of Bourke's history almost by accident – I buried the other two local historians! Alan Barton grew up on Western sheep stations owned by the legendary cattle king Sir Sidney Kidman, so the history of the region was in his blood. In the truest sense, he was one-eyed about Bourke history – he lost his right one in an accident, and was ferociously single-minded in his dedication to gathering local stories. Over a lifetime, he had painstakingly assembled albums of photos and notes – all written in longhand.

He was one of Australia's unheralded historians who did his work for the love of it.

If you let him, my friend Alan would talk for hours about Afghan cameleers, riverboats, pioneer aviation, early motor transport, artesian bores – the list was endless.

He infected me with his enthusiasm for tracking the narratives of his three poet-heroes – Henry Lawson, Harry 'The Breaker' Morant, and Will Ogilvie. I admired him as a model of quiet, persistent research, and I understood why he was jealous of his material. His consistent Presbyterian faith brought him to our non-denominational church, and being his pastor, the day came when I conducted his funeral. Alan's extensive research could well have been buried with him.

His rival was a 'blow-in', surveyor Bill Cameron, whose passion for Bourke history was ignited after he moved to the town in the 1960's. His home sat on a big bend in the Darling near the North Bourke Bridge – a major link in the stock route between Queensland and Victoria in the droving days. Like the drovers who had herded a prodigious number of sheep and cattle past his door, Bill had mustered a massive number of stories – his whole house was an archive of photos, artefacts, and documents all patiently catalogued in a card system. He spent hundreds of hours in the Mitchell Library in Sydney tracing references to Bourke and copying it all out by hand.

Here was a surveyor carefully mapping the contours of local history.

Bill was an atheist and never tired of telling me in his slow, sing-song drawl, "I read the Bible every day, Paul, but not for the reasons you read it – it's just good literature." He had the most extensive record collection of hymn music I can recall seeing, and when you visited Bogghi Bend, you were never sure whether you would be welcomed by a Bach chorale or one of the bawdy ballads that made up the balance of his collection. He was an enigma – a sceptic who loved the Bible and a dedicated historian who used quotes declaring that fossicking in the past was an exercise in futility. I felt that perhaps his long inner debate resolved the day I led his burial service under the coolabah trees, not far from where Alan was buried. The long rivalry was over, and the two competitors now lay silent together in the cracked grey river-soil of the Bourke cemetery.

Silent, but not quite muted. These two persistent eccentrics helped produce fourteen volumes of Bourke history plus two volumes of photos with the help of other enthusiastic members of the Historical Society – no small feat. Alan's daughter had completed her Dad's research on Henry Lawson in Bourke – but he died just before *A Stranger on the Darling*[42] was published. And now I was the last man standing. Only in a mirage could I see myself making the same journey as my friends. I wondered, 'What possesses people to make that kind of effort? Would their blood, sweat, and tears just evaporate?'

A few hardy family researchers and a handful of writers might appreciate their efforts, but who else was going to sit down and plough through sixteen volumes about an out-of-the-way corner of Australia? It seemed to me it was destined to be buried under the mantling dust of the bush, but an assertion from G.D. Richardson, which Bill put in the preface to one of the volumes, challenged me. 'The history of a country is more than the sum of the histories of its localities; equally clearly, the history of a country is not truly written if the history of its localities is ignored.'[43]

In other words, from little things big things grow.

Bourke was a town under siege towards the end of the eighties. The streets were filled with tension as the indigenous and white communities struggled to cope with serious social breakdowns. A strong police presence had failed to touch the core problems, and Sydney papers carried pictures of a main street that looked like a downtown Beirut war zone.

Community confidence was at a low ebb when the Shire Council initiated a community audit – a stocktake of assets as a way of looking for positives that would unite the town. It was Bourke's trove of stories that topped the list. Proposals to improve the face of the town were launched with varying degrees of success. Still the main task I felt was to engineer something that could mobilise those narratives to generate genuine social capital. It would be an exercise in redemptive storytelling.

What captured me was the quiet pride in many of the wizened faces telling me tales of droving cattle over thousands of kilometres of the backcountry. They told of the thrill of seeing a deep artesian boring rig pierce the aquifer to send water soaring hundreds of feet. Also of driving the first truck across country from Adelaide, or of forty years riding the dingo fence from Cunnamulla to Cooper Creek. I was deeply touched by their resilience. There were Aboriginal folk who had coped with racism and not got bitter, a mother on a lonely property who had buried her still-born baby 'and just got on', station owners crippled by drought who straightened their backs and kept going. There was also a reluctance to make something of themselves – as far as they were concerned, they'd done nothing heroic – that was just life. Few of them could realise the true value of their story because they had no vantage point from which to see the larger landscape within which it sat. Small fragments gain weight and value when placed in a bigger context.

My amateur efforts as a storyteller on radio gave me an inkling that there might be something I could do. History without interpretation loses its virility. Instead of creating a strong new generation confident of its identity, neglect leaves a forlorn group of orphans ignorant of their heritage. These life stories were like rough gems that could be polished and given a fresh lustre.Provided with the right setting, sound effects, and music, lost dramas could be brought to life, and sympathetic narration could remind Bourke of its infancy and the forces that had shaped it. I felt that if a mirror of burnished stories was held up, the community could see themselves with greater clarity and increase their sense of place. Healing might occur by painting an honest picture using snatches of the beautiful, the ordinary and the ugly.

Over and over, I witnessed a piece of magic as I led visitors through our local story during the time we worked in the Tourist Centre. Strangers absorbed chapters from the Bourke narrative and transferred them to their own because there were moments that touched on the hunger deep in their hearts for meaning. The feeling 'they've walked in my shoes' generated spontaneous companionship, and a genuine sense of shared identity grew during our brief meetings. They were on the road to find out, and these stories became a vehicle that created a wider community. As we made Bourke's neglected narratives accessible, tourists were persuaded to remain longer to absorb them. Then, as they travelled around the continent, they gossiped them at the campfires of other grey nomads.

The stories they gathered became transferable currency.

I was learning in practice that the reach of Australia's history could be made greater when its small provincial stories were brought to life and made accessible. And when we persuaded the more insular locals to share their particular experiences with travellers from Melbourne, Munich, Minneapolis or Manchester, it cracked their minds open to see that 'mateship' wasn't exclusive to the Australian bush. In the telling, they were not only contributing to the visitors' understanding of outback life, but also befriending their city cousins, and beyond them, embracing members of the global village. Almost unnoticed, they were gaining a better understanding of themselves in the process.

Cornerstone's effort to integrate more directly into the local community made national headlines. We had moved some of our teaching centre from the farm into town. We were astonished to find the front page of *The Weekend Australian* ominously captioned 'Fundamentalist Sect Takes over Bourke'. The article said that Cornerstone had got control of a heritage building and several businesses, and, according to some locals, it was a move with sinister designs.

Once I got over the shock, I laughed on two counts. First, because many fundamentalist churches wouldn't have readily owned us, and second because I had several locals immediately offer to sell me their businesses. One even said, "The sooner you take over the bloody town the better!" Considering the strong Christian presence throughout Bourke's history, including a couple of saints in the shape of Mother Theresa and Mother Mary McKillop,[44] it seemed slightly bizarre to be considered a menace. In fact, we were active contributors to the long spiritual narrative, which had underpinned the district from its beginnings. So I took heart from the thought that at least we weren't being ignored!

The threat we posed was colonising a vacant heritage-listed building as a base for our leadership school, opening a Backpackers lodge, and refurbishing a defunct indoor cricket centre for the town's youth. Council trusted us with the contract for the Tourist Centre, which became a platform from which to help animate the town's unique stories. Often a couple from somewhere like Melbourne, their rig cicatrised with stickers announcing the many routes they had travelled, would ask "Is it safe to stay in Bourke?" A fifteen-minute guided tour around our photo display with a live narrator led to the bewildered question, "Why haven't we heard this before? This is amazing!" Then they would head out with a 'mud-map' to discover more.

In this way, the Tourist Centre, perched on the disused railway station at the end of the line, became the training ground where we honed our skills in eye to eye, mind to mind and heart to heart storytelling. We realised as we test-drove Bourke's stories, we were handling an under used asset. People just loved them, and we had the fun of seeing dormant narratives bring wonder and surprise into our visitors' eyes.

Spurred on by consummate yarn-spinner Mayor Wally Mitchell, the town council called in experts in community renewal. Wally loved Bourke's story, and with his encouragement, I found myself part of a team uncovering key sites and establishing their importance. It was rewarding to help Bourke people seize on different ways to highlight their stories, and a fresh pulse began to beat as the rich maritime history came to life. A skilled local farmer was inspired to build a replica of the paddle steamer *Jandra* and passengers were journeying on the Darling once again. The wharf was repurposed as a centre for town celebrations, and the original North Bourke Bridge was restored. A pub themed itself around photographs of the riverboat days, and the character of other heritage buildings was revived.

Neglect was replaced by careful attention.

Bourke became a storied environment. For decades, Mt Gundabooka had lain asleep along the Western horizon of the Darling flood plain like a giant lizard. When it was declared a National Park, rangers stirred it to life by becoming interpreters of the Dreamtime legends painted in ochre on the cave walls. The town approach was made an avenue to celebrate the service of famous eye surgeon Fred Hollows around Bourke and across the world. A stone monolith in the cemetery declares his passion that all the world might see, 'The key he used to undo locks was vision for the poor.'[45]

At the entrance to town, outback artist John Murray, assisted by local indigenous artist Brian Smith, painted a large mural suggestive of two phantom swagmen disappearing through a gateway into the West. Nearby, a forgotten local hero was brought back into focus. Storyboards were erected celebrating Percy Hobson, the first Aboriginal athlete to win a gold medal for Australia. More recently, the two artists teamed up again to complete a spectacular piece of silo art capturing the instant Percy cleared the high jump crossbar at the Commonwealth Games. Hotels, caravan parks and farm stays sprang into new levels of hospitality and value-added experiences for travellers. This more immediate ownership fostered pride and generated a distinct identity.

Take big, hearty Phil Sullivan, the Aboriginal Conservation Officer, for example. He was raised in tough times on the government mission at Brewarrina and had plenty of reasons to be disillusioned and bitter. Instead, I've watched him develop into an expressive spokesman, not just for his Ngemba people, but for all the town's residents. I've also listened with admiration to his skilful blending of his traditional history with the accounts of Jesus' life that now shape his personal narrative. He is determined not to dwell on the offences in the past, but having acknowledged them, allow them to be reference points for moving forward. You can hear it in his voice.

> This is my camp… This land owns me… There's a great willingness
> to learn and understand our culture when people come out here. In
> Bourke there's a sense of ownership of the camp, from both black
> and white… Even in hard times people still honour and respect
> this town. We have our differences – it's always a challenge to see
> with your heart – but the reason we are still here is because we have
> faith in Bourke and faith in each other. There's a growing feeling
> we have to leave the past behind. That's why I urge people to come
> to Bourke – to learn about Australia today.[46]

The transport arteries, leading to Bourke from every point of the compass, were given character via an intravenous drip-feed of legend. Energetic work by the local Council had the Bourke section of the North-South highway connecting Melbourne to the Gulf of Carpentaria, not only sealed, but attached to the romantic tale of Sidney Kidman, the Cattle King. Similarly, the East-West connection between Brisbane and Adelaide was transformed into the Kamilaroi Way, where towns along the route helped celebrate Aboriginal history like the ancient fish traps at Brewarrina. The unsealed road running South-West became the Darling River Run - a thread on which villages like Louth, Tilpa, and Menindee could string yarns of the paddle-steamer days at pubs and farm stays. Pioneer settler Vincent Dowling, who carved Fort Bourke Station out of the wilderness, lent his name to the red dirt road heading North West to Hungerford on the dingo fence.

In this way, a mythical web was spun out wide, forming connections and drawing an increasing number of travellers to Bourke as its centre.

What gave me real heart was the regenerative effect in the growth of the arts. As a teacher, I knew this signalled that stories were stirring the local imagination. Poets and musicians took up local themes in ballads – yarn spinners did what they do best by making the stories vivid, while writers mined the archives and published books. Country singer/songwriter, Colin Buchanan, explained how the year he spent in Bourke taught him the dynamics of connecting incidental story and place in song. He had seen it cultivate people's engagement with their own stories.

> Because it was a small community, it was easier to write something that immediately connected with the people. I discovered that when you did this, you dignified an aspect or a moment that may not have registered with anybody as particularly significant before. You create a kind of memorial that reflects their lives for the future. As you celebrate local yarns in a musical form, you release the story in a different fashion – the locals begin to view it and themselves differently. There is a kind of spontaneous reflection that happens as they listen – they learn to observe themselves. It affirms their connection to the place and the lifestyle… When you articulate people's feelings, you provide a meeting place for them – a way of sharing their experiences. When they sing along with the words they are able to make a kind of collective vote about what has happened.[47]

There are other ways to capture the drama. The starkness of the bush, the character of the people, the texture of the rocks and soil, and the vastness of both landscape and skyscape provoked a different kind of storytelling by indigenous and non-indigenous artists. The region suffers periodically from devastating droughts, and artist, Jenny Greentree, set herself to tell the story of resilience in the face of despair in a series of exhibitions hung in a public gallery. These have become a source of hope to visitors and citizens alike, as she sees the hand of the Creator in the rugged landscape. She sat with an Aboriginal interpreter who explained the stories surrounding Mt Gundabooka before she painted its rocky outcrops. Her work has been warmly embraced by indigenous and non-indigenous alike.[48]

One Aboriginal visitor praised her aerial painting of Gundabooka as 'Deadly!'

The artist herself is emphatic that the story sells the painting. She delights in engaging with the visitors, connecting the scene to its narrative roots. As a result, she often sees them commit to acquiring an artwork as part of their personal biography. One of her works speaks from the wall behind Prime Minister Scott Morrison's desk. For nearly two decades, Jenny's gallery has been a vibrant space, articulating the primal narrative of the Darling floodplain using native colours and topography. She's in the tradition of landscape artists who give the bush a voice, and she's now experimenting with storytelling flights over Mt Gundabooka.

There's more than one way a picture can paint a thousand words. I drove hundreds of kilometres across the Bourke region with students and staff from Griffith University as they crafted an extensive photographic essay. Lecturer Peter Wanny was emphatic that giving them an experience of life beyond their urban area not only generated valued full-time courses, but had a maturing effect on the students themselves. In turn, they transferred the story of their visit to the Outback digitally to the world.

Outback Radio 2WEB maintained a steady stream of oral history and magazine spots that brought local archives to life while indigenous station 2CUZ broadcast programs in local languages. An increasing number of journalists and documentary makers began to appear, intrigued by the richness of the narratives, using the extensive archival material in the town library to expand the scope of their programs. In addition, national journals like *Australian Geographic* and *Outback Magazine* used these resources to help tell the Australian story. The phenomenon I witnessed firsthand was the way that, by a series of small steps, piece by piece, story by story, a collective memory was not only recovered but also set to work to rejuvenate a community.

I saw with my own eyes that from little things, big things grew.

As I explored the narratives of Jesus' life with the Cornerstone students, the thing that leaped out to me was that he too was a country storyteller. His mind was like a camera with a high-speed shutter, constantly capturing moments in the everyday lives of people around him. He showed the spiritual world was never far away, and his keen eye saw the activity of God in the most ordinary things. A remarkable crowd of characters appeared in his stories. Cambridge University classicist T.R. Glover, noted the way the immediate presence of his Father overshadowed them all.

> One of Jesus' great lessons is to get men to look for God in the commonplace things of which God makes so many, as if Abraham Lincoln were right and God did make so many common people, because he likes them best… When Jesus speaks of the highest and holiest things, he is as simple and natural as when he is making a table in the carpenter's shop. Sense and sanity are the marks of his religion.[49]

I was becoming more and more aware that there was a cast of characters primed and ready to speak in Australia. I became convinced that our stories, hewn from native timbers, sawn and mortised in our own workshop, had as much latent spiritual power as any that had gone before anywhere in the world. Unlikely as it may seem, even the players in the grainy history of Bourke had played a part in the larger narrative that had been unfolding since the human journey began.

During the 90's, it became clear that Bourke was strategically positioned to have an authentic Outback voice. Curators I met in my travels were unanimous that the heart of a good museum begins to beat when there is a passionate conviction that you have a story worth sharing. Testing the stories in every corner of the Shire proved to me that there was sufficient quantity and calibre to aim for something substantial – a high-quality storytelling apparatus of our own. The chronicles of Bourke, resting on the local library's shelves, or locked away in the memories of locals, needed transposition into a new key with a sounding board to match.

The ruins of the once-thriving Tancred's Abattoir, standing silent sentinel on the town's main approach from Sydney, signalled a message of decay and a lost cattle industry. Our challenge was to build something vibrant that flagged a different story. There was a chance to give substance to an observation author C.S. Lewis had made about history. 'Humanity does not pass through phases as a train passes through stations: being alive, it has the privilege of always moving, but never leaving anything behind.'[50]

5

LOOKING FORWARD, LOOKING BACK

Museum-making in regional Australia is based on a deep attachment to place and it is an expression of community self-belief. It is not just about celebrating the achievements of the past, but believing in the future.[51]

Kylie Winkworth

Broken Hill's famous 'Vegemite Artist' Peter Brown painted a picture for me depicting a bush yarn I once told to a rowdy pub audience in Bourke. Like every good tall story, its success depended on keeping the half-cut audience, half-convinced that it might be half-true. So, I had them visualising me astride a bolting 'sheemu' (a cross between an emu and a sheep), hanging on grimly as I headed west into the red country at an unbelievable speed. Its credibility swung on my experience of arriving in town as a city-bred bloke and trying to match it with locals on the lookout to take me down.

It was a bit of nonsense really, but the painting hangs on my office wall as a sort of milestone on my journey as a storyteller – making the locals laugh with me became a moment of heart connection with a more closed community. I wasn't taking myself too seriously. I was one of them. Linguist friends have told me that the critical moment in language learning is when you begin to think in the language you are trying to master. You no longer have to prop and search for the right word or phrase – the dialect has become native to you. So as I spun my yarn that night I knew I was speaking the local lingo – we were communing.

Living in the backcountry also taught me a non-verbal language. I'd call it bush-sense. It's a kind of alertness to all the signs around you. I learned to open my eyes, watch the skies, read the country, understand the wildlife, feel the coming changes of weather, and in particular, to take note of landmarks. Now, wherever I am in Australia, it's natural for me to look up at the night sky and take my bearings from the stars, particularly the Southern Cross. I've wondered if it's the reassurance of knowing where you're placed in the larger scheme of things, that profound longing in the human race to feel you're playing a part in a deeper narrative.

There's a vivid story that has stuck in my mind. In February 1937, dairy farmer Bernard O'Reilly, searching for two days without a compass or a map, located survivors from a plane that had crashed and burnt in impenetrable rainforest near the Lamington Plateau in South West Queensland. His herculean effort went down in Australian folklore as among its greatest feats of bushmanship. Bernard passed a particular navigational skill on to his children – it is crucial to train yourself to be observant. His daughter recalled, 'He taught us to turn around at key places so we'd remember them again. If you've been there before, you'll never forget them.'[52] For centuries, the Aboriginal people had developed their tribal song lines this way as mind-maps. The backward look informs your path forward and in this case, it saved two lives.

That's hard-won experience speaking and I've taken it on board as an essential life skill.

Two accomplished storytellers came to Bourke and promoted that kind of binocular vision – looking forward by taking an intelligent look back. The first was Peter Kenyon, whose bright blue eyes twinkled under bushy eyebrows as he recounted his experiences of helping hundreds of small towns across the globe to rejuvenate themselves. He lived out his watchword, 'The world is not made up of atoms, but of stories.'[53] His strategy was simple – to inspire vision with examples from the past. I watched him rekindle hope in an audience jaded by years of social conflict and vandalism. He catalysed the imaginations of Bourke people by reciting accounts of communities who had transformed themselves by realising their assets rather than being weighed down by their deficits.

Peter's story of a remarkable 'dunny-led economic recovery' springs to mind. He told of the perishing town that captured the traffic flowing from one large centre to another by building a state-of-the-art toilet block. Or the folk that successfully marketed themselves as 'the ugliest town in Australia – selling ugly petrol, ugly hamburgers, and Australia's Most Ugly Town T-shirts! By creating a narrative arc with his rousing yarns, he awakened self-belief and I watched his colourful rehearsal ignite optimism and help locals to look beyond the levee-bank that circled Bourke like a fortress wall. It was a masterful performance – we learnt a lot.

Peter was a kind of troubadour – a wandering minstrel trafficking in hopeful yarns. He urged people to familiarise themselves with the landmarks in their own topography as a way of navigating for the future. His infectious enthusiasm reinforced my conviction that the recovery of local memory could help restore a community.[54] He opened my eyes to see that it had the potential to generate the kind of social capital that would strengthen civic life, and re-energise the economy. It could create the pre-conditions for better schools, safer streets, improved health and most importantly, for spiritual renewal.

In conversation, I discovered Peter's roots were in the evangelical wing of the Christian world and that this fuelled his drive to generate positive change in neglected communities. The greater part of his work was simply awakening people to the God-given potential of the place in which they were living. To a large extent, they were the masters of their own destiny. Realise that the cavalry is not coming to the rescue – don't expect miraculous intervention by an outside group. Experience had taught him that vision had to be given impetus by the community's passion for its own place. It needed leaders who could articulate the dream and a team who could bring it home.

Brad Baker's specialty was making artefacts talk. As the Exhibition Manager for Sydney's highly interactive Powerhouse Museum, he had seen how it could influence, challenge, and inspire people of all ages to act on big issues and become more informed participants in a globalised world. Like Peter, he was a campaigner for looking backwards to develop a clearer vision of the future.

In the Port of Bourke Hotel one night, he triggered an idea in my mind with an audio-visual demonstrating how an abstract subject could be brought to life. A designer had been challenged to find a way of engaging his audience on the topic of mathematics. He did this by showing the range of innovations it had driven over time – incredible architecture, navigation instruments that mastered oceans and opened up continents, telescopes powerful enough to reach for the stars, and computers that created information super-highways. An interactive game based on multiplication made this non-concrete world tangible and entertaining. This demonstration of leading people from the known to the unknown even fired the imagination of a maths dyslexic like me!

I cornered Brad afterwards and discovered that he, like me, was shaped by activists wanting to give Jesus' message an authentic Australian voice. I confess I harangued him. "That's the primary task confronting the Christian faith right now. People are daunted by the swampy ground they feel they have to cross to begin a journey of faith. Too much abstract talk leaves them cold. We need to create a place filled with stories familiar to them as solid stepping-stones to the unfamiliar." The storyteller in Brad agreed and together we set out on a path to design the kind of authentic environment that would encourage this search.

In this way, backcountry Bourke became the testing ground for a larger dream – but that's a later story.

"People are fascinated by people" was Brad's designer's mantra. He assured us that Bourke's strong company of characters would readily animate a museum. His experience confirmed that this was the vehicle to transport Alan and Bill's dry volumes of history into a vibrant, accessible format that would be a working asset for the town. He insisted that if it was going to draw coastal Australians over the Great Dividing Range, it had to be a state-of-the-art facility – something exceptional.

He confirmed my thinking that Bourke was in a strategic position to be an interpreter of *the Outback*. This North-West corner of the State had its own collection of heroes and villains, adventure and exploitation, strange myths and tragic tales, which were a metaphor for all Australia. Even though I was city-bred, instinct told me that these stories were mine too. So a core group of us began to believe we could make this hidden chapter of Australia's story visible to a wider audience.

At the time, Bourke had hunkered down into something of a siege mentality. Defensive thinking can absorb energy and narrow focus. Some cynics declared talk of building something to articulate local stories looked like tuning up the orchestra on the deck of the stricken *Titanic*. There was a derisive chorus of "A sheer waste of time and money!" and "It'll never happen!" and "Solve the social problems first!" But there were front-foot thinkers who could see that sinking a bore deep into Bourke's hidden reserve of stories would bring a life-giving resource to the surface that could restore shrivelled hopes.

I once travelled from Cobar to the tiny village of Wanaaring with a flying padre, chatting amicably all the way. Conversation came to an abrupt halt, when, as dusk spread across the featureless plains beneath us, the pilot announced, "I'm not sure where we are!" Circling wide, he spotted the name *Urisino*, written large on the homestead roof, then he got his bearings and we landed at our destination right on dark. Reviewing his log, he found that being one degree out in his calculations had taken us 50 km off course. On top of this, he had failed to check for landmarks along the way. Minor navigational errors had compounded into a dangerous situation.

Looking back would have assured our path forward.

Jack Buster loved his blue and silver Tiger Moth and took every opportunity to throw us around the skies above Darling Farms. Complete with a leather flying helmet and aviator goggles, he'd loop-the-loop and stall turn until you were dizzy. It was a metaphor for the way he approached life. Nothing daunted him. As a pilot, he understood the importance of training people to keep their eyes out for landmarks to help stay on track. As a man with his finger on the pulse of current events, he saw the same need for Australians to check their national bearings and not fly blind.

This energetic Californian had a genuine affection for his adopted country, and he was passionate about history. So when the curve towards building an exhibition centre for Bourke began to steepen, he handed me Ken Burns' highly acclaimed documentary series on the American West, with one of his blunt directives, "Paul, you've got to do this for Australia!" Who was he kidding about attempting such a project? Burns had covered 160,000 km, conducted 72 interviews, and filmed 250 hours of footage for his seven-part series. I felt I was sitting in the front cockpit of the plunging Tiger Moth again!

It's an uncomfortable thing to have a visionary friend with such brash faith. Nevertheless, Jack was challenging me to reach for the sky, and before long, Robyn and I found ourselves on the way to the USA, where we barnstormed 28 museums in 29 days to learn how they went about the business of animating their stories. We hopped East to West across a dozen states from Washington DC to Los Angeles. First, we tackled the Smithsonian and then absorbed what we could on the Holocaust, Baseball, Pioneers, Mormons, Yellowstone National Park, Buffalo Bill, Plains Indians, Guns, Art – you name it.

We cut a swathe through American history in record time!

The sharpest impact for me came in the backwoods of New Hampshire from meeting historians Dayton Duncan and Geoff Ward at the Florentine Films Studio.

These were the men who had crafted the scripts for *The West* series. "Zero in on good first-person stories that evoke emotion," they told me. "We believe that history is biography. Historians make so much interesting material boring. People like stories, not lectures. We aim to examine the macrocosm through the microcosm to tell the big story through the little story. We use the chronological approach so that the audience can watch things happen in conjunction – let things bump into each other, accidentally or fortuitously."[55] This strategy became their signature. They created epic documentaries by simply allowing the troupe of characters from the past to speak for themselves through diaries, photos, and letters.

Geoff Ward said something that gelled with me. He explained that while the American West was a unique part of the country, it was also a symbol for the whole nation. 'With all its heroism and inequity, exploitation and adventure, sober realities and bright myths, it is the story of us all.'[56] Not only did it sound like our corner of the world, it also sounded exactly like the Bible to me!

While introducing Cornerstone students to the misadventures, half-attempts at goodness, comprehensive failures, and exhilarating exploits in the biblical narrative, it became clear that it had supplied markers for succeeding generations in Israel to look back to find their bearings for their spiritual journey. What was novel about this tangled chronicle was that it offered a path not just for Israel but for every nation on earth. For me, that added another dynamic to the storytelling business.

Israel's story offered a way out, a way forward, a way home.

Ken Burns himself took this a step further, pointing to the enchantment that canny storytelling generates. Larger understanding comes into focus as small stories are painted into a landscape on a wider canvas. This master storyteller offered me a keen insight into the craft.

> The secret of great storytelling is 'one plus one = three'. We live in
> a rational world where we are absolutely certain that 'one plus one
> = two'. And it does! But the things that matter most to us – some

people call it love, some people call it reason, some people call it God – is that other thing where the whole is greater than the sum of the parts... and that's the three! I think we do coalesce around stories that seem transcendent... Truth is the by-product of the best of our stories.[57]

I returned to Australia with a swag of tools to handle the brief of telling the Bourke story. I could see how minor events could take on major significance if viewed from a national perspective. For example, when the young, relatively unknown author Henry Lawson arrived in Bourke in 1892, he found its streets and pubs alive with radicals from the Shearers' Union. He was recruited as the voice of working men made desperate by the economic depression, and he fanned the flame of violent protest across the country.

> So we must fly a rebel flag
> As others did before us,
> And we must sing a rebel song
> And join in rebel chorus.
> We'll make the tyrants feel the sting
> O' those that they would throttle;
> They needn't say the fault is ours,
> If blood should stain the wattle.[58]

When I interviewed Henry's biographer Colin Roderick on radio, he confirmed that Bourke was the lens through which the young author viewed the Outback. Tramping long, waterless miles, carrying his swag from shed to shed looking for work, he met and immortalised the colourful characters that walked into the hearts of Australians everywhere, when his stories were syndicated through the pages of *The Bulletin*. As the colonies wrestled their way to nationhood, here was someone speaking with a voice they warmed to. Canadian professor of Literature Greg Bryan, a man who has given a lifetime to studying Henry Lawson's works, framed a succinct phrase, 'Henry gave Australians their own Mother Country.'[59]

Now when I held the dog-eared volumes of Bourke history that my friends had laboured over, they leapt to life in my hands. By tracking Lawson's meanderings, I could reveal that the apostle who popularised the secular gospel of 'Mateship' in Australia drew much of his sermon material from the wide country West of the Darling. He had mastered the art of telling the big story through the little story.

What intrigued me was that Henry knew he'd experienced a camaraderie that transcended the town itself. Looking back at Bourke from the other side of Federation, Australia's greatest bush yarn spinner made an extraordinary gesture.

> *And could I roll the summers back,*
> *Or bring the dead time on again,*
> *Or from the grave and world-wide track*
> *Bring back to Bourke the vanished men,*
> *With mind content I'd go to sleep*
> *And leave those mates to judge me true,*
> *And leave my name to Bourke to keep,*
> *The Bourke of Ninety-one and two.*[60]

So, why do I still get the feeling of 'one plus one equals three' when I recite his poems to wayfarers standing outside the Carriers Arms Hotel where he drank with his mates or on the board of Toorale Station woolshed where he toiled as a roustabout? Maybe it's what author Miles Franklin said about him. 'Henry Lawson gave us this kingdom for our own and wove it so we could fold it around us with the comfort of a blanket.'[61]

Tiny particles of a story can become significant markers on a shared journey. They can ignite feelings that draw us together and tell us who we are.

Like many Australians, I had inherited a cringe when comparing our history to that of the American West that's been told over and over in technicolour. But I returned from the USA with the quiet conviction that we should develop a top-class piece of apparatus in tiny outback Bourke because we had authentic, first-rate stories to tell.

The closer I looked, the more I realised that much of the material I was handling was grist for the national mill. We had no reason to shrink. An inner voice told me that all these could be made part of a cure for the spreading cultural dementia in Australia.

Ken Burns had said we coalesce around stories that seem transcendent. That's what fired me about the visionary men and women who had lived out lives of faith in our own West. None of them were perfect, but practical saints like Mother Mary McKillop, and Mother Theresa of Calcutta had mobilised women to care for children and outcasts. The heroic efforts of Rev John Flynn and Rev Stanley Drummond conquered the daunting isolation of the Outback. They spread a mantle of safety across the continent with airborne nurses and doctors. Energetic entrepreneur Samuel McCaughey used irrigation and sheep industry to further education, churches and hospitals across the nation.

Then there were the young Bush Brothers who journeyed from the comfort of Oxford University to push old T Model Fords through mud and sand hills, bringing pastoral care to isolated families. Civil rights activists Bill Ferguson, Bill Reid, Mark Davidson and Jimmy Barker carried the concerns of the oppressed indigenous population into the consciousness of the cities and the parliaments. Bush nurses brought security to isolated families. They drove and maintained ambulances, staffed lonely hospitals and conducted baby clinics in railroad cars.

Looking back on his droving days around Bourke, from the far-away Scottish Borders, stockman/poet Will Ogilvie shaped a hymn of praise celebrating the tenacity of the people with whom he'd rubbed shoulders.

> *Though poets have not yet sung you*
> *Nor writers your true worth told,*
> *I, who have wrought among you,*
> *I know you for Hearts of Gold!*[62]

I knew that by recovering the stories of these unsung heroes, we were doing something more than just being sentimental. Among the travellers I had guided, I found some who readily reached for stories to help them deal with questions of meaning, experiences of suffering and doubts about God. There was a call for the kind of stories that could supply wise counsel and inspire hope.

After nearly twenty years, the Back O' Bourke Exhibition Centre was officially opened in 2009. My friend Jodi has engaged visitors there with stories of her own. Pausing in front of a sepia photo of a family posed outside a rough camp somewhere West of Bourke in the 1800's, she puts herself in the position of the isolated mother raising kids a long way from anywhere. "That's my experience," she tells them. Tears well in her eyes as she recounts the serious accidents and chronic health problems that saw her boys rushed to hospitals by the Flying Doctor air-ambulance. Listeners are moved as she explains the sheer relief for a mother having that kind of emergency help, but above and beyond that, she has vibrant faith in God. She doesn't preach, she simply tells an authentic story and empathy does the rest.

One-plus-one-equals three.

The cluster of buildings alongside the town levee bank that make up the Back O' Bourke Exhibition Centre grew out of stories like hers. It sits under sweeping sails that glow at night. A team of locals joined with architects to design a complex that follows the meanders of an internal river. The narratives were arranged to lead visitors on a journey back into Bourke's past and give them room to graze freely on episodes that grab their attention. The displays cover moments where both people and the environment have soared to heights and crashed to lows.

These create spaces for reflection, remorse, celebration and renewal.

It's this steady backward look at the terrain already travelled which helps get bearings in the present. When writing the scripts for the displays, I felt poet Judith Wright's challenge to 'write no longer as transplanted Europeans, nor as rootless men who reject their past and put their hopes in the future, but as men with a present to be lived in and a past to nourish.'[63] I think she pinned it perfectly right there – *the need to nourish the past.*

Marshall McLuhan, the communications guru of my university years, warned us would-be educators to be careful of 'rear-view mirror syndrome' when preparing new generations for the future.[64] Fair enough – no point in being fixated nostalgically on a distant past. But I've learned that it is equally true in historical terms that absorption with the next turn in the road can rob us of wisdom already gained on the journey. Alertness to past misadventure can inform the eye when fresh opportunities for exploration offer themselves. Aboriginal trackers with long experience in reading footprints planted on the bush floor have always been prized members of outback communities when it comes to rescuing lost people.

We need forensic storytellers like that who can interpret the past with an eye to the future.

The preservation of the cultural DNA of nations has been given renewed impetus in recent days. Hostile forces in countries around the world have systematically vandalised the cultural sites of their enemies. The International Coalition of Sites of Conscience guides the strategic growth of over 300 museums, historic sites, and memory initiatives in 65 countries. It trains people to go beyond merely preserving the past. They want to transform these sanctuaries into dynamic spaces that promote action on pressing human rights and social justice struggles. They've seized on the transformative power of story.[65]

I believe our challenge in Australia is to counter vandalism of another kind – people deliberately severing present generations from their Christian roots. It is not solely a religious question but a matter of enabling the honest looking back at our foundational stories, which will foster intelligent progress into the future.

Returning to the strong sinews of faith I had found woven into Bourke's story, I reasoned that this must be true in every community across the nation. I had become convinced that the windstorm of negativity, weathering away at these markers in

Australia, needed to be countered by energetic storytelling that would unearth the spiritual topography strongly linked to that of first-century Galilee.

My conviction grew that this experience of setting story to work could be repeated at a macro-level in Canberra. There was reason to believe that men and women who had fostered the spiritual life of Australia had earned the right to speak on the national stage under spotlights. This included indigenous Christians who assured me their cultures had been built around a long-held belief in a Creator that fitted naturally with the meta-narrative they discovered in the Bible. They could provide tested experiences and accrued wisdom, which could shed light on present crises like the rising suicide rate and the breakup of families.

I'm sure I've been something of an irritation at times to those who know me, with my personal mission to resurrect stories of faith from the past. I pester people with the idea of creating places where the stories of our ancestors are blended with current intelligence as a way of breathing fresh spiritual life into Australia. It seems to me we need help in checking our bearings carefully when it comes to setting a course in our 21st century.

Looking back, I can see the markers, map the turning points, and track the twists and turns in the terrain that shaped my travelogue. My story is only one of billions, but I have had guides along the way who have shown me that my tiny particle of story can find meaning in the ultimate Big History that I believe God is writing every minute of the day on our planet. My mentors are an assorted bunch, believers and seekers in the tradition of the prophets of Israel, not afraid to take a long look back, astute at reading the signs of the times, and brave enough to make forecasts about the future.

Visionaries like this have fired my dream of training a band of dedicated trackers like Bernard O'Reilly, who can help new generations steer a sure course under the Southern Cross.

6

VOICES FROM THE WILDERNESS

Australia needs to be summoned to a larger destiny. The selfishness needs to be challenged by the idealism of Jesus. The fact of God needs to be placed down afresh amid the life of our people.[66]

Rev Sir Allan Walker

Her name was Consuelo Orozco de Orozco. She had the sweetest, most serene countenance I can ever remember seeing. She was a descendant of the fierce Aztecs in Mexico. Perhaps that is why, whenever I was about to preach in our church in Bourke, she would step up with her composed face shining, look me in the eye, and say in a quiet but firm voice, "Habla con denuedo Pablo" – speak with boldness Paul! She was rebooting the 2000-year-old request of my namesake, Paul of Tarsus, who asked friends in Ephesus to pray that he would be fearless in making the story of Jesus plain to the Roman world. Could that saintly senora have discerned that this Pablo was not particularly brave – just a pale gringo in need of some serious Mexican back up?! Strong, praying women like that have written an unseen back-story to Australian history.

She urged me on to be a storyteller with backbone.

I succeeded in flying under the radar at school. I think belonging to a small conservative church had something to do with me perfecting a low profile, and being a member of the Christian Fellowship at a boys' school didn't earn street-cred where so much hung on sporting success. I struggled to make any serious impact on the macho culture of our suburban High School at Epping. On the other hand, the somewhat cloistered off-campus world I grew up in fostered a closet activist in me.

My parents were unashamed about their faith, and I had a front-row seat to watch it tested through some tough times. My Dad, Allan, lost his job as a metallurgist, and there were a few years working other positions before he could return to his chosen profession. It was a hard blow and made for lean financial times, but I remember that whenever he faced a challenge, he'd remind us of Jesus' call to Peter that brought a miraculous haul of fish. "Push your boat out into the deep and throw your net on the other side!" Year after year, I watched my father choose the unsafe option as a reflex of faith. I witnessed Jeanie, my mother – a gentle palliative care nurse – walk the valley of the shadow with several close friends. She stamped some powerful impressions of faith on my memory as I watched her cope with her own painful injuries from a serious car accident.

Together, my parents pastored a large flock of needy people, and our home was often a healing sanctuary for wounded souls. Dad loved running camps, and contrary to everything natural in her about public speaking, my mother trained herself as a mobiliser of women. She, too, prayed for me as countless mothers have for their sons. I have never recalled my parents shirking opportunities to serve people in our neighbourhood or speak about Jesus. They had a habit of pushing out beyond their comfort zone – even in retirement, they volunteered to run a large aged-care facility. My parents were our staunchest supporters when Robyn and I left the security of Sydney and professional employment to launch out on our own adventure of faith in Bourke. They taught us not to flinch in putting our beliefs to the test.

So, when I sort through the bits and pieces of my growing years, I discover a collection of trust-exploits – some exhilarating, some naïve, some very moving, many plain ordinary – unrehearsed, but mostly real. The little church my parents helped plant flourished from their risk-taking, and from early teenage years we were encouraged to have a go at all kinds of music, public speaking, running youth groups and camps. We were exposed to many intelligent Christian activists whose stories were attractive and authentic. We heard from articulate women like Jean Raddon and Alice Chambers. Howard Martin, the Travelling Secretary for Scripture Union, lived with us for two years. He later became a Professor of Theatre in the USA. Doctors, lawyers, businessmen and a stream of missionaries from countries around the world sat at our dinner table. Of course, there were predictable patches of boredom and rebellion, but I can't argue that it was a dull, restrictive or hypocritical place to grow up.

By the late 60's, I was riffing in a rock band that seriously challenged both the older generation's hearing and the back wall of the church hall. But those gracious souls tolerated the high decibel level – often with a pained expression I recall! They knew that we were trying to translate our fledgling faith into the language of our generation. Somehow this random collection of early experiences lit a flame, which has burned in me since – a kind of restlessness that won't settle for a halfway faith.

A dog-eared card index sat up on my desk and looked at me as I was preparing to write this chapter. Shuffling through it was like entering a time warp – it was a kind of personal manifesto made up of random quotes from books, notes from lectures I've listened to, clippings from newspapers and magazines, plus talks I've given. I found myself walking through a long gallery listening to the voices of my heroes – realising with gratitude that these had been my companions on a fifty-year journey and gifted me a worldview to live by.

As those familiar cadences echoed out of my past, it dawned on me they were almost all activists – men and women of courage who, like my Mexican prayer-warrior friend, had come alongside a faltering young Australian and put muscle and sinew into his faith. Their life stories had steadily seeped into mine, reminding me that in reality, we are all composed of a myriad of story fragments not of our own making.

I borrowed the card index idea from my friend Laurie. He was an activist on university campuses and used it to collect and memorise strong statements he could wield when debating opponents of Christianity in the public square. For example, he electrified a group of us in Sydney by telling us the story of some students he met on a radical university in Mexico City in the early 70's. They got so excited about the pieces of evidence for the Christian case he had taught them that they ventured out to speak in a space where students had been shot in recent days by government soldiers. They were in full flight when a young Marxist stepped up and screamed in the face of the speaker, "Hypocrite! If what you Christians are saying about Jesus is true, then why haven't you told us this before? Don't you know the truth is urgent!"

Laurie used that story to stab a bunch of us Aussie students awake. At that time, my generation was walking away from traditional Christian faith and we felt the challenge to make the truth urgent in ways that grabbed their attention.

That's still the background music to my life.

Seeing people prompted to action by stirring stories and sharp-edged quotes prompted me to create my own cache. Wilfrid Grenfell, the doctor who pioneered medicine in the Arctic regions of Labrador, told of the transformation in his life when a preacher got him to see Jesus as the living leader you would want to serve with your very best. 'Religion, as the speaker put it, was chivalry, not an insurance ticket. Life was a field of honour calling for courage to face it, not a tragedy to escape from. What Christ called for was reasonable service, the service of our reason – but real hard service anyway.'[67]

Now here was a stirring call to galvanise the worldview I had taken for granted growing up! Passive acceptance was never going to prove to me a story big enough to live by. On closer examination, I realised the long Biblical narrative that had attracted me since childhood was in large part a logbook of people taking extraordinary gambles. It said loud and clear that faith was never a soft option.

From 'over the ditch' in New Zealand, I heard the voice of visionary author Winkie Pratney calling young people across the globe to roll up their sleeves and put their faith to work. One phrase of his penetrated like a shard of shrapnel. 'The world has never been moved by the mildly interested… If you want to move your world you must be prepared to pay the high cost of discipleship.'[68] From my reading of history, I knew he was right when he said the people who change things are the non-conformists who protest, prod, and probe out the things that hinder progress.

I felt a long way from being the firebrand type who hurled himself at the barricades. Still, something my rather sober university tutor wrote in an academic reference, made me square my shoulders a bit. 'Mr Roe has enough steel in his soul to succeed in what he does, though not necessarily in materialistic terms.' I could only recall the bruising I took from his Faculty superior, Professor Crowley – perhaps Dr Hudson saw that and wanted to put fresh heart into me. If so, I owe him a debt.

Another fortifying fragment was given to me by Dr Klaus Bockmuehl, a German professor at Regent College. One day after class, he presented me with a book examining the impact of Frank Buchman, the pioneer of the Moral Rearmament Movement. After watching the church in Germany gutted by liberal theology and bullied into silence by the Nazis, he had resolved to respond only to what he heard by daily listening to God.

I wasn't his star pupil – I struggled in his theology class. Some intuition must have prompted him to introduce me to this group who had set themselves to rekindle the faith of Europeans brutalised by war. It was steel forged in a crisis. Buchman made a call for a new approach to overcoming the numbness of the times. 'The greatest enemies of Christianity are so-called Christians who pay lip service. The Apostles were an offence to the world. Respectable Christianity is not… God must be made attractive. Your young men must become the prophets of a new age.'[69] His simple creed resonated deep inside me. I couldn't settle to rewarming old methods in my era where the world was busy restructuring itself yet again. The prayerful Klaus Bockmuehl was convinced of the same and I realise his gift had been chosen to spur me on.

Some of Buchman's trainees had already seized my imagination. They had found a familiar place in the centre of my thinking. Peter Howard, a British journalist and one-time captain of the national Rugby team, made a rousing call. 'I think a Christian revolutionary is meant to revolutionise the situation he is in. Every non-Christian in the world should be saying, "What are the Christians… thinking about now? What is their next move? What are they doing? What are they saying?" We ought to be the focus of attention at this time of crisis instead of being a pattern of disunity and ineffectiveness.'[70] Those words jagged my soul when I was a young student in the radical late sixties. I'd never heard this bold idea of Christians being in the forefront of change. Conventional church life had given me the impression that our job was to be conservators of the status quo.

The man who had turned Howard from being a cynical atheist joined him in my hall of voices. Journalist Garth Lean was the author of biographies of Christian activists John Wesley and William Wilberforce, men who had stood up for their beliefs under a hailstorm of hostile opposition. He voiced the opinion that Christians were too readily bluffed into a defensive posture. Boldness was called for. He challenged me to think hard about ways to intrigue the non-aligned and outmanoeuvre the opposition. He was adamant that nothing short of a Christian counter-attack would do.[71] The creation of Cornerstone in Bourke was provoked in part by this call to front foot thinking.[72]

Then a voice with an Australian twang cut in. The controversial Methodist broadcaster, founder of Lifeline, and constant social activist, Rev Alan Walker, summed up what I felt. 'Australia needs to be summoned to a larger destiny. The selfishness needs to be challenged by the idealism of Jesus. The fact of God needs to be placed down afresh amid the life of our people.'[73] My generation was being stirred by home-grown prophets like John Smith and Mal Garvin[74] who joined their voices with Alan Walker's, asking, "Advance Australia Where?"[75]

My card index soon pulsed with demands large enough to extend whatever gifts I had to the maximum. These influencers weren't armchair philosophers but combatants who had responded heart and soul to the call of Jesus to bring his story to the world. My catalogue of campaigners became creased and worn with use when speaking to my generation and the next. This habit of building the life stories of men and women of character into my inner sanctuary resourced my storytelling. Heroes I had never met loaned me their courage and put backbone into my faith. I told their tale to others, and I've since heard them passing it on in turn to new generations.

I learned that a good story is infectious and that a story of goodness can go viral.

These were the accents that stirred my blood as Robyn and I joined Laurie and Elvira to train young men and women to make Jesus' story visible and vibrant in our own time. We called our mission community 'Cornerstone', and we wanted it to be a foundation on which to build a force for change in Australia. I must admit I enjoyed the irony of working backwards from 'the uttermost part of the earth' in Bourke! Being over the horizon from Australia's population centres made us a bit of a mystery as far as mainstream theological education went and gave us a bit of a maverick reputation. I mean seriously – a Christian training centre that looked more like a set from a Western cowboy movie?

More than anything, we wanted to write an authentic Australian chapter into the grand story we knew God was unfolding all around the world. We were determined to transform rousing rhetoric and stirring phrases into life-deep changes won by doing some hard yards. We wanted these hungry hearted young people to leave with life messages that would make them game changers wherever they went and in whatever they did.

In a very real way, we wanted to become voices from the wilderness.

We set ourselves to be 'radical' in the original sense of the word – taking people back to the roots of the Christian story. Young people would walk in the gate at Pera Bore after a bone-jarring drive down corrugated Wanaaring Rd and stare bewildered at our ramshackle kibbutz style campus, sitting naked in the saltbush on the red country. Any romantic ideas they had evaporated in the January heat. Some came clutching tightly to a faith they had learned by rote like maths times-tables, others were nursing hurts from confused church experiences, some more bold types were looking for an adventure. The timid, the brash, the naïve, the sincere, the hopeful, the lost, the seeking, the idealists – we embraced them all. As we threw ourselves into the mix with each new group, we told them the year at Bourke would be like stripping a motor down to its component parts so that you understood its workings and then rebuilding it piece by piece.

The disassembling task could be unnerving. Pulling slap-dash worldview stories apart left bits all over the floor. Rebuilding workable models was painful and tedious at times. The daily schedule of farm work, serious study, and life in community meant there was nowhere to hide – a lot of blood, sweat, and tears went into the business of becoming real. But watching young men and women persist in piecing together a road-tested faith-narrative was very satisfying – even if it was rough around the edges. Authentic links were forged between the world of the Bible and their lives in 20th century Australia.

Central to the whole thing was the story of Jesus, who seized the task of bringing about worldwide change with the most unpromising advertising slogan in history, 'Take up a cross and follow me.' For many, the undiscovered Biblical narrative came to life daily – "like rewiring an old house" as somebody has put it. Colourful events filled our days in Bourke – every student left with a swag of memories. The fresh hewing out of those stories from raw timber fashioned the joists and rafters that built character in us all.[76]

I was poised to ask myself the question, "OK Paul, after reciting all that high-flown stuff that stirred your young blood – what really changed in the intervening years?" when my phone lit up with a call from a Pera Bore veteran from 30 years ago. It was a heartening conversation because my friend didn't just want to reminisce but to affirm that the learning experiences in our rough camp had readied him to weather many testing times. Renewed contacts like these encourage me.

Putting steel into the soul of another fellow traveller is a great reward.

My weathered card file looks pretty meagre and inoffensive sitting on the desk in front of me. Most of those voices that had awakened me to action are silent now. Lapsed atheists and converted cynics like G.K. Chesterton, C.S. Lewis. Douglas Hyde and Malcolm Muggeridge were among the most eloquent. Leading social activists like Mahatma Ghandi, Martin Luther King, Nelson Mandela and Desmond Tutu lifted my spirits by declaring Jesus their inspiration. Women like Elizabeth Fry, Florence Nightingale, Caroline Chisolm, Corrie ten Boom, and Catherine Hamlin had changed the world with their no-nonsense Christianity. These visionaries had gifted me hopeful stories and tuned my ears to listen for the voice of present day prophets summoning the faithful to mobilise.

That original wild man from the desert, John the Baptist, heralded his arrival as 'a voice crying in the wilderness, "Prepare the way of the Lord!"' The strident accents of these modern seers come from unexpected quarters, too, ringing out across the global village. John had demanded that his generation should repent. The Greek word 'metanoia' means to face the truth and change your way of thinking. It's been a valid call for every generation since then.

Historian Tom Holland has told the story of the ancient world to 21st century audiences. Now he is one of a number camped outside the church, calling for a halt to the ruthless removal of the Christian narrative from our collective memory. He recently jarred his secular audience by presenting a comprehensive case showing that Western culture was shaped by people with a robust commitment to the life and teachings of Jesus. He argues that the popular myth fostered by the Enlightenment thinkers that Science and Reason alone would lead us to the sunny uplands of Freedom, is looking increasingly threadbare as a story to live by.[77]

My 60's cohort had pretty much trampled the Christian chrysalis that had incubated us, but it gradually dawned that it was quite another thing to grow the wings to make a secular worldview fly. The wave of optimism that welcomed the new millennium was surfed by post-modern thinkers teaching the new generations they could live without any overarching story. In fact, they could be at ease with a multiplying range of incoherent narratives fashioned to suit their individual preferences. In a wide range of fashion colours, cheap life maps and dodgy moral compasses were freely available on eBay.

"Whatever…" doesn't guarantee a safe and happy passage through life.

Picture 5000 Perth teenagers swarming a tiny seaside town on 'Schoolies Week', loaded with alcohol and determined to celebrate the climax of their education. It's 2005 in an anxious post 9/11 world. Some parents had given their children $1000 and a packet of condoms and told them not to get into trouble. I saw a boy king-hit from behind. He ended up brain-dead. Predators raped several girls over the course of the week. Police on horseback did their best, but a riot still broke out, and shops were trashed. A friend observed, "This is like watching a tribe without elders!" When I asked some earnest young people what story they were living by? "Just believe whatever you think is true," they told me as I sat among them trying to get inside their world. I felt Manning Clark's stark prediction about Australia becoming a 'Kingdom of Nothingness' was happening right before my eyes.

It still is.

Returning through Perth, I chanced on a church advertising a lunchtime talk by popular social commentator Hugh Mackay. I was stunned as I watched him stand under a large crucifix announcing himself an unbeliever and proceeding to expound the humanist hope that morality would arise spontaneously out of the community. It was brave of him, I suppose, but his words rang hollow in the face of the days of chaos I had just witnessed. The fact was that the volunteers operating the casualty stations caring for those schoolies were mostly Christians who hadn't bought into his myth that there was no larger guiding story. So they weren't afraid to get down and dirty, quietly marching to the beat of an unseen drum.

There was something sad about that scene in the cathedral – the unbeliever's voice resonating off the solid stone, which stood as a witness to men and women who had lived lives of faith. But other thoughtful voices are reigniting the challenge I felt 50 years ago. For example, Foreign Editor for *The Australian,* Greg Sheridan, noting the rapid drain of people from the churches in recent times, has confronted Christians with the reality that they are now relegated to the wilderness.

The problem for the churches he sees is a lack of situational awareness – the nous to know that they are now a minority and no longer have their hands on the levers of power. Generations X, Y, Z, and Alpha, muffled by earphones, are staring into screens at a virtual world that doesn't include any Christian storylines. Greg Sheridan echoes the radical voices of my youth:

> Use your minority status skilfully
> Go on the front foot
> Become a bold sub-group
> Be ready to create controversy.

He argues, 'A minority is a guerrilla force and can choose its targets.'[78]

The gospels of Matthew, Mark, Luke and John record the most effective example of this in history.

Voices from unlikely places have shifted the world.

It took me a while, but eventually, I learnt important things from leaders of the minority group with the longest experience of guerrilla tactics in Australia – the indigenous community. The names Cooper, Ferguson, and Nicholls would mean nothing to most Australians. For a long time, I was the same, and it amazed me when I discovered that the pioneers of the civil rights movement in this country half a century ago were almost all humble men and women with bold faith. They were authentic voices from the Australian wilderness. They were following the world's greatest activist – a carpenter from backcountry Nazareth, who had audaciously pronounced that it was the meek who would inherit the earth.

Now that's a likely story!

7

SHARED SONG-LINES

*The path to Australia's future passes through its past. That past is **my** past. It is in the owning of our past failures that I find the way to our true national good, to the spiritual transformation we long for. But I need to be willing to see the whole truth first. See it, feel it and own it.*[79]

Graeme Cordiner

Racism came with the culture at school in the 60's. To my shame, derogatory words like 'Wops', 'Wogs', and 'Dagos' were part of our white middle-class slang, often prefaced by the descriptor 'greasy'. Down the main street, you expected to hear their parent's strangled English in the milk bar, fruit shop, or while ordering your fish and chips. They followed ethnic soccer teams like Apia and Pan-Hellenic on the weekends. Our Monday morning heroes were St George or Parramatta Rugby League players.

Solidly Protestant Epping left these 'others' to worship in the Catholic or Orthodox churches. The mildly derisive description 'New Australian' neatly bundled all the swarthy people into a job lot and divided us into ghettos. Our schoolboy meanness towards them was received as part of our culture, and nobody seriously tried to show us anything different – that's just how it was. It wasn't until I began teaching in a high school of predominantly Greek and Italian boys that my prejudices were exposed for what they were.

Scrambling to teenage years in North Shore Sydney, I didn't meet any original Australians until, at about 18 years old, I showed two Aboriginal boys from a remote town in Western NSW around the city. We sat down on a seat on the Manly ferry, and a woman instantly stood up and walked away. These lads had grown up as fringe dwellers on a steady diet of rejection, and I can still recall my shock when they murmured, "She doesn't want to sit with us." It left a shadow on a fun day. It was a while before it dawned on me that **I** was in fact, a 'new Australian' with a lot to learn about the deep racial divide in my own country.

Arriving in Bourke plunged me into an Aboriginal community wrestling with the newly-won freedoms granted by the 1967 referendum and expanded by the Whitlam government of the early 70's. My distant Sydney upbringing had stifled the anguishing story of their struggle for recognition in their own country, and so I arrived in Ngemba territory in 1978 naïve and unprepared. If I'm honest, I started as something of the caricatured pith-helmeted white missionary coming to help the natives. Unconsciously, I felt alienated and distanced by the alcohol-fuelled instances of rowdy public behaviour and belligerence. I quickly formed the opinion they were the 'problem element' in town.

My initiation took place at the top of a steep flight of wooden steps in a rickety old building that looked like the set of a Clint Eastwood Western. Cornerstone ran a drop-in coffee shop there and, for several years, it was the lone option for the street kids who filled the upstairs rooms and wide veranda of *The Cocky's Joy* drop-in centre on Friday and Saturday nights. They turned it into a theatre with a fair amount of, 'Go ahead, make my day!' about it.

I learned to strum Slim Dusty songs, play endless games of cards, negotiate with drunks, placate police and relate to street-wise teenagers. It was a rough and ready setting that rubbed your nose in reality. Mostly, white kids told me they didn't come because of 'the Abo's', and those restless Aboriginal kids were constantly testing to see whether you really liked them. I soon realised many were too scared to go home and that our simple cafe was their sanctuary. They taught me some important lessons about myself.

What did I know of their story?

Nowadays, a cheerful face belonging to one of them will surprise me in the Dubbo shopping mall with the query, "Remember *The Cocky's Joy* brother? They were some of the best days of my life!" Visualising all the fights and mischief, I smile and think to myself, 'It wasn't always fun… but yeah, I'm glad I was there to listen and learn.' Now fresh chapters are being added because the story we are writing spans generations. We have met their children and grandchildren in RE classes in West Dubbo and watched their faces brighten when we hold up the beautiful indigenous artwork telling the ancient stories of the Bible in *Our Mob, God's Story*.[80] At last we were learning to speak their heart language.

One sweltering night at North Bourke, a few of us stood feeling very intimidated as the only white faces in a crowd of Aboriginal people angrily venting their feelings about the decades of degradation. Finally, one young man poured out his rage in verse that left no doubt about his contempt for the European invaders. As a boy, he had stood with his Dad Terry Doolan and his uncle Duncan Ferguson when they were preaching in Bourke's main street. Now Frank had chosen political activism as his gospel. The long history of injustice and despair drove him to look for radical answers to the hurt in his soul.

The passivity he saw in the churches to the plight of his people jarred with their talk of Christian love.

Murrawari elder Jimmy Barker opened my eyes to the kind of experience many of the native people had on the Government mission at Brewarrina earlier in the 20th century. They were more confused than hostile. Too often, the Christian message was delivered lovelessly.

> Many types of preachers came around to convert us...They did not try to teach us carefully and gently; there was no discussion, and we had to accept everything they told us. Our own religious beliefs were a subject of ridicule and we were told we were useless humans and must forget our Aboriginal religion...We were forced to attend all services – if we didn't, our rations were stopped. We were willing to accept Christianity, but few of the preachers set an example of kindness; it was confusing to both the old and the young people. The preachers knew nothing of our beliefs or religion. We had never worshipped an image or an idol, yet the evils of idolatry were drummed into us.[81]

It took some time for me to understand why there was so much anger and pain in the people I met daily in the place I had made my home. Frustration fuelled by alcohol scarred the streetscape. Men and women, their lives broken by years of living neglected at the 'Bottom End' of town or on the Reserve, drifted around the parks. The 'Back Lane Boys' gang harassed the streets, keeping one step ahead of the law by using a set of coded whistles, boasting, "Us blacks own the night."

Being on the receiving end was challenging, particularly when you felt you had tried to hear and help. I stood gritting my teeth in the police station as the Constable took down the details of my stolen and damaged car while telling me there would be no legal consequences. The teenage thieves and their parents laughed about it in the background. Both traditional tribal law and Western justice were rendered impotent. They were living in a no-man's land without a guiding story. Tragically, the mocking turned to mourning a few months later when some of the same children died in another stolen vehicle. I felt sadness and frustration and that I was somehow left with my hands hanging. Textbook answers and Bible verses weren't enough.

The word 'shame' was written indelibly into the thinking of the indigenous young people I taught in school over the years in Bourke. They used it freely to say they weren't going to attempt anything in public in case they failed. It meant they felt crippled by their colour, sense of inferiority, their past, and fear of ridicule.

Repeated often enough, these ideas shape your story.

But the reverse was true too. I had arrived ignorant of the wrongs done to them, and as a result, I felt no shame. The Jesus I had set myself to follow had identified with the poor and imprisoned. He belonged to a race who had been invaded and oppressed for five hundred years, so he understood what it was like to be abused and subjugated. He came to lift up the heads that hung with shame and to turn their mourning into dancing. If I was going to be faithful to his call, I needed to develop an honest understanding of the disgraceful treatment of the indigenous people who were my neighbours. I needed to take the blunt advice of Diana Williams, wife of West Australian Ron Williams who brought a fresh, positive spirit whenever he visited Bourke as an Aboriginal evangelist.

> Most whitefellas are used to taking the lead, walking into the room ahead of the others, taking charge, speaking their mind first, getting their say in as quickly as possible. Indigenous people sit back, waiting patiently for leaders to emerge from the group interactions that take place. Relationships are established, the lines of generations are acknowledged, trust is recognised, and everyone has their say. No tall poppies are wanted.[82]

Billy Williams, an articulate Aboriginal pastor of the Kamilaroi people, taught me an important piece of lore. He said if old and new Australians were going to make a strong future, "We need to share our stories, accept our stories and write a new story together." I learned to do this by sitting down and really listening to the stories of some unsung heroes. Let me tell you some that I heard around Bourke:

Frankie Faulkner's fruit run never made any money. He gave everything away. I only met him briefly, but his story was written into hundreds of lives. I was told of a quiet, thoughtful son of a preacher ploughing everything he had into the Aboriginal community of Bourke for over forty years. This 'white fella' earned their respect by giving it, and so they called him 'Brother Frank'. He surrendered his home to a young Aboriginal couple who had moved to town and lived most of his life in a tin shed, freely distributing the fruit and vegetables he grew to anyone in need. Over and over, I heard stories about Frank and his Ford pick-up, packed with kids from the Reserve, headed out to North Bourke for Sunday School and a swim.

Others heard him pumping out hymns on a pedal organ in the reserves, at shows, or in the main street, while people like old George Mungindi the drover spoke of witnessing many of his people shot down by white men when he was a boy nearly a century before. But this Wanggumara tribesman had let go of bitterness because the story of Jesus had shown him how. His favourite song was *For God So Loved the World*.

Frank also sponsored Kamilaroi man Bill Reid to pastor the United Aboriginal Mission church he helped build. I was challenged by the way these strong men had refused to let racism make them sour and how together, they set about writing a new story into Bourke. At Frank's death, the town's agnostic doctor testified, 'He never witnessed to me, yet he affected me more than any other person. That little man lived out Christ in my presence.'[83]

Sometimes wordless stories speak loudest.

I have two lasting memories of Pastor Bill Reid. I see him striding out alone, straight-backed, carrying a swag, Akubra hat tilted stylishly over his blind eye, full head of white hair – the solitary Aboriginal in the town street parade. He silently declared his story – proud Kamilaroi man, shearer, pastor, and citizen of Bourke – Australian to the core. And I see him framed against the Ngemba people's cave paintings on the red rock walls at Mt Gundabooka, standing in the shade of the ghost gums, big working man's hands clasped to his lips, playing *The Old Rugged Cross* on a gum leaf. The quivering notes of his music brought two ancient stories together – one born in Gondwana Land and the other on a hill in faraway Israel. His exquisitely carved emu eggs spoke volumes of his love for the bush and his family.

In the 1930's Bill had helped pioneer the civil rights movement when the going was tough for his people, and you can hear his gentle voice spell out his part in the struggle for justice in the documentary *Lousy Little Sixpence*.[84] It was one of the greatest honours of my life to be asked to help write the final paragraph in Bill's story when I conducted his funeral. Twenty years later, a significant footnote was added by an agnostic Jewish doctor when he placed a beautiful headstone on Bill's grave into which were carved his favourite words from the Bible, 'I am what I am by the grace of God.' That was the life lesson Bill Reid left in Bourke.

When I first met Peter 'Chicka' Gibbs from the tiny settlement of Weilmoringle – broad-shouldered, athletic, a gifted Rugby League player – he had every reason to be embittered.

Years of painful experiences climaxed in 1997 when his sister Fiona died in police custody in Brewarrina. It was almost ten years to the day after a young indigenous man had hung himself in the same lockup, provoking a riot that pitted the Aboriginal community against the police. Peter told me that after Fiona's death, furious locals came to the Gibbs family ready to trash the town. But her brother, along with her father, insisted that they wanted something different to mark her death.

Twenty years later, at the TAFE College in Dubbo, I sat and listened to Peter tell this story. He spoke to a classroom of young people entering an intensive academic, fitness, and leadership program he had devised called IPROWD (Indigenous Police Recruiting Our Way Delivery). He told them that this is his way of building a positive legacy for his sister – to prepare them as recruits for the NSW Police Academy. In his words, "What happens when there's a blackfella in a blue uniform, there's a message that just transcends like no other… It's really about crime prevention because it's about our police work with Aboriginal people, and nobody can do that better than Aboriginal people."[85] Peter is a man of Christian faith, and his determination to write a fresh story out of a bleak past inspires me.

"We don't serve blacks here." Wiradjuri elder, Aunty Pat Doolan, told me that was her reception in a shop in Bourke's main street when she first arrived as a young bride in the late sixties. "I was shocked," she said. "I walked out the door, and I prayed that God would help me change that attitude in this town."

Born at the Talbragar Mission, on the banks of the Macquarie River in Dubbo, Pat's early education included being shown where to run and hide if Government people and police came to take the children away. As a child, she didn't quite understand why the train stopped on the edge of town where the indigenous passengers clambered down onto the tracks. Later she learned that the humiliating exit was to avoid offending white citizens at the main station. An early encounter with the story of Jesus through a travelling missionary had birthed the resilient faith that has sustained her in her journey with endemic racism – from both black and white people. For years her husband Terry took the gospel to the streets of Bourke where he had once wandered drunk and despairing, and together, they gathered kids for a Sunday School at the Reserve.

True to her word, Pat worked hard to become a qualified teacher and engineer her own quiet revolution, helping to create education programs in the Bourke TAFE College for indigenous people. She partnered with the High School Principal to launch a public-access radio station 2WEB as an innovative means of equipping young Aboriginal students with communication skills. The Doolan family were often seen on the tennis courts and became champions in more ways than one. After some twenty years in Bourke, she brought the same energy back to her native town, pioneering initiatives, which have swung open doors of opportunity for scores of Aboriginal young people in Dubbo and beyond.

Terry appeared by my bed in Dubbo Base Hospital, where he was a much loved chaplain. How moving to have this Aboriginal brother minister to me, reading from his well-worn King James Bible and using the 'thee and thou' of Elizabethan English when he prayed for me!

Terry and Pat's tools for writing this new story across troubled communities in the North West have been the willingness to listen, the determination to put bitterness aside, the heart to act courageously, and the humility to serve both white and black communities. Chairing meetings of all the educationalists involved with indigenous students, Pat boldly declared her source of strength, announcing, "You all know I'm a praying woman!" I've had her sit around the campfire with schoolkids from Sydney and tell her story and watched their faces melt. Her enduring faith, love and optimism continue to inspire the whole Dubbo community.[86]

The Doolan family have written a fresh chapter into the story of Western NSW.

Aboriginal people rarely darkened the door of our church in Bourke. Despite our sincere conviction that the good news didn't discriminate, there was a social barrier that kept them away, even though it was invisible to the primarily white middle class congregation. One exception was Uncle John Ferguson, who would stand quietly aloof under the olive trees after the service – his rejection radar alert. One Sunday, he placed a book in my hands, explaining this was his father's story. His eyes told me this was precious to him and that he wanted me, as a historian, to do something with it. The title, *Bill Ferguson: Fighter for Aboriginal Freedom*,[87] warned me that this would be a confronting read. Jack Horner's biography of this remarkable indigenous leader opened my eyes wide to an epic struggle about which I was ignorant.

Unbeknown to me, Uncle John had once marched his nephew, Frank Doolan, across to the Dubbo cemetery and stood him in front of Bill Ferguson's simple grave. He wanted the angry young activist to realise he stood in the shadow of the truly radical leader of the Aboriginal people. Here lay the son of a Scottish Presbyterian father and a Wiradjuri mother. They had declared their determination to write a new story in racially divided 19th century Australia by hanging their marriage certificate conspicuously on the wall of their home for every visitor to see.

They wanted to declare this was no convenient 'shack-up', but a commitment of equals. William Ferguson senior was a hard-fisted pioneer of the Shearers' Union and a lay preacher along the Murrumbidgee River. He trained his son not to take a backward step when it came to fighting, either with his hands or his words.

After years witnessing his people living in squalor, underpaid, exploited, and abused on stations across the backcountry, young Bill decided to harness his Christian faith to the Union training he had gained in the sheds to mobilise the justice movement in Australia. He stood up for the rights of working men, regardless of their colour. He called his people together to form *The Aboriginal Progressive Association* in the Masonic Hall in Dubbo in June 1937.

His abrasive voice startled hearers awake all across the State. 'We must educate the minds of the white people – otherwise the thrusting back of my people which began 150 years ago will continue until they are swept off the face of the earth!'[88] Working alongside Melbourne-based activist William Cooper – also a man of Christian faith – he organised the first Day of Mourning on Australia Day in January 1938. They launched the civil rights movement on a national scale. Together they presented a petition to the Prime Minister, pleading for equal recognition of their people, on the grounds that the Bible said all men were God's children.

I was astonished when I realised that they had anticipated Mahatma Gandhi and Rev Martin Luther King by several years in the quest for humane treatment of their race and yet both were conspicuously absent from Australia's Hall of Fame. And to my shame, I realised that these devout Christian leaders were also missing from the ranks of the churches' heroes.

All this came into sharp focus when I met Frank Doolan in Dubbo again after 30 years. He was now 'Riverbank Frank', poet and community worker, living alone on the former Talbragar Mission site on the Macquarie River. A measure of understanding had replaced my ignorance, and Frank's anger was tempered by wisdom forged from hard experiences. We stood together on new ground, as brothers with a common faith. We realised that Uncle John had trusted his father's story to both of us. In telling Bill Ferguson's story, Frank and I wanted to honour his dual heritage. And so, we set about doing that side by side – I descended from my Scottish grandfather's Baird clan, and Frank came from the Wiradjuri people whose song lines covered the country between the Murrumbidgee and the Macquarie rivers.

When we stood together in front of school and university students, church congregations, and community organisations, we wanted to present a hero that both white and black communities could embrace. We've tried to embody the spirit of this Ferguson family by modelling the new culture that Jesus had envisaged. It's like a campfire where people of every race gather to listen to each other's stories, to confess their short-sightedness, and embrace one another genuinely. Frank frames our task using the words of the old Jewish prophet, 'To do justly, love mercy and walk humbly with your God.'[89]

That is a heart language that everyone can understand.

These humble people convinced me I had work to do to square up to the realities of their narrative. Apologist C.S. Lewis had taught me to think with both my head and my heart. He was adamant that, in spite of an honourable legacy of good works, the repeated failures of Christian history demand a '*mea Culpa* – I am guilty' component in the telling if they are to generate hope. He called for, '... a full confession by Christendom of all Christendom's specific contribution to the sum of human cruelty and treachery.'[90] Having witnessed two world wars at close quarters, he could see that having the courage to own the dark chapters could make the rest of the story shine brighter. Australian historian John Dickson has gained a wide hearing by doing this in his recent book *Bullies and Saints*.[91]

It moved me to read Diana William's account of her extraordinary wedding to Ron at Skull Creek, the site of a massacre of his people. This was a dedicated Aboriginal evangelist, not only making a life commitment to a former Wall St businesswomen, but a moment where their two different narratives were transformed by the gospel story. 'I watched Ron bring symbols from all over Western Australia into a creek bed at Laverton in preparation for a day to celebrate a union, of a man and a woman, black and white, in a place where years before there had been killing.'[92] It was their way of changing the dark narrative. Diana wrote later, 'reconciliations of the heart occur when the story is revealed and understood. They occur when we enter the space that is created by the other, when the book on the past is opened up and we walk into its pages and allow them to penetrate our thinking.'[93]

I've witnessed this.

Billy Williams is a Kamilaroi man from Collarenebri in NSW who announces publicly his pride in the English part of his ancestry. I was standing beside my friend Laurie talking with Billy after he had poured his heart out to an audience in Melbourne. Laurie normally doesn't display his emotions, but I was moved when he looked his Aboriginal brother in the eye and apologised for deep offences committed by one of his ancestors against indigenous women in backcountry Victoria. As they gripped hands, time and pain slipped away. Reconciliation was distilled into that single moment for the two of them. Laurie explained to me that as an anthropologist, he felt regret over the shameful saga of atrocity in every culture, including our own, but that he could sensibly only confess guilt over the ugliness that he felt party to through his forefather.

Likewise, I shook hands with my brother Frank after church one day. I expressed the sadness I felt over the stories of massacres and maltreatment and also confessed the guilt of my personal disdain at times for the Aboriginal people I had lived among. The bonds between us continue to deepen as we write a new story together in our hometown.

Thirty or forty years ago in the Central West of NSW, people used to call Gilgandra 'the Holy Land'. It was said that if you went there you'd probably be converted by William B. Naden, a fearless indigenous preacher whose shearing teams were respected as the 'guns' in the woolsheds of the district. His grandson Neville travels the country with Bush Church Aid to help field workers speak the heart language of indigenous communities. At an ordination service made up of stories, prayers, and hymns spanning 3000 years of Judeo-Christian history, I heard him deliver a Welcome to Country, which spoke of an inclusive new story being written.

> As a descendant of the Wiradjuri nation, I would like to welcome you to this land and acknowledge our God, the creator, and sustainer of all things... I recognise that he gave custodianship of these lands to our first nations' people. I recognise that in his sovereignty He has allowed other people groups to migrate to these shores. We give thanks and praise to God for those who have exercised godly leadership in this nation over the past 230 years and... that he is raising up a new generation of leaders that will faithfully serve him.[94]

We were in Dubbo's Holy Trinity Anglican Church about 200 metres from St Andrew's Presbyterian Church. Bill Ferguson had led his wife and ten kids to worship each Sabbath and served as an elder some eighty years previously. Bill had been fiercely proud of his Wiradjuri song-line, but willingly joined it to the clan-story of his Scottish ancestors. The vivid stories of freedom fighters like Moses and Jesus had fuelled his quest, as they would Martin Luther King's in the USA, Mahatma Gandhi's in India, and Nelson Mandela's in South Africa.

I heard in Neville's words an invitation for all of us to understand the different journeys our feet have taken to bring us to the present and to walk together into a future with a promise of hope. Confession can be a fresh wind blowing away the ugliness and bringing the promise of a stronger future. Forgiveness, as Jesus taught us, is the circuit breaker.

Our storytelling can then build bridges to our common humanity – new lyrics for shared song-lines.

8

FORGETTING TO REMEMBER

Our endeavour is to preserve for the nation in measured narrative, a great episode... I regard our work as something like that of a photographer who must fix certain pictures... else they will be lost forever... What we have to do is 'fix' that history for posterity.[95]

Charles Bean

It's strange how swiftly you can move from a street jostling with people on busy individual agendas into a silent space that sobers you with a shared sorrow. With two young friends, I passed the Eternal Flame burning outside Melbourne's Shrine of Remembrance and climbed the wide flight of steps to stand on the pavement of the Sanctuary. Under the stepped pyramid roof, we felt the weight of a great granite shrine designed to impress on the visitor the cost of war. We'd been talking about the power of museums to multiply the impact of a story, and they decided we should make the pilgrimage to the King's Domain on St Kilda Road.

Signs reminded visitors of the need for quiet in respect for the fallen. The marble block sunken into the floor at the heart of the sanctuary caused us to bow our heads to read the simple inscription: 'GREATER LOVE HATH NO MAN.' We stood reverently as the guide explained that at the 11th hour of the 11th day of the 11th month, a beam of sunlight would pierce the gloom from high in the roof and single out the word 'love'. You couldn't help being impressed by the genius of this silent one word sermon to mark out the moment when the slaughter stopped in France in 1918, with 37 million dead. Then as a requiem for the 19,000 Victorian service-men and women who had died, the guide recited *The Ode for the Fallen.*

> *They shall grow not old, as we that are left grow old;*
> *Age shall not weary them, nor the years condemn.*
> *At the going down of the sun and in the morning*
> *We will remember them.*

The well-worn words hung briefly in the silence. What came next startled me and has remained with me ever since. When I asked about the origin of the words engraved on the rock, she replied confidently, "Oh, they come from the Bible, but they're not religious!" She professed not to know that it was Jesus who actually said them. For me, that moment distilled into the conviction that there are cogs and gears in Australia's story that have stopped meshing.

There are foundational things we are forgetting to remember.

Outside, the Shrine was anchored at the corners by heroic statues calling the nation to aspire to Justice, Peace, Sacrifice and Patriotism. It seemed sad to me that this guide had bent over backwards to avoid connecting the powerful words in the floor to the one person who, it could be argued, had done more to lift the world's under-standing of justice, peace, and sacrifice than anyone in history.

Many of the ANZACS knew that. I once handled a worn New Testament that a Light Horseman from Bourke had carried into battle in the Sinai desert, and research confirmed he was not alone in prizing it. Forty million Bibles, Testaments and Prayer books flooded the battlefields along with the torrent of armaments.[96] William Ewing, a chaplain at Gallipoli and in Mesopotamia, described some telling moments among the young Australians plunged into war:

In hospital, it was a common thing to see a lad on his stretcher, quite unobtrusively, but with evident appreciation, reading his New Testament. I handled a great number of these books, and found them not, as a rule, simply dog-eared from carrying in the pocket, but well thumbed, which sufficiently testified to the use made of them.[97]

I sensed that here was one of the neglected small stories that carried the DNA of our larger Australian story. Surely here was a major source of our much talked about Anzac values. While I felt the tug of national pride visiting the shrine, I knew that patriotism alone could never produce a story big enough to embrace the deep questions facing humanity. I asked my friends, "Why do the signs declare this memorial to be 'a sacred space' if we are a secular society that believes a human being is merely an accidental collection of atoms and life a free-for-all where only the fittest survive?"

In effect, it seemed to me that we are borrowing from the Christian narrative to dignify a painful chapter of our history. It had sprung from the life of Jesus. It was a story that not only outlived a myriad of wars but, even in the carnage, displayed the power to inspire moments of genuine human kindness. I felt certain Melbourne's city fathers had chosen Jesus' words to inscribe into their memorial because they reminded us of a higher loyalty and a deeper love that was at the very heart of our national ethos.

It's a story that simply won't go away. In 2019, the bronze statue of Australian Light Horseman Jack Pollard was unveiled on the shores of Lake Galilee, honouring the one thousand indigenous troopers who served in Palestine in World War One.[98] He is kneeling beside his horse, both of them with their heads bowed over the grave of a newly buried mate. Jack was a man of faith, so in his hand is a New Testament telling the story of the one the world remembers as having laid down his life for both friends and enemies. The carpenter from Nazareth had walked that same ground in Northern Israel. I was very moved when I saw it. In talking about it with an Aboriginal mate, we agreed that this sculpture expresses the power of the story of Jesus' brave self-sacrifice to transcend the pain of any racial prejudice and the horror of any battlefield.

To my mind, the real tragedy about World War One was, that the nations locked in the bloodiest slaughter of history to that point, with the exception of Turkey, publicly championed Christian faith and behaviour as the spiritual drivers of their culture. Clergymen on both sides assured the young men, marching off to war from Munich, Melbourne, Madras, Mafeking, Montreal, Moscow, and Marseilles, that God was on their side. (No doubt the mullahs of Turkey assured their soldiers that Allah was with them.)

It was astounding to discover that between 1914 and 1918, *The Bible Society* put 40 million copies of the story of Jesus into the hands of Germans, Austrians, Russians, British, French, and Commonwealth soldiers and citizens, confident that they would all be familiar with it.[99] I pictured men and women on both sides seeking help from the same source, despite the nationalist rhetoric of the church and state-leaders that confused divine blessing with state policy.

Here was a phenomenon worth examining. In 2009, Robyn and I visited the battlefields of France. We read reports of the brief Christmas truce on the Western Front where enemies met in no-man's land to sing carols, exchange gifts and play soccer. We were struck by the effect of this story on those battle-weary soldiers. It had raised 'peace on earth and goodwill' out of the mud and blood of the trenches, no matter how momentarily. Was this evidence of personal faith an anomaly or a sign of a deeper story at work?

I was intrigued to discover, when I returned to Australia in 2000 after visiting museums across the USA, that our Canberra War Memorial ranked 23rd on a list of the planet's top man-made shrines. After nearly a century, it remains the number one landmark in the country, boasting one of the finest military artefact and document collections in the world. I wondered how it had managed to go beyond being a sentimental retreat for an ageing population to grow a connection with younger generations. Naturally, images of young men falling in battle connect to deep emotional springs. But I saw part of the secret of its longevity was vivid story telling that enlivened imaginations and the continuous strengthening of the narrative by research.

They were ensuring Australia was remembering not to forget.

The real genius though, lay in joining the saga of human violence to higher aspirations. Museum Director Dr Brendon Nelson replied to a friend who told him he was wasting his life trying to rearrange history. He said that remembering actually had more to do with the future than the past. He counted it a grave responsibility. He was clear that it was not about the building or the artefacts but the stories of the men and women and the values they fought for. 'I ask myself what's important for us in this and it is to never lose sight of who we are and what we believe as Australians. What are the values that define and bind us as a people, truths by which we live?'[100] The Memorial was to be a place where people found emotional resonance and meaning. He was talking about purposeful myth-making that harnessed nostalgia's power to shape thinking about the past, present and future.

The Anzac Day 2020 'Driveway Services' in streets across the nation while under COVID 19 lockdown, along with the widespread social media circulation of the stories of family members who had served in the military, illustrated how past events could help nerve a nation in crisis. Veterans reported a sense of community being enhanced by this whole experience.

They recognised the power of a constitutive story to touch people in the present.

A museum expert has commended this wistful looking-back as 'a crude form of historical consciousness that at least fosters dialogues between past and present.'[101] I believe it does more. It links us directly to the story behind the phrase carved into the floor of the Melbourne War Memorial and the matchless courage of the man who said it. Fathers and sons from both sides were buried under a cross – the Roman torture instrument transformed by Jesus when he freely laid down his life for others. That's a deeper dialogue that needs to be pursued in Australia.

One recent redemptive story is of Ali Ammar, the Lebanese youth who tore down and burned the Australian flag at an RSL club at the height of the Cronulla race riots in 2005. He was described at the time as 'a potent symbol of the rifts in Australian society and a lightning rod for anti-Muslim sentiment across the nation.'[102] Though he was vilified in the media in the heat of ugly events splashed across national television, the RSL decided on a radical strategy for the teenager. They sponsored him to climb the punishing 110 km Kokoda Track in Papua New Guinea with a Youth Leadership Challenge party. This exercise connected them directly to stories of the underprepared 39th Battalion's valiant fight against the more experienced Japanese jungle forces in 1943.

An ABC television team documented Ali's transformation, as he came to understand the narrative and the symbolic meaning of the Australian flag. Values like *mateship*, *self-sacrifice*, and *courage* carved into monuments along the trail took on fresh meaning for the 17-year-old and his peers as they struggled up the Owen Stanley Range to complete the pilgrimage. The trek changed him profoundly. "Before I went on the trip, all I cared about was myself, and when I got back, I was thinking a lot more about other people."[103] Ammar went on to help young people like himself realise the opportunities they have in Australia.

I took my hat off to the RSL! Here was the perfect example of how skilled interpreters could touch the heart with stories that animated core values and fired aspirations. In the same way, I saw the team at the Australian War Memorial had become adept at finding fresh ways to project fading memories into the national consciousness. In doing so, they located themselves as popularisers of the Heroic Myth. They understood Charles Bean's intuition that the story must be told graphically, boldly, and with integrity if it was to remain fixed in the popular imagination. What was admirable was their expertise in generating it widely through a network of grassroots connections across the nation.

Once I stood in a tiny graveyard about 80 km from Bourke to help lead the celebration of ANZAC Day with the entire population of the village of Byrock – all twenty of them! This was in spite of the fact that those on the Eastern side of the highway weren't getting on with those on the Western side at the time. ABC television had singled out this moment as one of twenty thousand happening in towns and cities across the country because locals had discovered more decorated war heroes in their district than anywhere in Australia. So for a few moments, the pathos of war, fading family memories, the flag and the haunting notes of the Last Post brought young and old of a community together, there in the lonely mulga scrub.

That's the power of a well-maintained mythology.

All my life, I've seen the fresh waves of documentary story, broadcast in April each year, fix iconic images of the Diggers in the national imagination, and so keep the drama alive. The story of battle has been embedded in the daily life of every town and suburb in the shape of a central monument and RSL Clubs, each with its own displays of militaria. At the going down of the sun each evening, patrons pause with heads bowed or hands on their heart at their poker machine or their meal table. They stand in reverence while the 'Lest we Forget' Ode reminds them not to neglect the sacrifice of the Anzacs.

So, when political leaders seize on the 'Spirit of the Anzacs' or call out for the 'Anzac values' in their speeches, pretty much everyone knows exactly what they mean. In the aftermath of the widespread wild fires and the global pandemic in 2020, the figures of ANZAC's merge seamlessly with firefighters and front-line medical workers.

Each year, as the ranks of veterans thin, new generations are being encouraged to swing into step in their place. For the first time, Robyn proudly pinned her father's and grandfather's medals on our grandsons' chests in a recent parade. They were proud too. This struck me because balladist Eric Bogle had assured my Vietnam War generation that soon, no one would march at all.[104] But, fifty years later, schools are making epic journeys to the Western Front in France for remembrance services, and young business people are setting out with backpacks to prove themselves worthy descendants of the Anzacs by tackling the rugged Kokoda track in New Guinea. Growing numbers stand shivering in the dawn listening to hymns at Gallipoli and Villers Bretonneux, to connect to transcendent moments of bravery.

The trained storytellers at the Australian War Memorial have used the apparatus at their disposal to stir the nation to action with ceremonies, sentiment, strong images and evocative symbols.

Lest we forget.

My journalist sons, Chris and Jonathan, have recently surfaced lost chapters from the archives of their grandfather's and great-grandfather's war experiences. It's deepened our family's understanding by researching our shared heritage. Part of the genius of the Australian War Memorial has been to connect families to their ancestral history, tapping into the recent phenomenon of genealogical research. The fact that it's become a billion dollar a year industry, second only to pornography on the net, signals to me that family connection is a powerful driver in bringing meaning in people's personal lives. The staff has engaged school children in this exploration with stimulating information packages, travelling exhibitions, online connections, essay-writing, study scholarships, involvement in wreath-laying ceremonies, writing stories on commemorative crosses, and singing in travelling choirs. The fact that Australia's greatest annual pilgrimage is made by school children and families to this story-telling apparatus in Canberra speaks of its genius.

Over the years, interpreters have broadened the scope of the original ANZAC epic to celebrate the part played by women, Aboriginal servicemen, Vietnam veterans, and non-combatants. It's even included former enemies. It has helped rescue the genuine stories of self-sacrifice from degenerating into shallow patriotism and propaganda. The promotion of pilgrimage to battlefield sites, where the story is coupled to place, has added a spiritual aura to the visit. By utilising imaginative recall, they bathed the locations with cathartic emotion and helped visitors purge some dark chapters of pain. In some cases, forgiveness has been made possible and reconciliation has replaced rancour.[105]

This is a formidable extended performance and the War Memorial has set the benchmark for mythmaking in Australia. The annual investment of $40M by the Federal Government signals that they consider this is our defining legend. But is it big enough to answer the deeper questions facing present-day Australians? I can accept Brendon Nelson's argument that the exemplary courage, devotion, and selflessness of many ANZACS transcended the horror of war. But I have a nagging feeling that while the story justifiably remains loaded with profound significance for Australia as a nation, by its very make-up, it would always be bound by severe restrictions.

First, it dwells on an obscene waste of life. No amount of outstanding bravery can mask the ugliness of the slaughter, the bending of human ingenuity to inhuman destruction, and the pointlessness of so much of it. I have personally heard few participants report any glory in the struggle and felt uneasy at the recent bent to make war veterans into secular saints. The ANZACS fought mostly on foreign soil away from their native land, in several intense periods. The danger is that the story can become so cherished as a heroic legend that it is almost beyond critical examination.

Other questions press for answers. Does it demand an understanding of manhood purely in terms of the warrior? Is war to be singled out as a principle means of defining character? Does it unconsciously reinforce the myth of redemptive violence? Does it suggest our soldiers were braver and nobler than any others? Does it, by its nature, lack the breadth to adequately embrace women, children and non-combatants? Is it possible that its Anglo-Saxon flavour distances indigenous people, immigrants, and former enemy cultures, who also have a stake in Australia's future? Will the voices of pacifists and conscientious objectors always remain unwelcome? Does it look point-blank at the question of PTSD and suicide among veterans?

I'm the first to admit that engaging with the great deeds of our ancestors has often fired my imagination and strengthened my purpose. I've learned that love of family has taken me the first step beyond self-love and that love for my countrymen can take me a step further. Inspiring tales can train our spiritual muscles for the call of higher service and even provoke a willingness to forgive. But they have also taught me to appreciate that other people have a deep affection for their homeland's language and culture. True stories of the redemptive effect of forgiveness between enemies in successful movies like *Railway Man, Blood Oath, Unbroken,* and *To End*

All Wars, can challenge us to face the dark chapters of our own history honestly and to make amends for cruel and unjust behaviour.

I sat with a group of teenage boys outside the Darwin War Museum and told them about the Japanese commander who gave the battle cry 'Tora, Tora, Tora' to launch the bombing of Pearl Harbour in 1941. Captain Mitsuo Fuchida[106] also led the attacks on Darwin, where ten times more bombs were dropped on the city. A visit to Hiroshima in the aftermath of the Atom Bomb, convinced him that the Japanese warrior code he had lived by had failed to answer his deeper questions. Then he read the story of an American airman, who crash-landed after a reprisal raid on Tokyo, survived solitary confinement in a POW camp by reading a New Testament, and returned to Japan to teach the forgiveness Jesus offered. It deeply touched him. His culture had built a commitment to unrelenting revenge into him that was destroying him. Here was the circuit breaker he had been searching for, and he responded to the message of pardon and compassion. As I watched the boys' faces taking this remarkable story in, I thought, "What could this teach young Aussies in schools across the country about real reconciliation?"

Suppose stories are the glue in our nation's self-awareness. In that case, I believe the time has come to step in alongside the ANZAC myth with an equally courageous, but largely forgotten story capable of generating answers to spiritual questions. This is not to denigrate the dauntless actions of the Anzacs. Still I know the Christian community has a lengthy record of sacrificial deeds, which could deepen the national conversation about identity. It would present a different kind of narrative, also written in blood, sweat, and tears, shed in seeking justice for all peoples.

The two could lend strength to each other by asking the tough questions together.

Bourke and Gallipoli had shown Charles Bean that the real theatre was located in the lives of regular people. He developed a deep affection for these unpretentious young men who endured the severest challenges. Journalist Michelle Grattan phrased it perfectly. 'He saw and portrayed heroes, making them grander by making them ordinary.'[107] I have found story after story of quiet achievers, buried in all corners of Australia, whose courageous faith had won victories every bit as important as the yardage gained and lost in the Great War. Cambridge historian Herbert Butterfield voiced my feeling, that if people could be drawn to consider, 'the spiritual work done by humble men…they would find it the most moving spectacle history presents and would see how the spread of piety does mean a growth in charity.'[108]

I surprised a church congregation one ANZAC Day service with the question, "What do we mean when we repeat the refrain, 'Lest We Forget'"? They gave the predictable reply, "Remember the brave men and women who laid down their lives for us."

"That's a noble idea", I told them, "but not what Rudyard Kipling had in mind when he wrote those words in The Recessional."[109]

I recalled for them singing these words each year as a boy standing in the schoolyard on Armistice Day, November 11th. We had only the vaguest idea of what it meant. They had a haunting, lonely effect. I can still feel it – a kind of patriotic emotion welling up inside me. The poet had written those words in 1908 as a reminder of a higher calling. He was challenging the leaders of Great Britain not to forget that God was holding them responsible for the honourable treatment of peoples under their rule in an Empire, which, at that time, circled the globe. 'A humble and contrite heart' before the Creator should always be the rule for rulers, captains, and kings that would, in Kipling's judgement, outlast the ambitions of empire builders. But, ironically, like the source of the ANZAC values, that original message seems to have got lost.

A passionate call from wartime leader Winston Churchill reinvigorated the yearning in me to tell the stories of the many Australian men and women of faith that I had come to admire. He was well placed to sound a siren warning. He wrote in the aftermath of the second massive slaughter in the twentieth century, hoping to pre-empt yet another. It was a summons to commit to the kind of storytelling that spoke of things that mattered.

One of the signs of a great society is the diligence with which it passes culture from one generation to the next. This culture is the embodiment of everything the people of that society hold dear; its religious faith, its heroes…When one generation no longer esteems its own heritage and fails to pass on the torch to its own children, it is saying in essence that the very foundational principles and experiences that make it a society are no longer valid. This of course, leaves that generation without a sense of definition or direction, making them the fulfilment of Karl Marx's dictum, 'A people without a heritage is easily persuaded.'[110]

Charles Bean is my historian hero! He lived through five years of frontline action as an eyewitness of the mind-numbing carnage on the slopes of Gallipoli and the moonscape around the trenches in France. He painstakingly sifted through the battlefield litter and returned home in 1919 to a newly federated country with a boatload of artefacts and a swag of war journals. He was determined that Australia should never forget what the ANZAC soldiers had done. Over the next two decades, he wrote and edited five million words recounting Australia's deeds of war and was the creative genius behind the Australian War Memorial in Canberra.

Almost single-handed, Charles Bean crafted the ANZAC myth, and for that alone, I rate him as our nation's most successful storyteller. With passion and imagination, he blended a sacred space with a storytelling device that, a century later, draws pilgrims in increasing numbers. It is myth-making at its best, and generations of archivists and interpreters have ensured that the War Memorial continues to define the image of Australia.

This challenges me because Australians forget to remember hard-won yards and heroic deeds of our spiritual history. I am convinced that we urgently need to engage in some strong-minded storytelling in a dedicated space to rectify this neglect. A steady barrage over the past few decades has radically altered the spiritual landscape in Australia, and familiar landmarks have been obliterated. Churches have suffered casualties, leaving many who had looked to them for help numbed and groping for guideposts to the future.

Charles Bean has left a plan of action. The record of sacrificial deeds carried out by Christians in Australia deserves a world-class facility that matches their significance. What do new immigrants know of this journey and how will they find out? Will they really understand Australia if the Judeo-Christian epic is merely presented cafeteria style as one of the thirty-five flavours of religion to choose from?

Will this story simply be allowed to drift away?

Salvage will require storytellers saturated with the same vigorous spirit of inquiry Charles Bean commended a century ago: 'The ultimate bedrock on which we must build the new order, is the freedom of every citizen to discover the truth and proclaim what he finds.'[111]

9

MUSCULAR FAITH

For some Australians, sport is life and the rest is shadow.[112]

Donald Horne

I am a sport tragic. Along with many other Australians, physical contests have been the background story in my life since boyhood – a sub-narrative that ebbs and flows with the seasons and sets weekly rhythms. I sense this shared mythology all around me, drawing people from every walk of life into cultures and sub-cultures, each with their own specific languages, nostalgic memories, heroes and villains, agonies, and ecstasies. It's a passport that permits me to connect immediately with the pain of a total stranger wearing a Parramatta Eels cap – "Things are looking more promising this year" is our tentative pre-season mantra. Renewed hope haunts our eyes.

As near as I can recall, the opening paragraph of this part of my narrative was written by a rotund, moustachioed missionary who kindly took my mate and me to watch the mighty West Indians in combat with NSW at the Sydney Cricket Ground in 1961. I can still smell the fresh-cut grass and see the lithe Wesley Hall striding in from somewhere near the boundary fence – gold necklace flying, hurling the ball at batsman Brian Booth with an arc of fielders poised behind him. In the heart of that young boy perched high in the stands, a flame was lit and a life-long passion was born.

Further paragraphs were added late at night, lying in bed listening to eloquent British voices relaying the drama of an Ashes Test at Lords through the static of a transistor radio concealed beneath the covers. The Aussie successes exhilarated me and I felt their failures keenly. I lived and breathed those stories. On the steeply sloped wicket in our backyard in Orchard Street, I became my cricketing heroes – carrying Australia to glory against the Poms!

Winter brought the Rugby and the joy of a flying Woodies winger blitzing the opposition down the muddy touchline at T.G. Milner field at Eastwood. Then came the adrenaline rush when watching the gold-jerseyed Wallabies do battle with New Zealand All Blacks, the South African Springboks, the Shamrock of Ireland or the Red Rose of England. (Here I confess the delusion of being a very mediocre Rugby player who harboured the secret ambition to one day swerve and goose-step my way to the try-line like the legendary Aussie winger, David Campese.)

Tennis and a host of other sports filled the gaps, and of course, the Olympic Games supplied the periodic dose of national euphoria as our swimmers left the world in their wake. Again and again, I rose to my feet to celebrate with the rest of Australia as our medal tally 'proved' us to be a sporting people who punched well above our weight on the international stage. Indigenous athlete Cathy Freeman not only lit the cauldron at the Sydney games, but she also lit a flame in the sporting heart of the nation as she sprinted to a 400m gold medal. I felt validated by these moments too, as if we were co-authoring chapters of the Australian story together.

Sporting terms embedded themselves in my speech – currency readily exchanged in conversations. A linguistics expert has estimated that one in thirty of our words has vaulted into our vocabulary straight out of the sporting arena. Apparently, I'm not alone when I feel that I've been 'hit for six' or 'caught on a sticky wicket'. And it's entirely understandable that I should 'put the ball in the scrum' at a business meeting or protest that I've been 'blind-sided' by a decision. And when the prestigious

Australian of the Year awards are handed out, why am I not surprised that sporting achievement remains a key measure of greatness in our culture? In fact, captaining the national cricket team ranks second only to winning the Nobel Prize in terms of public profile and probably rivals that of the office of Prime Minister![113]

I'm one of the great majority who wouldn't know a trifecta from a trotter but, since Primary School days, it's been hard not to feel at least a twinge of the excitement that swirls around every corner of the country on Melbourne Cup Day. For over a century it's been called 'the race that stops the nation' – even our national Parliament pauses to share the ritual of the two-mile horse race. Jockeys and horses share the adulation of a worldwide audience nearing a billion people. The massive adrenaline injection it makes into the national veins registers as a steep spike in workplace morale. Despite millions of lost work hours, the national economy benefits from the annual flutter.[114] Perhaps it's because Australians secretly entertain the thought that given a chance, we'd conquer a treacherous slope astride a mountain pony, like the legendary Man from Snowy River!

It's a phenomenon woven into the national mythology.

I realise I am not a lone pebble on our sporting beach. Historians say the passion for sport stowed away in the cultural baggage that our ancestors brought from England. Getting together to kick and hit balls of various descriptions, gambling on anything rideable, and being stirred by the spectacle of people driving their bodies faster, further and more furiously actually brings us together as a nation. Overseas visitors find it remarkable that the ABC shuts down nearly all other regular radio broadcasts to cover five-day cricket games blow by painstaking blow.

For decades, the murmur of the commentators makes a drowsy background narrative that shapes our summers. So, it doesn't surprise me that a cricket bat and stumps glow in coloured glass inside the sacred dome of the ANZAC memorial as one of the symbols of our ancestry. Statistics tell me I am definitely not the odd man out – over half the people I rub shoulders with daily will spend eight or more hours a week absorbing four or five different athletic contests on their screens.

Sport can be far more than mere amusement. It has become the defining story in many Australian lives – just talk to any supporter of our homegrown Aussie Rules football!

Snatches of conversation I've overheard on Mondays reveal the weekend's results are the conceptual base around which we organise many of our attitudes. For some, it's a great escape from the drudgery of routine work. The gloom that descended when the Covid 19 pandemic drove every sport from the field, endorsed the conviction that for many Australians, 'Sport is life, the rest is shadow.' The proliferation of Fox sporting channels proves that these weekend contests remain a powerful adhesive in Australia's national narrative.

Growing up in suburban Sydney, my mates and I wiled away many hours in the waters of the local baths. I broiled in the sun at swimming carnivals run by our mainly White-Anglo school at the Ryde Aquatic Centre. These days, I watch my granddaughter being coaxed into the pool by an instructor whose family probably lives in Delhi or Mumbai. The parents jammed together on benches could have been texting photos of the grandchildren to Suva, Peking, Abu Dhabi, or Buenos Aires. For a moment, race, religion, language, and culture seemed to dissolve in the chlorinated atmosphere and the shared experience of seeing our kids learning to swim. Clearly, sport also acts as a sacred ritual where new immigrants are baptised into the life of the 'Land of the Long Weekend'.

I knew I was seeing a new Australian story emerging from the pool.

Everywhere I look, I see the appetite for recreation weaving different strands into our national narrative. Lanky Africans, bulky Pacific Islanders, wiry Middle Easterners and agile Asians are being grafted in alongside players of our familiar English-Irish-Scottish and Indigenous stock. I feel the sway of the argument from ABS research that our high level of physical activity personifies Australia and that sport is the most important element contributing to our feelings about our nation. At the peak level, men and women of very different racial backgrounds stand side by side and sing passionately of the rich and rare beauty to be found in a fair Australia. Digeridoos welcome strangers to tribal country and remind us of an ancient heritage.

The call to write new stages in our history's pages is most often heard resounding in our great arenas as hundreds of thousands lift up their voices in song at sporting events. More lately, listening to the haunting bugle notes of the Last Post echoing in the stands, I heard the music of two of the country's most powerful mythologies – Sport and Anzac – merging. The significant amendment to Australia's national anthem announcing 'We are one and free' was launched at an international Rugby match.

Some observers have gone further to pronounce sport as our national religion. Joining the families that swarm weekend soccer and netball fixtures definitely makes it seem so. When I was young, the summons to worship in the sun and surf was always far more alluring for me than the call to sit in pews inside church buildings on Sundays. Family SUV's and 4WD's have expanded our horizons for recreation. Colourful communal events complete with rituals, symbols, clothing, and song offer a cathartic rhythm of excitement and release. Even the uninitiated can feel the euphoria of Grand finals in cathedral-like stadiums.

As a pilgrim, I've stood respectfully in the Bradman Museum in Bowral, viewing cricket legend Don Bradman's cricket bat and other relics, reliving the life of the humble champion who radiated hope to Australians in the Great Depression. His career conveyed that a 'battler from the bush' could rise to sporting immortality.

I've listened to Fox Sports 'evangelists' expounding on various sporting contests, pondering the significance of the wounds of the gladiators and prophesying both doom and hope in equal measure. The success of Australian athletes at the Athens Olympics caused a spike in the National Wellbeing Index at home. The Tokyo Games may possibly have driven it higher given the lockdown due to COVID. It confirmed my suspicion that sport somehow links body and soul. It weaves a tapestry of heroic feats that captures the imaginations of kids watching rapt in front of the television. At times like this, it's hard to deny that, for many Australians, sport functions as an overarching narrative for life.

But I baulk when I hear the turf of the MCG being declared 'sacred', football grounds elevated as 'spiritual homes', and some very flawed sports heroes being declared 'Immortals'. Borrowing these religious terms calls for radical re-definition. I don't think our sporting bodies seriously contemplate that they can even begin to meet the deepest needs of their followers. There is nothing more sobering than listening to elite athletes report that excellence alone has failed to provide them with a life-defining story. It puts a reality check alongside the mantra repeated to young aspirants to 'dream the dream and become whatever you want to be.'

Every sporting code has an ugly underbelly of corruption, gambling, drug taking, and violence that reveals serious shortcomings. The growing demand from clubs for both psychologists and chaplains to deal with disappointment, anxiety and depression in athletes reinforces the reality that sport on its own is incapable of answering the questions of meaning and purpose. The pretence can be a delusion.[115]

Sinew and muscle were never meant to carry the weight of the spirit alone.

Just the same, I realise it was sportsmen who set vigorous impulses in motion in my life. The first clear call came from English cricketer C.T. Studd, whose name was engraved on the original Ashes urn, which has defined Australian/English rivalry for over 150 years. As an adolescent, I thrilled to his exploits with the bat and to his feats of bravery as a pioneer missionary in India and Africa. His biography laid a foundation in my thinking because his sporting prowess was overtaken by a higher calling to give his very best in a wider arena.

Leaving his promising career behind in the mid-19th century, he shook a whole generation awake when he toured England with evangelist D.L. Moody. He challenged young men and women proclaiming, 'If Jesus Christ be God, and died for me, then no sacrifice can be too great for me to make for him.' A century later, I felt the impact of his voice reminded me of priorities.[116]

Biographies like his made it clear that stories of faith lived out on the playing field of life were worth being part of.

Both Moody and Studd were caught up in a worldwide movement that became known as 'Muscular Christianity'. It stemmed from a college in Rugby, England. In 1827, an energetic Headmaster, Thomas Arnold, was called in to tackle the problems of bullying, bastardising, drunkenness, and gambling, which were crippling the school. His strategy was to prioritise the spiritual growth of the boys, believing that kindness would promote moral character and that intellectual development would follow. When harnessed to physical activity, he believed these would breed men of Christian character. A compelling driver in this transformation was the way it turned shambolic schoolboy games into orderly activities. It launched an educational reformation that spread across the world, and a century later, its ghost was haunting the corridors of my High School at Epping.[117]

I had no idea until recently that the strain of men that shaped organised sport in Australia one way or another was fashioned by this remarkable experiment. I grew up on the myth of young William Webb Ellis seizing the football and running with it as the genesis of Rugby Union. But for another graduate, Thomas Hughes, the real hero was Dr Arnold himself. He preached his Headmaster's Rugby gospel in the popular novel *Tom Brown's School Days*.[118] Published in 1857, it sold 28,000 copies in five years, and so this educational philosophy became international by the skilful use of fiction. Along with another popular novelist, Charles Kingsley, Hughes argued Arnold's core conviction that Christianity should breed the kind of men given to the service of others.

Both authors were Christian Socialists bent on alleviating the suffering caused by the Industrial Revolution. Kingsley expounded a sporting gospel I had never heard.

> The least of the muscular Christians has hold of the old chivalrous belief, that a man's body is given to him to be trained and brought into subjection, and then used for the protection of the weak, the advancement of all righteous causes... He does not hold that

mere strength or activity are in themselves worthy of any respect or worship, or that one man is a bit better than another because he can knock him down.[119]

As these layers were peeled back, the narrative hidden beneath the surface of much of the sport that I had grown up with was laid bare. The instigator of the modern Olympics, Baron de Coubertin, was inspired to declare that, 'Arnold gave the precise formula for the role of athletics in education. The cause was quickly won. Playing fields sprang up all over England.'[120] And all over the world! Watching the 2020 Tokyo Olympics coverage, I wondered if the frequent use of Christian virtues like humility, grace, courage, belief, faith and perseverance to describe some of the athletes' performances reflected this root connection.

It never occurred to me when I ran out onto a suburban footy ground or walked through the gates of the SCG that I owed something to a visionary Christian Headmaster from Rugby. In every continent, people seized on the idea that sport should be hitched to the highest purposes. Organisations like the YMCA, which introduced basketball and volleyball as competitive sports, were devoutly Christian. Although sport could never claim religious status legitimately, there was no question it had a spiritual DNA that determined its laws and nourished its values. It was drilled into us that being a 'good sport' meant playing fair.

This ideal has risen out of the ashes of many sporting disgraces when young athletes are reminded that they are role models for children. Along the way, much of this spiritual energy drained when replaced by adherence to a surface morality. This meant not being 'too religious', loyalty to 'the old school tie' or 'being a good chap'.

A string of Christian sportsmen spoke to me as a boy approaching manhood and as a young man hungry for a vocation. I was stirred by the story of Wilfrid Grenfell and his heroic adventures as a pioneering doctor in the frozen wastes of Labrador in the late 19th century. He was a young London intern who loved outdoor recreation and was fascinated to hear evangelist Dwight L. Moody speak of Jesus as a noble living Leader who calls out the best in us. Life became a field of adventure where his gifts were put to use in the service of others.

This challenge stirred the University world of the mid-19th century. Seven of England's elite athletes travelled across the country summoning young men and women to follow Jesus in practical missions across the world.[121] Grenfell was prompted to action. 'The decision to fairly try out that faith, which has challenged and stirred the ages, in the laboratory of one's own life is, I am convinced, the only way to ever obtain a fixed heart on the matter. The prize is to be won not swallowed, as is everything else we know that is of permanent value.'[122] As I matured in my own faith, men like Grenfell became the Immortals of my personal 'Hall of Fame' and provided a store of narratives to stir the young people I was teaching.

Behind them was the figure of a carpenter from Nazareth who had faced down the most powerful men of his day in single combat.

Risk-taking faith often triggers a chain reaction. C.T. Studd's challenge launched Grenfell to Labrador, where he took initiatives to meet the medical and social needs of people living in isolation. His daring inspired my home-grown hero, John Flynn, to turn bi-planes into ambulances, stretching a mantle of safety across the neglected Inland of Australia. I could hear C.T. Studd echoed decades later in 21-year-old Flynn's letter to his father. 'If it be true that Jesus is God's Son and that through him "whosoever will may approach the Father himself", what more honourable calling can a man follow than getting his fellows to realise this fact and act upon it?'[123] I have read these words to many young Australians and seen it light a fire in them.

I once interviewed Australian Test cricketer Brian Booth at 2WEB in Bourke, asking for some highlights from his career. He named captaining Australia, scoring a century against the West Indians, and being part of an Ashes-winning team. There was astonishment on the face of a group of teachers listening on the other side of the glass when he went on to say that all these ran a distant second to the day he decided to take Jesus seriously. Brian fleshed out what I had seen in my heroes and reinforced the idea that sacrifice, commitment, and excellence displayed on the sports field should be translated into the rest of life as a calling. I use Grenfell's words, 'Faith is just reason made courageous'[124], to encourage bravery in developing an intelligent, spiritual life.

Bruno is one of those who has been seized by that spirit. He's a chunky Tongan mate of mine in Dubbo who has coached a local Rugby team. It is believed that Methodist missionaries brought not just religion, but rugby to Tonga. He told me that at home, footy training always began with singing a hymn (the boys knew the whole Wesleyan hymnbook by heart) and a prayer. Their faith drives their football, and they are joyfully transplanting this onto the playing fields of secular Australia – and who's going to jeer at a 120kg Islander for being too religious? Bruno knew nothing about Thomas Arnold's goal to produce well-grounded men through sport until I explained it to him. He was amazed. But he's been modelling it to people all around him who've lost touch with faith. He's begun a group called Tradies in Sight, 'a mental health and wellbeing organisation dedicated to supporting tradies in regional NSW'[125] This was his response to help the many he had seen struggling with issues that were destroying them.

I see the Rugby Headmaster's legacy living on in Bruno.

Rugby's boast has long been that it's 'the game they play in heaven.' As I watched the flood of footballers from the Pacific Islanders storming the sporting fields of Australia, it strikes me that they are awakening us to priorities we have forgotten. Fans should realise that many of these men and women are playing rugby the way Dr Arnold purposed it for his pupils – as an exuberant expression of faith in the Living God. To me, the hearty hymn singing and prayer at their games are more than a quaint social custom. It's a rousing reminder of rugby's spiritual roots – exactly the kind of game that you might expect to light up the playing fields of heaven! The back story of those who first ventured from Europe and Australia to bring the transforming story of Jesus to the ferocious people of the South Seas, needs to be told, alongside their feats on the football field. Islanders have told me that many of these missionaries lost their lives in the process, and they are deeply grateful to them for it.[126]

I'm not arguing that sport owes everything to the Christian faith. It doesn't – not by a long shot. What energises me is the thought that valuable social capital can be generated by placing sport in the context of all of life spirituality. Then faith is not seen as a competitor but as an ally. People of genuine faith have a great opportunity to nourish the spiritual root-system that keeps sport from declining into egotism, brutality, corruption and ruthless competition. Leading coaches have agreed that the sports chaplain has an important role because they are there to assist players in building a narrative that goes beyond sporting success.

Betty Cuthbert, the 'golden girl' who gripped the imagination of my generation by winning the 100m sprint at both the Melbourne and Rome Olympics, spoke of a deeper need fulfilled in her. 'Winning my medals was superb, but six hours afterwards you would have thought I'd lost. I was so tired, so drained, and I got thoroughly sick of talking to people about it. But when you win Christ, so to speak, it's so different. You get excited about it all the time, and you're eager to tell everybody.'[127]

Storytellers who weave fleeting moments of athletic success into a fuller narrative could help prevent sport from becoming an emotional cul-de-sac. In his day, cricketer Steve Waugh was one of my sporting heroes. After retirement he distilled the lessons that had not only helped develop his renowned mental toughness as a batsman and captain, but gave him a vision of a fruitful life beyond sport. The most impactful were the brief meetings with Nelson Mandela, Mother Theresa and Rev James Stevens, the founder of *Udayan* refuge for leprosy sufferers in Kolkata. What impressed him was the way these three people of faith had laid aside personal ambition to live out a larger story than their own narrow narrative. The words on Mother Theresa's business card worked a profound change in the heart of one of the world's most successful sportsmen and inspired him to work at giving disadvantaged children greater opportunities.

The fruit of silence is prayer.
The fruit of prayer is faith.
The fruit of faith is love.
The fruit of love is service. [128]

A friend's little daughter Emily, who is suffering from cancer, was welcomed by the Sydney Swans team at training – the family are fans. One of the players carried the frail little girl onto the SCG through the banner at the start of their AFL match – it brought out the best selves in those muscular heroes. The humbling effect on the players and the joy the moment brought to the family transcended the result of the game. Emily's father Jono reported it was the genuine interest of the players in their whole family that touched his heart. The team's ongoing concern signals it was more than a gesture – it was part of their culture. I sensed not just Dr Arnold's values surfacing there, but also the presence of the Jesus of the gospels who raised a young girl from death. It lifted the spirits of participants and spectators alike as a reminder of what is really important in life.

Likewise, it's inspiring to see an Aussie crowd wearing pink at the Sydney Cricket Test each January in support of breast cancer nurses, as a dynamic memorial to champion Glen McGrath's wife Jane who died from the disease. Watching footy players visiting children's hospital wards or hearing that tennis players are funding orphanages and schools in third world countries widens the world's lens on life. When sporting heroes use their strengths to serve those less fortunate, they provide reality checks in the hyper-charged world of professional sport. That would make the Rugby Headmaster proud! In my calculation, without realising it, they are resurfacing the spiritual musculature that lies beneath the surface of Australian sport.

They are writing chapters in a larger story that speaks of real immortality – something that provides us all with direction and hope. President Nelson Mandela's master stroke in using the Rugby World Cup to inspire healing and reconciliation in South Africa was the story behind the movie *Invictus*. I think he saw that Thomas

Arnold's idea of muscular Christianity could be lifted to the level of statesmanship if harnessed to Jesus' vision of true humanity.

> Sport has the power to change the world. It has the power to inspire, it has the power to unite people in a way little else does. It speaks to youth in a language they understand.

> Sport can create hope, where once there was only despair. It is more powerful than governments in breaking down racial barriers. It laughs in the face of all types of discrimination.[129]

10

A COMPASS, A MAP AND A HARBOUR

A person without a story is a person with amnesia. A country without its story has ceased to exist. A humanity without its story has lost its soul.[130]

William Bausch

Stories weather our world. Day and night, they sweep across the surface of our inner lives, sculpting our ideas and values. Some we are glad to remember, others we would rather forget. For example, hearing my family repeat shared memories since childhood, steadily built a picture of the tribe I belonged to and gave me some sense of place in the physical world. I've learned that stories breed stories, and so every day, we are adding to the cluster of anecdotes and reminiscences that become our worldview.

I can now see they were the everyday ingredients that gave texture and tang to the years spent under my parent's roof. I regret that adolescent collisions with my stern Scottish grandfather robbed me of the opportunity to sit with him and hear stories of my Celtic ancestors. I'm sure we would have been better friends if I had – but they're lost. It makes me realise how fragile these tiny story spores are and how swiftly they can be blown away unless they are rooted in a seedbed bigger than themselves.

Robyn and I like to walk at Dubbo's Taronga Zoo. As far as I can see, despite Walt Disney's efforts to persuade us otherwise, animals don't pass stories around or recite history. The apes and elephants, meerkats and tigers seem content to simply respond to whatever is in front of them. We human beings, by contrast, are remarkable in the way we expend so much energy relaying folklore and creating sagas. There is something that drives us to seek out meaning in our small narratives, and when we struggle in this, we borrow other narratives, both real and artificial, to strengthen our own.

I am grateful to the varied host of storytellers who have stepped alongside on the journey with compelling tales to tell. The best of them made every sentence count – filled them with images that were inviting, informing and inspiring. They set a rhythm to my stride because they spoke of purpose. They became prized possessions, stored in my pack like waybread to be shared with fellow travellers on this pilgrimage we are making.

Let me introduce a few.

Illustrators captured my childish imagination with drama. Sunday School teachers who got us sticking simple figures to a flannel board got me repeating larger-than-life stories that have attached like burrs to my inner world. One gifted lady made biblical scenes vivid with chalks that glowed under ultraviolet light, while her husband painted the story with his violin. Filmmakers opened our eyes wide to the wonders of Creation – taking us soaring into the vault of stars above us or plunging us inside ingenious cities built by bees. Extrovert acting-types engaged us with joyful singing, hilarious tales, puzzle parables, puppets, and ventriloquist dolls, teaching us serious things while we laughed.

Because these people loved the stories, they awoke and nurtured the responsive soul of a child, affirming feelings of right and wrong, tuning my ears to listen for the voice of God in his world. Dedicated mentors patiently built foundations and scaffolding into the inner world of a restless boy that gave me a frame for manhood. These sacred storytellers shape the destinies of future generations.

I fear they may be a dying breed – I hope not.

Modernist storytellers had been busy dis-enchanting the 20th century world. Cynical voices told my generation that science could assure us there was no hope of anything beyond the hard, 'proven' realities of our present physical environment. Anyone reporting an immanent spiritual world was accused of peddling outdated nonsense.

Then the masters of 'true myth' appeared, building fantastic bridges that transported us beyond our parochial world where things can become blurred by familiarity. Somehow old truths and traditional values became vibrant when they were part of fabled adventures happening to schoolchildren in Narnia or through a heroic conquest of evil by humble hobbits in fictional Mordor. Science Fiction was offered as an anaesthetic to ease the pain of severed religious nerves. Intelligent story-wizards like C.S. Lewis and J.J.R. Tolkien called their bluff by inviting us to surrender to the possibility of a secondary belief in things not seen under a microscope. Instead, they re-enchanted our world by appealing to the shy, persistent voice within us that whispered of greater realities and supernatural spheres. In doing so, they charmed us into reconsidering the soaring biblical narrative with its mind-blowing storyline of the Creator invading our planet.

In time, I chose to become one of the tribal storytellers. I was taught that we historians were detectives, carefully sifting through the fragments of the past to construct a framework in which people can function with reasonable certainty. We were to delve into the lives of our forefathers with an eye for clues to our collective identity. But, at the same time, there were limitations to this craft.

The final decision as to what our storied journey means is a highly personal one.

Over time, a troupe of interpreters crowded in – artists, poets, musicians, filmmakers, prophets, apologists, theologians, scientists and philosophers – whose voices have blended into a choir in the background of my life. They sing romantic ballads that make my spirit leap or my heart melt. They provide pilgrim songs with sturdy lyrics and steady cadences that keep my feet moving when the going gets tough.

Standing in St Peter's Cathedral in Rome, I asked myself what exactly inspired Michelangelo to capture the pain in Mary's heart as she cradled her crucified son in Carrara marble. Surely it was the touch of a Master Craftsman that enabled him to transcend the physical boundaries of solid rock? Similarly, who gifted my friend Jen Greentree with the eye and the hand to make her canvases sing of the glory of God written across the cathedral skies and burnt-red plains of Western New South Wales?

And where did the inspiration come from for my daughter Alison to compose a patchwork quilt with painstaking care, featuring our family tree complete with photos? The clue was in the embroidered words, 'The Lord will provide.' Robyn used this picture of our family story to encourage a classroom of children to trust in a God who cares for them. My youngest son Pete has a genius for hilarious recital that generates a climate of warm connection where stories flow easily. Laughter is a gift that disarms and heals.

Storytellers all. Our world is story-rich if only we have eyes to see.

Poets and musicians have helped me develop insight by using the eye of the mind that looks for cogency and the eye of the heart that warms and transforms by love. They made words pulse with meanings that have touched my emotions. Their skill was to use words to interweave truths I had come to understand with my reason and feelings that came from deep within. They freed me to approach storytelling with the academic rigour that demands the concrete and the passionate faith that seizes on the unseen.

One such man, who has captured my attention, penned a poem in the trenches of World War One in France. Chaplain Geoffrey Studdert-Kennedy wrote about a furnace-tried faith. Crouched beside him in the stinking, bloody mud were young soldiers struggling to reconcile the daily obscenities they were witnessing with the things they had heard about, when sitting safe in the pews at home. He explained his own decision in verse.

> *I have to choose. I back the scent of life*
> *Against its stink. That's what Faith works out at*
> *Finally. I know not why the Evil,*
> *I know not why the Good, both mysteries*
> *Remain unsolved. And both insoluble.*
> *I know that both are there, the battle set,*
> *And I must fight on this side or on that.*
> *I can't stand shivering on the bank, I plunge*
> *Head first. I bet my life on Beauty, Truth and Love…*
> *I bet my life on Christ - Christ crucified.*[131]

Reports were that those men loved this 'Bible-basher' because he was willing to bet his life the same way they did, by going over the top into the teeth of machine gun fire to rescue the wounded in 'No-man's land'. That's why, after the War, battle-hardened veterans filled the pews of any church where he told stories that helped them rekindle their faith.

I know his resolute voice still speaks to me and gives strength to others I know.

Whenever country singer Slim Dusty came to town, nearly the whole population of the Bourke district, black and white, flocked to hear him sing ballads celebrating life in the bush. The simplicity of his home-spun sketches drew the community together. Australian wordsmiths like Slim and Paul Kelly have understood the way songs can become living links between our spiritual world and us. They intuit that melody and memory can create space for those sacred, 'That's us!' moments. For forty years, I've worn grooves into my faithful Maton 12-string guitar while singing songs like theirs to folk in every situation and proved this true.

The long tradition of the troubadour as the teller of a people's heart-stories is alive and available.

Over centuries, hymn writers have carried potent biblical stories into the consciousness of the nation. I was taught them from childhood – some ordinary, some majestic. I sang them with my widowed mother as we walked together down a bush track through the gidgee trees in Bourke. They were the threads that knit our souls together. They were the last things she remembered as she slipped away into dementia – the musical anchor point for her spirit.

Skilled filmmakers have invited me to plunge into the lives of others and created celluloid worlds that offered a temporary escape. So much of it has been sheer entertainment, but the lasting moments were when teams of scriptwriters, producers and cinematographers fixed images and phrases that have sharpened convictions that I live by. The Scottish blood stirred in me in the scene from *Chariots of Fire*, when champion runner Eric Liddell explained to his reproving sister, "God made me fast Jenny, and when I run I feel his pleasure." Nobody knows whether he said those exact words, but they sent me on a journey to discover the man and what made him tick. Internees in a Japanese prison camp recalled his courage and unselfishness in the years following his 400m win at the 1924 Olympics.[132] These created the image of a tried and true man of faith in my inner gallery, and the electricity was still there when my grandson sat me down to give me his impressions of this brave Scot, after reading his biography.

A story well told can awaken curiosity and expand the spiritual horizons of both older men and young boys.

I've come across a few prophets in my time – strident voices unsettling me with warnings that things were not as they should be. God Squad founder Rev John Smith, straddling a Harley Davidson motorbike, shouted a warning at us about our frantic materialism and careless pleasure-seeking.[133] Psychologist Ronald Conway sketched scenarios predicting social chaos unless we vacationers in the 'Land of the Long Weekend' woke up to ourselves.[134] Social commentator Hugh MacKay pleaded with leaders to supply narratives that offered new generations some direction.[135] Clergyman Bruce Wilson punctured our complacent 'Christian Country' thinking with the blunt question, 'Can God survive in Australia?'[136] His research drove him to argue that for most Aussies, God is an ice chest in a world that has invented the refrigerator. He issued an urgent call to overhaul the whole Christian narrative.

Sharp-eyed lookouts like these have challenged me, again and again, to take my bearings, check the compass, familiarise myself with the map and recalibrate my course. It's all too easy to drift with the tide in the Lucky Country. But, like the prophets of ancient Israel, with one voice they declared this was no time for lazy storytelling. A vigilant recounting of the journey that has brought us this far is imperative to set an intelligent course for the future.

All my young life I heard preachers who mined the biblical narrative to explain the human dilemma – I confess some were way better than others! I've alternately dozed and squirmed through my fair share of painful sermons, but most tried honestly, and there was enough genuine material to keep me listening. I'm particularly grateful to those unassuming Bible teachers able to cast a backward look to explain the past and also peer ahead to inspire me to envision something better. In a despairing world, it's good to realise that even the most ordinary people can paint pictures that are both believable and bright with hope.

Hard-nosed thinkers have battered my worldview into shape with some solid intellectual punching. Bible stories were embedded in me in a fragmentary fashion but what I needed for the long haul was a narrative strong enough to make sense in the present. These were the apologists who taught me to be more tough-minded and helped me build a plausibility framework with tested evidence. I then had to do my own research. Again, my mentor Laurie opened my eyes to the sturdy platform that upheld the historic Christian faith and provided reasoned answers to my questions about meaning and purpose. When I watched him match arguments with various philosophers on a university campus I thought, 'This is story-telling with grunt!'

Modern technology has brought brilliant scientific minds to my door who unravel the mysteries of our universe and the genius of our minuscule DNA. These master-dramatists have unleashed narratives that take the breath away. David Attenborough's camera has delved into the soil of every continent. It has crawled beneath the leaves of every jungle plant and submerged to the murky depths of our oceans in pursuit of the life-story of our planet. He has delivered a blockbuster, mind-blowing in its scale, intricacy, variety and design, enabling us to be eyewitnesses to more natural wonders than any generation in human history. While he struggles to acknowledge that this grand Story has an Author, he is reluctant to say there is not. Others, like Anthony Flew, rated as the world's leading atheist at the turn of the new millennium, have bowed to the weight of evidence that speaks of a Creative Mind.[137]

As we pilot through life, these are constant navigational decisions. In each of us a silent figure sits listening, sifting through the stories, and making judgements about what is true north. This quiet adjudicator decides what I will adopt as reliable data to steer my course. Like the tales told by old salts with a lifetime of experience at sea, tested narratives have supplied longitude and latitude, explained tides and currents, warned of shoals and reefs, as well as preparing me for storms and becalming.

Most important of all, they've helped me fix a destination – a harbour, a homeport.

In the past few decades, postmodern thinking has turned the world into a confused tournament of narratives. Not all those who have wrestled for the helm in our culture have contended fairly. Instead, they select the story lines that support their worldview, and readily discount any competitor. There is no room for discussion. They dismiss the lingering nostalgia to be reunited with something at the back of creation as irrational fancy. But talking with Australians of every description, eyeball to eyeball, it's clear to me that eternity was written on the tablets of our hearts in the same way Arthur Stace chalked it into the heart of Sydney in an elegant copperplate script.[138]

They work hard to ignore the monumental witness of graveyards, mausoleums, temples, and pyramids, which shout mankind's suspicion that we are all embedded in a larger mystery. Instead, they recite cheerless tales to convince new generations that they are just a random collection of atoms destined for eventual extinction. Their stories say that the best our species can look for is the slim hope that we can do a little good while we're breathing and leave something for our children. The leading atheist of the 20th century, Bertrand Russell, drove this storyline to its logical conclusion. He commended building our lives on 'the firm foundation of unyielding despair'! Here, and here only, he prophesied, the soul's habitation could be safely built.[139] Stoic words, but hardly the kind of news to make you leap from bed each morning!

Given that as an interpretive guide, is it any wonder the statistics tell the sad story of a rising suicide rate among young Australians. This challenges me to recount the experiences of people who have found the Bible a useful compass to guide their journey. Yet I cringe when I see the feeble effort to unpack Australia's Christian archives. If the churchgoing population were sat down to a test on their history next Sunday, I doubt many would pass. It tells me Christians are either ignorant or ashamed of their heritage. Has the focus on the tragic failures of some robbed us of our heroes? Do we realise there are great faith adventures of ordinary people on our island home that could energise our families? Are we relating the memories of brave and visionary ancestors with the same vigour the press details the failures? Was Moses right when he commanded Israel to relay their unique history to succeeding generations, to avoid the peril of sliding back into pagan practices. Is our voluntary amnesia in Australia damning our own children to ignorance?

It should not surprise us when the present generation of Australians blithely declare themselves 'secular' when the custodians of traditional faith have such a feeble grasp of their own story. Justifiable shame at recent accounts of failed clerics has bullied many of the faith community into fearful silence.

But we wave the white flag too easily.

A university student sat in our lounge, and her posture reflected her defeat. She told me she was worn down by lecturers laying the blame for many of our society's failures squarely on the shoulders of the church. She felt she had no way of returning fire. Her head came up, her back straightened, and her eyes became bright as I offered her some of the noble elements of her history. Finally, she asked in a puzzled voice, "Why aren't we told these stories?" Moments like this convince me it's strategic to set the story straight.

Young Christians need to know their heritage.

I love the challenge of this contest – it makes my nostrils flare, and I urge fellow Christians not to shirk the opportunity to take our faith-based stories into the arena ready for combat. Contrary to popular opinion, the positives far outweigh the negatives. The greatest single resource for determining the future of any nation is the storehouse of shared history at the centre of their tribal identity. In Australia there are many fine stories of faith filed there. It can be a powerful corrective when people honestly explore the origins of their own mythology.

One morning near Teen Ranch on the edge of Sydney, I sat with a group of young leaders on the gravesite of Yorkshire born Thomas Hassall[140], resting in the shadow of the chapel he built in 1822. I painted the picture of a child who had survived the dangers of his parent's pioneer missionary work in Tahiti and grown up in the infant colony of NSW. At 19, he began Australia's first Sunday School in an effort to teach the first generation of Currency lads and lasses to read and write. The adventures of this lone man riding tirelessly around a vast area, bringing spiritual encouragement to soldier and convict, Aboriginal inhabitants and white settlers alike, made a heroic tale. It explains why he was widely loved. These moments were native to our history and I used them to fire those leaders with pride in what they were doing for the six thousand or so children who swarm around the camp next door every year. Like the orphaned generation of the first settlement that Thomas Hassall cared for, they too need stories to live by.

Inspiring material just like this is currently gathering dust on bookshelves, wasting away in back rooms or standing voiceless in public spaces. It could be set to work to explain the spiritual journey of Australia to the varied faces that are filling the streets of our cities and towns. This came fresh to me as I chatted to a young Australian – an engineer of Indian background as he and his Vietnamese friends explored the Royal Flying Doctor Experience in Dubbo. The story was completely new to them, and he was very open to searching out John Flynn's vision. I've seen this stir faith in numerous groups of young people.

Contrary to the public perception of church, recent research by psychologists and sociologists has confirmed that the support generated by a genuine religious community promotes substantial well-being.[141] Enormous social capital is produced when people are provided with existential meaning, a sense of purpose, a coherent belief system and a moral code. I have found that animating the record of lives inspired by Jesus can touch any Australians, whether they attend church or not. People embrace stories which confirm true north. Successful rescue operations demand a reliable compass, a proven map, a safe harbour – and a lot of courage.

I never fail to be moved when I read the story of *The Snow Goose*. Paul Gallico's graceful prose transports me to the perilous days of May 1940, when sailors, in a motley collection of small boats, headed across the English Channel on a mission to rescue British soldiers from slaughter on the beaches at Dunkirk. That rag-tag flotilla pulled off an unlikely operation that turned a disaster into a celebrated redemptive story.[142] It stirred wartime Prime Minister Winston Churchill to his most rousing speech. 'We shall not flag or fail … we shall go on to the end … We shall never surrender!'[143] His words gave courage to a nation on the brink of defeat.

It may sound way over the top, but I visualise a task force of storytellers in every corner of Australia, mobilising the resources at hand with creativity and compassion. Their assignment will be to recover the forgotten deeds of the many men and women who followed Jesus and helped to make our country a safe harbour.

Their mission (should they choose to accept it!) is to tell Australians another story – one that could help them find their bearings.

11

ROOT STOCK STORIES

The story behind the story of Western literature... is inconceivable without the Old and New Testaments. A Christian story line inhabits our imaginations whether we are Christian or not.[144]

Imre Salusinszky

My friend Russell is a citrus grower who makes horticultural stories rise out of the ground. I've witnessed his skill at coaxing magnificent grapes, mandarins, and oranges from the sandy red soil of Bourke that buyers from city markets compete to pay top dollar for. Previously it grew only stunted saltbush. Like many farmers, he doesn't believe he has much of importance to say, but when you get him talking, you realise he has an amazing store of wisdom – a crop of stories born out of a lifetime's experience.

When I quizzed this reticent storyteller to reveal the secret to producing an abundance of fruit from unpromising native ground, he said, "The governing point is choosing the right root-stock." He first tests the soil to determine its makeup and then searches for an original old tree that had adapted to these conditions. This tested specimen then becomes the root-stock into which he grafts new varieties. His skill lay in connecting hardy roots to a healthy crown. Like most people, I enjoyed the fruit from Russell's trees, oblivious to the careful choices that had taken place in the background.

In the last forty or more years, there have been repeated attempts to deny the existence of Australia's significant spiritual root-stock. In 1988, editors of the landmark bi-centennial history of Australia decided to drop a chapter entitled, 'A Country Not So Christian', tacitly dismissing the role of this ancient faith in determining the national mythology. One academic explained that Europeans in Australia have not been religious people in contrast to the Australian Aboriginals and asserted that a secular attitude had been predominant in the past 200 years. I recall Prime Minister Bob Hawke – a preacher's son – declaring at the time that the new Parliament House in Canberra would open without prayers. I was present with 30,000 Christians from across the nation – indigenous and white – who voted against him with their feet when we circled the centre of government for an all-night prayer vigil.[145] A much smaller number attended the official opening the following week.

In 2005, I came across the article by journalist Imre Salusinszki in *The Australian*. While not claiming to be religious, he was honest enough to admit that the philosophical, legal, and literary framework of Western society had grown directly out of a rootstock that was distinctly Christian. The piece was titled *Hitching a Ride on Faith*[146] and he suggested that these stories had supplied the consensual framework of ideas that had enabled immigrants to survive the shock of being displaced from Europe and transplanted into soil half a world away.

He seemed to be trying to wake his fellow countrymen and women up from the pretence that we had somehow created modern Australia without help from any spiritual source. He said it bluntly – that we were actually freeloaders on a very powerful vehicle that had carried the Western world forward for centuries. Recent publications by respected British journalists Peter Hitchens and Douglas Murray have widened this call to European countries denying their Christian heritage and been echoed by psychologist Jordan Peterson in North America.

In 2011, I was surprised to hear Julia Gillard – another Prime Minister who had walked away from her family's faith – make a public call for the Bible to be taught in schools for the same reason put forward by Salusinsky. This seemed doubly strange because she had overseen the virtual removal of Christianity from the national history curriculum. Equally astonished was Chris Berg, Research Fellow at the Institute of Public Affairs. While holding an atheist viewpoint, he responded with a call on ABC television to teach 'good history' that fully identified the religious origins of modern society – in particular the Christian contribution to the West.[147] That accords with the 2016 Census finding that Australia still remains a predominantly religious country[148]. I'm all for that sort of good history!

To my mind, these added up to a strong plea for an intelligent 'Hitchhikers Guide to Australia' to be made readily available in the marketplace for believers and non-believers alike. The good news is that some highly qualified writers have done just that.

Three decades ago, John Harris, an acknowledged expert on Aboriginal culture, delivered an honest account of the extensive impact of Christianity on the indigenous peoples of Australia.[149] He didn't airbrush the picture. Few seem to realise that, contrary to public opinion, the most recent census showed that 54% of the indigenous population declare themselves as Christian, and only 2% align with their traditional religion. How many have read Dr Harris' 900-page book which explains this anomaly?

More recently, lawyer Roy Williams presented extensive proof in his book *Post-God Nation* that Christianity still plays a vital role in Australia.[150] In conversation, he agreed with me that more needs to be done to help our fellow Australians understand and value this substantial legacy. Historian Meredith Lake followed this up with a vivid account of the Bible's mostly unremarked journey in the Great South Land. The fact that her book won the Australian History Prize in The Prime Minister's Literary Awards signalled it was a serious piece of work.[151]

Close behind, fellow-historians Stuart Piggin and Bob Lindner delivered a monumental two-volume work detailing the remarkable contribution of Christians to pioneering everything from the trade unions to the vote for women. Volume One argued that this faith was the fountain of our country's public prosperity and was recognised as the Australian Christian book of the Year in 2017.[152]

Next, Foreign Editor for *The Australian,* Greg Sheridan, spoke out for embattled believers highlighting the unrecognised contribution that people of faith make at every level of society in his well-received book, *God is Good for You.*[153] Hitting the shelves in 2021 was his highly commended companion volume, *Christians, The Urgent Case for Jesus in our World.*[154] Combined, they present a formidable body of thoroughly researched evidence to counter the popular assumptions I hear parroted like, "Religion is to blame for all the evils in society" or "Science and technology have proved religious faith irrelevant."

What I like about these long overdue books is that they are honest and plain-spoken. The authors are not beating a triumphalist religious drum, trying to prove that this is a 'Christian country', but have simply been seized by the urgency to explain Australia's spiritual DNA to all comers. They detail failures as well as successes in the religious world, working hard to redress the balance in telling the faith history of our country. They should be welcomed both inside and outside the community of faith as a critical contribution to understanding the forces that have brought us to this point in our history. They identify Australia's spiritual rootstock.

But will all this eloquent defence be drowned out by a wall of secular noise?

There have been enough cultural shifts in my lifetime to sheet home how an accurate understanding of our past can give us something to set against the uncertainties of the present. Too often, we've listened to spin-doctors who have created fictions for us, only to discover we were grafted into a trunk without roots. The high-flown dreams of an era of Peace and Love in the Age of Aquarius generated by my 60's generation had evaporated in a whiff of marijuana smoke by the 70's. The Beatles' imaginings and mystic mantras were soon replaced by hard-nosed 'Greed is good' hymns from Wall Street in the 80's.

The wistful hopes of the new millennia refreshing the human spirit with sophisticated high-tech salvation, collapsed in a mammoth pile on September 11th 2001, replaced by a worldwide paranoia about terrorism. Superannuation nest eggs cracked under the pressure of the Global Financial Crisis in 2008. The global pandemic of 2020 has made a dent in the Teflon- coated myth of Science as our saviour. Passionate warriors of the Green gospel continue to urge us to look only to the future. We can save the planet for our children by joining a monastic movement committed to disciplined, eco-friendly lifestyles.

I'll be the first to admit that I have felt the tug of some of the noble aspirations of these movements. The best of their heroes remind me that religion does not have a mortgage on truth. But what irritates me is that many of these protagonists appear to have had little time for an honest examination of the spiritual root system, which nourished the social and legal systems that have allowed them to thrive or the sciences that have equipped them to explore their world. They freely edit or have simply forgotten their past and all the time they are hitchhiking on the faith of their forebears.

The real tragedy I have found is that many of those who call themselves Christians have so poor an understanding of the rootstock they came from. They barely know how to relay the extensive history of their faith, and few seem to appreciate the richness of the sacred ground they grew from. Too often the result has been that they have projected a pale portrait of the robust personality at the centre of their faith. Too many have fixed a remote Sunday School picture of Jesus wandering through the villages of Israel in their inner gallery. Few have seen him in the vital figures striding the Australian landscape from coast to coast, hard at work among our people.

It astonishes me that our governments seem bent on removing any exploration of Jesus from our schools when, after 2000 years, he remains at the top of surveys listing the most influential leaders in human history. A large percentage of the other contenders were his followers. On these grounds alone, he merits intelligent attention. Yet, curiously, there seems an emotional readiness to blithely accept Aboriginal Dreamtime mythology, but an unwillingness to examine the Biblical narrative which similarly tracks our footsteps back to the dawn of time when the Creator called all things into being.

Why are these deep, deep, roots so carelessly dismissed?

I've always watched the public celebrations that preface major events as a window into our self-perception as a people. At the 2018 Commonwealth Games on the Gold Coast, indigenous performers danced and sang their Dreamtime stories to a worldwide audience as a ceremonial expression of Australia's spiritual heredity. It struck me that Jesus was not welcome, even though he had had a strong part to play in the spiritual formation of nearly all the participating nations, including our Aboriginal people. He was just edited out! To me, it signalled that we were denying a foundational story that helped grow modern Australia and continues to sustain a sizeable portion of our people.

Followers of Jesus have been struck mute.

As a mainland Australian, I feel rebuked when I see the Torres Strait Islanders' joyful celebration of 'The Coming of the Light'. It's an annual reminder of the arrival of the gospel of Jesus, which turned them from sorcery and cannibalism in the 19th century.[155] Where they gladly give voice to their redemption story, we hang our heads and shuffle our feet when it comes to any mention of Christian spirituality.

Analysts like those from Pew Research Centre are showing that in recent times, more people than ever are following Jesus in Africa, the Middle East, China and South America. Extensive initiatives to assist poor countries with health, education and housing, or to intervene on behalf of the exploited, have been driven by his teaching. Yet in Australia, Christianity has been reduced to an unconscious pattern of thought, best left buried somewhere beneath the secular surface of the country.

It's evidenced in the increasing numbers of children being sent to religious schools because parents have a lingering sense they can gain some 'good values' there. They need to go further than looking for a moral deodorant. I think it's fair to say that anyone wanting to understand the Australian psyche needs to get more serious about understanding the influence of Jesus. During the length of our country's modern history, his biography would have been the most frequently repeated and perhaps the least understood. Yet, I have found it written everywhere in the lives of women and men who have shaped our culture.

Jesus' footprints are embedded in every corner of the land.

I don't think it's too far-fetched to say that when measured by the breadth and depth of his impact, Jesus is the most successful storyteller in history. I've spent a big chunk of time developing an understanding of both his life and the story of Israel. I made these a lens to help my students in Cornerstone get to the core of our own art, music, industry, science, enterprise, literature, mores, ethics, and law. The cluster of skills in redemptive storytelling we discovered in the gospels has rarely been equalled over the past 2000 years. They've been tested repeatedly in the laboratory of individual lives and proved effective. It made me believe there is an urgent need to recover this foundational story and recast it in the imaginations of 21st century Australians. A fresh image of Jesus needs to be crafted for our multi-cultural population.

What impressed those I've taught about the people who gathered the fragments of story to form the Old Testament, is their remarkable candour in retelling Israel's meandering journey of faith. Far from delivering an air-brushed tale of a noble tribe of saints, they gave us a rough-hewn epic composed of dysfunctional families who argue, flawed leaders who doubt, heroes who made massive mistakes, justice-fighters who were martyred, and prophets who at times question God's integrity. It doesn't hide the strife, incest, rape, murder, theft, deceit, prejudice, slavery, and bloody warfare. To a large degree, it is a catalogue of repeated failures, long excursions into unbelief, and outright rejection of their calling to be God's people. It's not a pretty picture, but it was this fundamental honesty about shortcomings that particularly appealed to the Australians in my classes. We found we could identify with their struggles because it's not a whitewash.

It's important to tell it like it is.

The side of the Old Testament saga that heartens me is God's reported determination to redeem his people despite their mistakes and then the exhilarating moments when they repent and the partnership is renewed. Thanksgiving soars above the moments of dismal disaster. I find hopes rise when we tell it as the drama of battlers like ourselves inching towards a workable faith. Along with the New Testament, I've learned to see it as the extensive root system that daily sends nutrients into the lives of 21st century Australians.

As a juror, I've stood in the impressive courtroom at Bourke under the penetrating gaze of the judge as I swore to give a true verdict according to the evidence. Underneath my hand on the open Bible, I read an ancient Jewish poem calling on God to establish righteousness in a corrupted world. I remember thinking, "It's not a frozen law code in a holy book that is magically going to make either me, the judge, the lawyers, the witnesses, or that prisoner in the dock better people. It's a handbook on forgiveness that offers hope for us failed human beings."

More than anything, I would argue that it's these grounded case histories that made the Bible a benchmark for honest evidence giving in the first place. Right now, these need to be unpacked and revitalised in settings beyond church buildings so that Australians can become familiar with its whole truth and nothing but its truth. What's the use of swearing on a history book that you've never read, let alone tried to understand?

We castrate the Bible when we make it a talisman.

As a teacher, I delight in seeing people grasp the fact that the biblical epic is not fixed in a remote past but is an unfolding spectacle connected to the present, complete with chapters from our own history. Such a powerful narrative needs to be attached to a strong backbone. Jesus launched himself into Israel's history as a crisis of cosmic proportions and knocked it into a fresh trajectory. Since then, the episodes reported in the four gospels have served as the criterion against which all other efforts to give meaning to human existence must be measured. It's impossible to deny that Jesus' story has been an integral part of nation building in Australia, whether or not you believe it's true.

One of my favourite stories features a sign-writer student of mine who had begun to get a hold on big-picture thinking. Visualise him standing beside his work shed in the back lane of a country town with a paintbrush in hand. He got yarning with a mate and in an effort to depict the Bible's panoramic view of human history to the newcomer, he began sketching a timeline of events on the corrugated iron. It was such an eye-opener, the next day, he discovered his friend had brought another bloke with him and was busy explaining the blockbuster painted in bold strokes on the shed wall.

Not quite Michelangelo's Sistine Chapel roof painting, but the same effect!

Jesus understood that soil conservation was an essential part of the storyteller's skillset. To yield a crop, a field needed determined preparatory work. That's why he spent time mulching nutrient-loaded stories into the hearts of his hearers – readying them for the right rootstock to be planted. He sketched scenes of shallow and rocky ground in swift strokes, resistant to even the best seed. He knew neglect would allow weeds and predators to debilitate and destroy the work of centuries. When a testing wind arrived, the topsoil would blow away, leaving the country barren and fruitless.

That's why I'm so insistent we train storytellers determined to engage modern Australians with animated pictures drawn from our buried store of faith-stories. In this way, we create worlds and open up new vistas for our hearers. By telling them with skill, we can crack open the worldviews of our fellows and provoke them to reconsider the large slab of history they may have too easily written off.

Jesus intrigued men and women to rethink God by gathering a supply of colourful human-interest material drawn from the everyday doings of people around him.

His natural instinct was to reach for a story when the opportunity offered.

The genius of his strategy was to concentrate on preparing a team of itinerant storytellers. He then commissioned these ordinary men and women to carry the report of all they had seen and heard to every corner of the world. He never wrote a book but chose to trust these eyewitnesses to convey his life story.

So, they set about the conquest of the Roman Empire by chatting around meal tables. They swapped news at wayside inns, met on hillsides, gossiped in markets, and spoke in village squares and civic meeting places. They told of Jesus' miracles, his many acts of kindness, his teachings about life, his courageous death, and above all, his astonishing resurrection.

In a remarkably short space of time these stories overcame the iron fist of Rome!

And as they were repeated over and over they swelled into a torrent of narrative, gathering colour and richness from the soil of every country along its path to the present. That river continues to gain momentum across the globe. I grew up inside a tiny molecule of the Christian community in suburban Sydney. It was church historian Dr Ian Rennie at Regent College who opened my eyes to the liveliness and richness of my spiritual legacy. He led me on a journey from the moment news of Jesus' resurrection first exploded in Jerusalem, step by step across continents and into the 20th century. The evidence was sitting alongside me in the form of students from every continent on earth.

I went from Vancouver to outback Bourke. Over the next forty years I taught Tongans, Fijians, Papuans, Koreans, Mexicans, Chileans, Norwegians, Swiss, English, Americans, Indians, Pakistanis, Bangladeshis, Nepalis, Chinese, Timorese, Indonesians, Filipinos, Ghanaians, South Africans, Zimbabweans and a slew of others. They all reported the Jesus story as having taken root in their cultures. Their stories all had different pigments and textures that added depth to my own.

A couple of West Papuan students insisted I return with them to the home of their people in the highlands. In a dramatic mountainside setting, a thousand Danis in tribal dress acted out the watershed moment when Australian missionaries brought the story of Jesus to them only fifty years previously. Older women held up hands missing most of the fingers and mimed that tradition had required them to cut them off to appease the spirits when someone died. "This was before the gospel came," they repeated, smiling. They were part of the largest people movement in history when hundreds of thousands turned from animism to faith in Jesus. I also came to see that in every culture, there are always complexities in a shift like this. Nevertheless, the changes brought by being grafted into this rootstock have brought real and lasting benefits. Australians have played a part in carrying out this task worldwide. Collected, their stories would surprise the country.

I found an unexpected story in my own backyard. The former steel city of Newcastle had been revamped in recent years. Underneath the new Novotel built on the original hospital site, there's a chic restaurant named Bistro Dalby. It had been named for my great-grandmother Marianne Dalby who arrived in the colony as a child from Plymouth in 1855 on the barque *Lady Anne.* When I eventually read her story I laughed, because the photos of her in middle-age, dressed in sober black, made it plain she cared nothing about chic!

For half a century, this energetic little lady worked tirelessly raising funds for the Newcastle Hospital, the Salvation Army, the Benevolent Society, and the Seaman's Mission. My Dad told me stories of walking the streets with her as a boy, distributing food and clothes to people in need. Predictably, she was at the centre of the action when the lethal influenza epidemic hit the city in 1919. I was moved when I read that the news of her death in 1924 caused the masters of all the ships in the harbour to fly their flags at half-mast, recognising her care for their crews. Seamen and dockyard workers rubbed shoulders with the city fathers as the mayors of three districts carried the coffin of this simple lady from the cathedral. The many tributes paid to her painted the picture of a kind of Mother Theresa of Newcastle.

Her son described her in his eulogy as a true follower of Jesus Christ. As she trekked across a whole city on errands of mercy, my great-grandmother grafted his story into our family tree. At the same time, she left the footprints of Jesus on the streets of Newcastle. The Dean of the cathedral had remarked at her funeral that every city needed a woman like Ma Dalby and predicted she would never be forgotten. But the intervening years have crowded her memory into the background. The response to a press article I wrote during our recent Covid 19 pandemic, telling of her work during the 1919 influenza crisis, affirmed that new generations could be inspired when they realise they are standing on the shoulders of women like her.[156]

I was a proud great-grandson in telling her story.

Moses, when shaping the unseasoned tribes of Israel over 3000 years ago, urged his people to pass their rootstock story to succeeding generations. He was convinced this narrative of grace would hold them together and against the odds, it has. I'm pretty sure the old veteran didn't mean drumming it into your kids by wooden repetition, but the kind of storytelling that refreshed the spirit as they went about their work or sat around the meal table. In this way, it became a living, breathing narrative, season after season putting out new shoots. Whether we like to admit it or not, there's a wealth of case histories to show that much of our culture has flourished by being grafted into the same stem.

Environmental activists urge us to rescue precious trees from vandals. It seems to me that the same applies to the deep-rooted Judeo-Christian story, which is in imminent danger of being woodchipped in Australia. We're talking about a grand old-growth giant of the forest that has earned the right to have its story told in the public conversation about the shape of future Australia.

If my orchardist friend Russell had a chance to speak he would say, "You need hardy roots to grow a healthy crown."

12

ON THE ROAD TO FIND OUT

So, what happens is people are breaking away from the institution but they are still asking the big questions, and that's exactly where pilgrimage fits in. Because a pilgrimage is at its core a gesture, or an action. It's saying that I'm going to take a step. I'm going to figure out what I really believe and I'm going to determine for myself how I want to live my life.[157]

Bruce Feiler

Their bus had broken down outside the Tourist Office in Bourke. So, there they were – 30 or so bright-eyed, intelligent young exchange students on a journey of discovery across Australia, with time to kill. They came from countries like France, Germany, Brazil, and others I forget. As the resident storyteller, I did what I loved to do – I walked them through the saga of the West, trying to meet their energetic inquiries about our history as best I could. After a while, one sharp lad looked me in the eye and said, "You're not like most other Australians we've met – you know your own story! Why are you different?" I explained that I believed the effort to trace the journey of our own people led us on paths that connected to the journeys of others. When these roads merge, we can find ourselves walking side by side on a highway we all share. And once there, we often discover others searching for answers to the big questions about meaning in life that besiege us all.

An hour or so later, a dozen or more were still seated in a semi-circle peppering me with questions about God, suffering in the world, the reliability of the Bible, the reality of Jesus, and more. The Tourist Office had morphed into the Interpreter's House imagined by John Bunyan in *The Pilgrim's Progress*. Here were modern day wayfarers from across the globe, their hearts alive with queries about the spiritual world. We parted friends, having walked a mile together with some promising to read the story of Jesus with an open mind.

Census statistics suggest that this is not the norm. The picture they paint is of a growing number of Australians walking away from church and declaring that they have no interest in religion. Alarmists suggest this forebodes a wholesale plunge into atheism and unbelief in our country. Much to the dismay of my clergy friends, churchgoing seems to have lost its charm. However, hundreds of conversations with tourists, backpackers and hitch hikers have convinced me that many of those Aussies who have walked away from the institutional church, have opted for the road as a way of finding answers.

It's a worldwide phenomenon, accelerated by cheap airfares and general ease of mobility. A couple of years ago, the United Nations estimated that a third of all tourists were, in fact, on a spiritual odyssey – that's 330 million pairs of feet questing across our lonely planet annually![158] The recent Covid lockdown has only increased the restlessness – the questions of meaning have deepened, and people are impatient to travel. James K. A. Smith, a North American philosopher, has gone beneath the surface of this global disquiet trying to fathom the source.

> We leave because we're looking. For something. For someone. We leave because we long for something else, something more. We leave to look for some piece of us that's missing. Or we hit the road to leave ourselves behind and refashion who we are. We hit the road in the hope of finding what we are looking for – or at least

sufficiently distracting ourselves from the hungers and haunting absences that propelled our departure in the first place.[159]

The tread of pilgrims' feet has echoed in my mind since childhood. In a real sense, the Bible stories I learned as a boy were a spiritual travelogue. Abraham took his family on a mysterious journey, leaving permanent footprints in the sand all the way from the Tigris-Euphrates valley to the fabled Promised Land. In doing so, he launched his descendants on a pilgrimage of cosmic proportions.

Centuries later, Moses marched across the Sinai desert at the head of a column of Hebrew slaves on the long road to freedom in Canaan. Almost a millennium passed before Jewish exiles turned their faces west from Babylon to begin their emotional return journey to a shattered Israel, bent on rebuilding Jerusalem and its spiritual centrepiece – the Temple.

Four hundred years later, Jesus appeared, striding the length and breadth of his native land, calling disciples to take the dangerous option of following him on his mission to Israel. His parable of the prodigal son's long excursion back to his home has become a classic tale of a redemptive journey. It's no surprise to learn that his disciples chose to be called 'followers of the Way' before they were nick-named 'Christians'.

In a short time, Paul and his team began hiking 10,000 miles on Roman roads, determined to bring the gospel to the Empire. Other apostles spread to every point of the compass. From the very outset, the kingdom Jesus launched was mobile and adventurous. He never designed it to be static.

Subsequent history has shown that when it stalls, it loses its dynamic.

As I ventured further on my own journey, I was inspired when poring over tales of missionaries who trekked far and wide on reckless expeditions of faith. While studying at Regent College I was stirred by the carefree, Celtic monk, Columbanus, who reminded his disciples, 'Let us, since we are travellers and pilgrims in this world, keep the end of the road always in our minds – for the road is our life and its end is our home.'[160] It was especially rewarding to learn that some of this breed of spiritual adventurer had eventually crossed the oceans and tramped the plains and ridges of the 'Great South Land of the Holy Spirit' where I lived.

In Social Studies at primary school, we painstakingly traced the courses of mariners like Columbus, Magellan, and Cook across the oceans of the world and drew dotted lines on the weathered face of Australia as we followed the explorations of Mitchell, Sturt, Eyre, and the ill-fated Burke and Wills. British poet Rudyard Kipling detected a divine call in this lure to discover something beyond settled existence.

For better or worse, empire building and the spread of the gospel became co-extensive.

> *Till a voice, as bad as Conscience, rang interminable changes*
> *On one everlasting Whisper day and night repeated – so:*
> *'Something hidden. Go and find it. Go and look behind the Ranges –*
> *Something lost behind the Ranges. Lost and waiting for you, Go!'*[161]

There were many well-trodden paths in my mind. I had been walking in the steps of other pilgrims all my life, and this faith I followed was no mere by-path. Over centuries and continents, hundreds of thousands of souls, reckless and resourceful, timid and tentative, had worn a network of highways and tracks across the world. Whatever the motive, I developed the distinct sense that these faith-inspired journeys had brought us to the present.

I learned that story must provoke the growth of wings and roots to fulfil its inspirational function in a culture. Thomas Cook is a prime example. While working as a Tourist Officer, I discovered that the modern tourist industry was birthed, almost accidentally, by this young Baptist preacher. While tramping thousands of miles across English counties carrying the gospel, he had his eyes opened to the road being a school.

Largely uneducated himself, he seized on the exhilarating possibilities of bringing pilgrimage within reach of ordinary folk. 'Travel is to feed the mind and rub off the rust of circumstance… to travel is to have Nature's plan and high works simplified… to travel is to dispel the mists of fable and clear the mind of prejudice taught from babyhood and facilitate perfectedness of seeing eye to eye.'[162] The popular success of his cheap train trip for 500 mainly working-class people to a Temperance meeting in 1841 launched a worldwide phenomenon. Since childhood, I heard 'Cook's Tours' used as a byword for getting people on the road to find out.

More often than not, this road-hunger was a pilgrimage without a particular destination, where travellers tried to convince themselves that the road was life. The ambition of my restless 60's generation was fired by American author Jack Kerouac when he sold us the romantic Road Trip as the pathway to freedom. It promised us a transformative rite of passage where we could shrug off the dull routine of suburban life and become active participants in a journey of self-discovery – easy riders with the wind of the open road blowing through our shoulder-length hair.

The Australian version was leaving Sydney or Melbourne to follow the overland route through Asia to the ultimate destination waiting beyond the horizon – London, the rock music capital of the world! It was not unusual for a spiritual hunger to surface, and along the way, hippies joined the ashrams of Indian gurus who promised magical enlightenment. Many experimented in liberating their minds with the hallucinogenic drugs they found in plentiful supply and bequeathed the idea of 'tripping' with new meaning. With sexual freedom thrown in, it was a heady package for young Aussies, weary of respectable urban life and the damp blanket of routine religion. With the Beatles as the pop-evangelists of Eastern mysticism, what could possibly go wrong?

Well, a lot, as it turned out. I've talked with friends who ran a Dilarim House in Nepal, salvaging the lives of young Westerners for whom the warm-fuzzy dream of the 'peaceful East' had become a nightmare reality. This couple had followed the trail from Amsterdam through Kabul to Kathmandu to see first-hand what many young pilgrims were experiencing as they drifted rudderless. For seven years, they were part of a team that provided a sanctuary for this flotsam of lost souls – an Interpreter's House set in the Himalayas. The restoration process involved not only detoxing and healthy food, but also reviving stories of the Christian faith that for many had been bleached of meaning in the materialistic West. New spiritual journeys were begun.

Road-hunger has been described as some sort of leftover evolutionary habit from our ancestors – the herd instinct to migrate. The tug that drew friends on that pilgrimage was never strong enough to get me on the road, yet I confess it stirred the blood. It wasn't my brilliant navigational skills that kept returning the needle of my moral compass to True North, but the store of guiding stories I had been gifted.

It wasn't long before I too, met disillusioned casualties who had failed to find the enlightenment promised by the prophets of LSD and transcendental meditation. Not all had been burned, but many came home with spiritual blanks unfilled. They had widened their experience of the world – but I've yet to meet anyone who returned from the hippy trail with all their questions answered. In time, most of the pop-gurus limped away from that path themselves, having sent many young Aussies on a trip to nowhere.[163]

Meeting different travellers showed me that your personal experience can be meaningful or meaningless depending on the interpretive tools you are given. Nearly all hopefuls seemed to be in a stage of transition – experiencing some seismic shift from one stage to another. Long ago, St Augustine jabbed his finger on a deep spiritual nerve with his famous prayer, 'Our hearts are restless, until they can find rest in you'[164]

Theologian Alistair McGrath confessed he wrote his book *The Journey* specifically because he felt there were people like himself, 'fed up with being fed trite and shallow answers to the big problems of Christian living.'[165] He was calling them to step out on a dangerous journey, away from the safety of inherited religion, to go deeper and explore further. That was the type of voice that mobilised me.

During my studies at university, the idea surfaced that many take to the road, driven by an age-old hunger for connection to the sacred, seeking blessing, forgiveness, healing, and even immortality. Geoffrey Chaucer's motley band of pilgrims, swapping tales on the road to Canterbury, has fixed this kind of travelling theatre in the Western imagination for the last 700 years.

Recently, Australian broadcaster, Sheridan Voysey, pulled on walking boots, slung a pack of broken dreams, and set out to retrace the steps of Anglo-Saxon saint Cuthbert along the shores of England.[166] The beautiful, painful, reflective journey brought fresh insight and healing. Others I've met were eager to learn, some sought regeneration, others longed to touch greatness or revitalise their family heritage. Whatever the reason, they were on the move and hungry for experiences that might assure them of where they belonged.

The call to pilgrimage is a powerful tide when harnessed for spiritual renewal. There was a considerable shock in secular Sydney when half a million mostly Gen Y kids from 200 countries hit town for Catholic World Youth Day in 2008. Local economic indicators registered an impressive spike in spending, but those involved spoke of a less tangible surge – something genuine on the spiritual scale. I recall the astonishment of Sydneysiders at the time who were pretty much convinced that religion was on its deathbed. Puzzled faces asked, "What on earth motivated such a mob of young people to trek here on Christian pilgrimage?"[167]

Good question. Could it have been the same insistent urge that sent Abraham 'looking for a better country – a heavenly one'?

Some shrewd observations from an American journalist with a secular Jewish background went a long way to answering that query for me. Spurred by the apocalyptic events of September 11 in New York, Bruce Feiler decided to 'walk the Bible' to get inside the seminal story of Abraham – the reputed father of Jews, Christians, and Muslims. First, he studied the original source documents, and then secured an archaeologist as a guide for a physical odyssey through the locations of the biblical stories. His lengthy quest drove him to list some conclusions about the inner workings of a pilgrimage.

He was convinced it most often originates with a call – for Westerners, an elusive yearning to escape the over-scheduled lives that smother spirituality. He found the step away undid the certainties he depended on – those offered by family and culture and especially those pledged by our rational education. The blisters he acquired on the trail became a significant part of the experience – enduring hardship and pushing beyond his physical limits had a humbling and purifying effect.

It also created community with fellow sufferers struggling on the journey with him. Unhurried trekking through the natural world, in particular the deserts, allowed time for reflection on deeper questions of existence. The climax, which amazed him, was an encounter with the supernatural – he hadn't set out with that in mind. On return, to his further surprise, he discovered that the meaning he had found in foreign territory had been quietly residing beneath the surface of his own backyard.

Feiler explained the profound effect of a pilgrimage in terms that resonated with things I had learned about connecting story to place. He summed it up by saying that his learning went from his head to his feet.

> So, the big transformation was being on the land… and finding the story in the geography itself. I don't think I ever realised that the Bible consisted of real stories that happened to real people. I think I always thought of it as happening in some kind of mythic time and place. So, I think what happened to me… was that I just became really grounded.[168]

This aligned with what I had witnessed happening to people half a world away from the Middle East, on red dirt roads at the back of Bourke, connecting travellers to Australian stories. Learning not only shifted from head to feet – it also went to the heart. Observers of human behaviour have labelled this transition from a secure place into the unknown as entering a 'liminal space' – a kind of borderless in-between area that allows for psychological progression of the spirit. In Australia, there is no more liminal zone than the Outback.

Travelling these lonely spaces west of Bourke, I watched the eyes of locally born poet Andrew Hull open to his home territory in a fresh way. It galvanised him to put the things he saw into music and verse. In his words,

> … the real strength, the inherent reason for stories, is to connect us to places, to identify who we are and where we fit in the narrative of our community… This to me is the reason to write, the reason to listen, the reason to look… It is a reason to try and understand a place, a story and most of all, your place in that story.[169]

I knew I had stumbled onto something significant with the Poets' Trek when well-known historian Bruce Elder declared it 'the most significant literary journey in Australia.'[170] Then a retired professor of Australian Literature reported that this journey in the steps of Henry Lawson had rekindled his love for research, and he was back in the library writing. Finally, a city-bred musician, who had accompanied him, returned to Melbourne fired up to compose a Lawson musical, which he has, would you believe, taken on the road. The magic of tracking footprints!

I felt I really hit the jackpot when a reserved fencing contractor, with hands calloused from running a thousand kilometres of wire, confessed at the end of the journey, to writing his very first poem. It sprang from hard-won experience cutting timber in the bush – "you can tell a lot about a bloke by which end of the log he picks up!" I winced at the clever way he applied it to some religious people he'd met. I began to see there is a universal music and deep wisdom embedded in the country. It reaches the heart through the feet, whether trekking in the Middle East or the Australian Outback.

One plus one equals three.

Aboriginal friends have painted a vivid picture of their ancestors scattering words and music along the line of their footprints, weaving a web of 'Dreaming tracks' across the country. If you knew these songs, you could, in theory, sing your way across the whole continent. One bushman told me he'd been shown scars in trees that marked a trail through tribal territory, so the landforms became an encyclopedia, and the storytellers were the guardians. If the tribe failed to sing its musical score, the land would die, and the next generation would be left without a guide.

As the clan walked together singing, the song-line merged their daily activities with the unseen world of the spirit. Travel-writer Bruce Chatwin confirmed this essential connection from his journeys among Aboriginal people across Australia – if you didn't know your song-line, you simply didn't exist.

> The temporal melody and the spiritual melody interpolated each other, combining to form the song-line of the tribe's pilgrimage; the daily narrative made no sense if separated from the Dreamtime narrative. The dislocation from the material world was in a very real sense, a cultural death sentence.[171]

That reverberated with the energetic pilgrimage songs of the ancient Israelites I had heard from boyhood. There was an echo of this in the wistful spirituals of black American slaves who identified with them marching on the long road to freedom. Generation after generation of Israelites had recited chapters from their past – candid about failures and successes – and celebrated the links to the Creator who supplied navigational information.

This was the music that Bruce Feiler heard as he followed the steps of his ancestors with his archaeologist companion, reconstructing the narrative of their epic passage. It was a startling encounter – more than snapping a series of 'selfies' in front of famous shrines. The story he had previously consigned to the dustbin of history came to life. 'This is not a book with black covers and gold on the edge of the pages. The Bible is literally a living, breathing entity, is what really comes through if you travel the route, and read the stories along the way.'[172]

Insightful author G.K. Chesterton could have been describing Feiler's journey when he wrote a century ago that all of us feel instinctively that life presents us with a riddle to be solved. 'Every stone and flower is a hieroglyphic of which we have lost the key; with every step of our lives, we enter into the middle of some story which we are certain to misunderstand.'[173]

In other words, we need interpreters on our journeys.

History without interpretation is drained of its virility. Instead of creating a new generation confident of its identity, neglect produces a crop of orphans ignorant of their heritage and wasteful with entrusted resources. Daily, Australians are scuffing over the footprints left by earlier generations, deaf to the voices of ancestors anxious to tell us about their leg of our shared journey – in particular those who have walked the Christian faith into our history.

That's what prompted me to embark on an odyssey from Dubbo to Darwin with a busload of year nine boys from the Central Coast of NSW. Their Principal was keen to overlay the topography of Australia's heartlands with heart stories – in this case the saga that unfolded with the men and women of the Australian Inland Mission. Strung along the 3500 km route were interpretive centres, churches, hospitals, distance education centres, statues, and markers straddling the hundred years of AIM's innovative service to the people scattered across the Inland. Sadly, very few of the staff that manned them understood that the story of Jesus had ignited the vision, but there were some notable exceptions.

A flying padre in Broken Hill grabbed the boys' attention when he explained that he was an active part of the second 'mantle of safety' John Flynn had cast over the Inland alongside the Flying Doctor network – bringing spiritual care to the lonely corners of the country. The elderly guide, who explained the symbols of Flynn's church in Alice Springs, did the same when, in a quiet voice, he revealed he had been a flying doctor for forty years. The boys sat riveted as he called on them to consider a life of service to the Outback.

My job was to join the dots in the narrative, hoping to impress on these young students the fact that most of these men and women who joined Flynn's adventure were followers of Jesus. It was poignant to stand with these lads at the great ochre boulder near Alice Springs that marked his grave among the Albert Namatjira ghost gums in the shadow of the blue McDonald Ranges. I painted the picture of him as a 16-year-old youth from backcountry Victoria, hungry to make his life count. I explained how he became conscious of a call to a life of service – to walk in the steps of Jesus. The pilgrimage he took over the next half a century gifted Australia with a medical and educational network unparalleled anywhere in the world.

Those lads captured their responses on camera – mostly genuine longings to make their lives count. With interpretation, the humble school excursion had taken on the characteristics of a spiritual pilgrimage. It doesn't mean the Stuart highway to Darwin magically became the road to Damascus, complete with a divine voice and a radical conversion. But from conversations with them, I learned that most of the boys returned changed by a trip that connected stories to places outside their existence on the coastal strip. I saw myself in them. I realised that various kinds of pilgrimage have helped me join my small story to a credible, over-arching narrative that explains the past and gives me confidence in planning the future.

Like Thomas Cook, Bruce Feiler decided to use pilgrimage as a device to look for truth in the stories he had only heard. In effect, he used the liminal space provided by a purposeful journey to test the belief systems handed down to him. The result was a learning curve that moved him from ignorance to an intelligent affirmation of the biblical narrative. The same phenomenon hit me sitting high above the Sea of Galilee in a Roman ruin at Tiberius in 1995, with a map in one hand and Luke's eyewitness account in the other.

I could see how the topography of Israel was the mould into which the story of Jesus' life had been poured. It became more believable because the hand fitted the glove. The narrative became a vital 3D epic. It convinced me that thoughtful excursions of this kind can build up the credibility of the Christian story. The fact that millions over centuries have been drawn from their homes to connect themselves to sacred sites in the Holy Land proves to me the power of the stories embedded there.

We are free to ask whether ideas, traditions and beliefs can be reasonably entertained away from cultural boundaries. So I like to unpack words – some are like babushka dolls. The word 'entertain' describes three distinct activities – being charmed, welcoming guests, and openness to consider an idea. I knew pilgrimage was at its best when all three of these intersect – when theatre, warmth, and persuasion work together to lead you to a new understanding.

A journey like this appeals to truth, not only in the cerebral sense, but it also invites you into an experiment to see if it has congruence in real life. If you encounter a plausible, embracing story, you are likely to adopt it as part of your worldview. With careful thought, I believe the growing movement of people taking to the road in search of meaning could be channelled in this way.

The surf that pounds the coast of Australia generates powerful currents that sweep along our beaches. I learned early that you need to read where these rips are and work with them, not against them. I know because I nearly drowned a couple of times fighting them! The volunteer Lifesavers who set the safety flags, warn of dangers, and train themselves for rescues have become an iconic part of our culture. But patrolling safe zones and issuing warnings can put you in an unwelcome position – swimmers take to the sea as a way of escape and don't readily welcome policing. They signal for help only in extremity. I've felt our churches have been pushed into a similar role as guardians in our society – perhaps not quite as chiselled and bronzed, but heroic enough at times!

Skilled surfers use the rips to get out beyond the white-water to access the breakers. In the same way, I think the tide sweeping people out of Australia's churches may well be used to some advantage. Instead of fighting against the current, why not set ourselves to serve these travellers as they vote with their feet on what they see as static church safety zones and restrictive whistle-blowing by the clergy? The call to the road trip in the younger generations could become a highway to genuine discovery.

Pilgrims need wise interpreters, welcoming way stations, and trustworthy maps. When I have fallen into step with fellow travellers, it's natural for conversations to follow and, bit-by-bit, deeper questions rise to the surface. The hard yards of the journey wears away pretence so that only the road-tested stories will get a decent hearing. You can add colour, depth and meaning to their adventures by researching the stories native to your own region.

I'll drop my guard here and speak to those of you who follow Jesus. I visualise you, in every Australian town, suburb, and village skilling yourselves to serve the pilgrims – overseas tourists, backpackers, grey nomads, schoolkids on excursions, interest groups, sportspeople, bike-riders, car clubs, photographers, hikers and trek-kers. You can assume they are on the road to find out and help them to see the invisible stories. I see you offering yourselves as guides. You could provide hospitality, design trails, lead walking tours, spin good yarns, tell some of your own narratives, recite poems, sing, paint pictures, dance – whatever your gifting!

You can be the interpreters who help these travellers understand the music hidden beneath the surface of our culture. You might discover that, as you intertwine the spiritual melody with the secular, you could open their ears to ancient pilgrim songs – songs of experience. You could open their eyes wide to see traces of a well-trodden trail that winds all the way back to Calvary and beyond.

13

THE INTERPRETER'S HOUSE

Nobody can change stories unless an alternative story is made richly available with great artistry, love and boldness.[174]

Walter Brueggemann

In terms of popularity, John Bunyan's 350-year-old tale *The Pilgrim's Progress* was the *Harry Potter* best seller of its time. As a boy, I was riveted by the dramatic telling of a desperate man's adventure in search of hope and salvation. I read it so many times that the characters still people my inner world. But what intrigued me as an adult was what lay behind the gate that the hero was first directed to on the distant horizon. Exhausted after struggling through swamps and precipitous side tracks, he was welcomed at the house of the Interpreter who prepared the pilgrim for the next leg of his adventure using parables that opened his spiritual understanding.

That made me consider. Why did Bunyan give priority to the Interpreter? My solid evangelical education suggested the poor man should have been sent straight to Calvary and the Cross. I've decided that this was rather a shrewd insight from a master storyteller.

It was one of those eye-popping moments that sneak up on you. I was researching the Muslim Museum that had opened in Melbourne in 2010, funded and feted by the State and Federal governments. A YouTube clip followed four young men in a 4WD traversing the continent in search of stories to demonstrate the contribution of Islam to Australia – in particular the 'Afghans' who pioneered the camel trade across the Inland. To my astonishment, I saw these young seekers in Bourke cemetery, prostrated in prayer before a tiny tin shed. They were ecstatic at discovering what they thought was possibly the first mosque in Australia.

The shock for me was that I had rescued that rusty corrugated iron shed and had it placed there. I'm pretty sure I was the only one who knew its identity at the time, having interviewed the ageing Mrs Perooz somewhere in the 80's. She had pointed down her backyard and said, "That there shed was where they used to say their prayers" – 'they' being her husband's fellow cameleers who lived in a camp nearby. According to his custom, Morbine Perooz had purchased Myrtle as a girl-bride, and she had been carefully shielded inside their community for decades. I have to admit that my initial thought was, "Oh no, what have I done? I should have left the shed in obscurity!" Then as I thought further, I said to myself, "Paul, you're a historian – get real! You can't edit things out of your history just because you're uncomfortable with them."

Another emotion followed. Shame.

Shame first because of my prejudice, but then, mortification that my own family of faith failed to prize its story with the same passion. I was familiar with the story of the Far West and knew that hut constituted pretty much what that close community of Muslims gave to the district in terms of anything spiritual. They came to operate a carrying industry and they served the country well. After a time, many returned to their native homeland – today, we would call them FIFO's – fly in, fly out temporary workers.

By contrast, wave after wave of men and women had come West, motivated by their Christian faith and left a living legacy of pastoral care, medical services, educational facilities, charitable institutions, and business enterprises. I knew from my research they had, more often than not, given hard-driving European colonisation a more compassionate touch.

Then the voice of the Interpreter asked over my shoulder, "Who is telling their story? Don't they deserve to have it told too?" Instinct warned me it couldn't be a matter of chest-beating or grandstanding – there were enough sad instances to keep the Christian community from bragging. But I had discovered a welter of honourable stories that lifted the spirits – stories of faith that had generated genuine social capital for both indigenous and white populations for nearly two centuries. And the Afghans, for that matter!

So, I asked myself, "Where are the parties of young people, scouring the country, eager to uncover their lost Christian history so that it could be relayed to modern Australia?" Already, tens of thousands were flocking to hear the Muslim story being told in their Melbourne museum. They valued their story, and their pride was being rewarded.

The absence of the Christian story from the marketplace, I think, has something to do with being bullied. Over the last fifty years, secular academics and media figures have dominated the ring with a flurry of punches – some definitely below the belt – and the church is on the ropes. Any real contribution from men and women of faith to Australia's defining story has too often been derided or dismissed. I've named some hardy researchers who have come up off the canvas in recent days – trained historians and articulate writers who have swung some heavy counter-punches. It has turned the contest into a much more even affair. But how many are aware of this? No matter how convincing the evidence or how brilliantly written the books are, the overall message in the wider community remains that religion has caused most of the problems in the world.

For years I waxed eloquent to students in our dusty classroom on the rim of the Outback, about the discovery of the Dead Sea Scrolls in 1949. I would tell them breathlessly, "How amazing to find the ancient book of Isaiah carefully copied by scribes a century and a half before Jesus still intact!" Not only that, but it was virtually identical with a copy made a millennium later and spoke volumes about the reliability of the transmission of the Hebrew Scriptures. I wanted them to be confident in the documents that underpinned their faith in these cynical times. This discovery was one of the greatest news stories of the 20th century.

The moment came in 1995 when I found myself standing in The Shrine of the Book in Jerusalem, gazing in awe at that very parchment. There it was, the lines of immaculate Hebrew script preserved behind Perspex, only a few feet away! Wow! Here I was, in the presence of one of the most important archaeological finds in history. As I moved reverently around the circle, I came across a woman staring at her reflection in front of the scroll, lips pursed, doing her makeup! I had to stifle a laugh – all that scholarship and painstaking reconstruction from scraps of parchment that impressed me as a historian, made a nice backdrop for her to powder her nose!

That quirky, very human moment is locked into my memory bank as a wake-up call on capturing popular imagination.

The sanctuary housing the scrolls had been crafted by architects to copy the lids of the earthen jars in which they were found – a theatrical element that, on its own, drew overseas visitors to a landmark in our shared human story. Inside, scholars had worked tirelessly to establish the scrolls' authenticity and reject the bogus copies. This intense process presented a powerful endorsement of the biblical narrative. I was trained to see that Christianity, in particular, had embraced reason as a primary guide to religious truth. So far so good!

But it dawned on me that artefacts + brilliant architecture + rational argument alone was never going to be enough to touch the heart of people like my lipstick-wielding friend, with the deeper mystery wrapped inside the scrolls. Surveys indicate that modern generations are hungry to hear first-hand accounts of those whom the Bible had given meaning to their existence. They are eager for living evidence that might help them make their way in the world.[175]

Whether scribed on papyrus, or encoded on a computer memory stick, truth is still truth. Truth fleshed out in biography is even more potent. I am convinced that rolling out a broad sample of human experiences, tested in real-life across time, will capture imaginations and open minds. An engaging Interpreter's House, en route to Calvary, could have a powerful cumulative impact on shaping Australia's future.

Live stories told eye to eye, would take things to another level.

One trick I'd learned when visiting museums was to watch the behaviour of the visitors. It was always intriguing to see what engages them. One afternoon, I stood next to a cluster of restless teenagers in the Jewish Holocaust Museum in Darlinghurst, Sydney. They were examining a photo of survivors from a grim Nazi concentration camp. Their guide picked out one particular face. "See that girl there?" she asked them. "Well that's the lady standing behind you." The group pivoted and drew in close around the old woman like iron filings to a magnet. Those millennials were riveted as the survivor began to relate her harrowing story.

I was fascinated as I watched time and distance, age and gender, evaporate.

Flashes of real connection like that have cured me of a lingering impression from childhood that museums have to be dark marble halls that mute speech to a reverent whisper. I have musty memories of butterflies transfixed in glass cases and scruffy stuffed animals in frozen postures. Current surveys tell of present generations flocking to sites of memory, hoping to rekindle a warm connection with their past. One Australian study detected the paradox. While there is shrinkage in history taught in our classrooms, the media has churned out successful dramas and documentaries foraged from national archives.[176]

Genealogy is now a booming industry, with Ancestry.com evolving into an online powerhouse, driven by women in the 50 + age bracket, combing the records for their family's root system. Archivists, museum experts and historians, invisible in the past, have now been transformed into heroic detectives, leading people through a jungle of documentation, tracking long lost relatives in television shows like *Who*

Do You Think You Are? Almost without exception, the seekers reported being made wiser by connection to their past.

Interpreters helped deepen their self-understanding.

It's a rude awakening for both clergy and teachers to hear that museums now rank above churches and schools as sources of reliable information. Interviewees said these tended to be one of the first ports of call in critical times when rapid change caused people to lose their bearings.[177] That slap around the ears got my attention, even more so in the face of a global pandemic that has shaken our certainties. It says to me the need is urgent to design attractive spaces that encourage intelligent dialogue, where important issues are explored and controversial points debated with respect. Pulpits where preachers speak down to a passive audience in voices shrill with certitude have a limited appeal to modern generations. In my experience, interpreters who fall into step as guides are almost always welcomed.

I felt a complete ignoramus when I walked into the Baseball Museum in Coopersville, Michigan. I knew next to nothing about this American sporting obsession and stared blankly at portraits and cabinets of equipment. An eager baseball fan on duty must have seen my bewilderment and took pity on me. For the next hour, that patient young man unravelled the mysteries of the game he loved, warming me to its intricacies as he fielded my naïve inquiries. I walked away feeling just a tad wiser about what gripped him, and not only that, I felt that I had been befriended. Similar experiences on that museum crawl from East to West in the USA convinced me that unrehearsed conversation, in a relaxed and stimulating environment, makes for great learning.

As I continued my research, an improbable thing called a 'Christian ashram' presented itself as a template for re-engaging Australians with their spiritual roots.[178] It was a response by an American missionary, E. Stanley Jones, to the tumultuous events of 1930s India. At a time of great hostility to both colonial rule and the Christian faith, this initiative was reported to have helped pave the way for Independence in 1948. Jones was nominated for the Nobel Prize for Peace.

His original idea was to replace the large-scale evangelistic rally with safe spaces designed for followers of all faiths to make intelligent inquiry about Jesus. The dialogues centred on transparency, courtesy, honesty, and a determination to seek for truth. Jones reported that friend and foe alike agreed on the character of Jesus Christ. Remarkable changes were triggered by bringing Jesus' unique Beatitudes into this marketplace of ideas. For example, the biography Jones wrote of his friend Mohandas Gandhi, inspired Martin Luther King Jnr to employ passive resistance as a weapon in the American Civil Rights movement.

With the current push by some in Australia to 'decolonialise' our history and to cast the churches as instruments of repression, it seems to me that Jones' spaces for honest engagement with our faith stories, is a viable version of the Interpreter's House. A fresh portrait of the historical Jesus could emerge, showing that he has always been a robust and honest contributor to the shaping of good things in modern Australia.

The leader who preached, "Blessed are the peacemakers" has earned the right to be a voice in deciding our future.

I have a store of distinct museum experiences that lifted me above the ordinary. Floating by the wharf at the Maritime Museum at Darling Harbour, I found a tiny fishing vessel, the *M. V. Krait*. Leaning over the rail, I was transported back to boyhood, sitting riveted by the radio, reliving every moment of the daring raid made by a small band of commandos on the Japanese stronghold of Singapore Harbour. The sheer courage of that Special Operations Group gripped the heart of a young boy, and it still moves me now. Over the lapping of the water, I heard again the call to put your life on the line for something bigger than yourself.[179]

I would challenge any Australian to walk through the brutal story of the convict prison at Port Arthur in Tasmania and the site of the 1996 massacre, without being driven to some deep deliberations.[180] The only bright moments that I found relieved the dark pall that broods over the sandstone ruins were the stories of Christian kindness embedded like opals in hard rock. Hope shone, even in that dark place.

Visiting the Australian War Memorial as a boy, the lasting impression was the sculpture of Private Simpson at Gallipoli, his arm supporting a wounded ANZAC slumped on his donkey. Jesus' fictional character of the Samaritan who rescued an abandoned assault victim took solid shape wearing a familiar Australian uniform.[181] When I stood before the stained-glass windows in the Hall of Memory, I understood why signature Christian values like loyalty, chivalry, and comradeship were etched there to remind future generations of what rose above the carnage of war.

In 2006, the first Australian Christian Heritage Forum drew a large crowd to the Great Hall of Australia's Parliament House. It was hosted by the Prime Minister and a number of politicians from both sides of government. Spearheaded by Professor Stuart Piggin, it was a powerful challenge to secular fundamentalists in the media and academic institutions who, he said, had to a large degree silenced Christian opinion in the discussion of the nation's future. He declared that their creed was, "…the dogmatic received conviction that all religion is irrational, unhelpful and harmful, or that it has no right to speak in the marketplace of ideas…This is why the Christian voice in Australia has been so muted, so tame, so lacking in prophetic power."[182]

I could have cheered. Here was a gifted historian throwing down the gauntlet, with his feet astride a lifetime's research on Australia's Christian foundations. The panel of highly qualified speakers then spent two days presenting hard evidence that gave substance to his assertion that Christians had earned the right to speak in the national debate. Deputy Prime Minister, John Anderson, made a strong call for a visible expression of Christian faith in our National Capital.

> I am often struck as I approach this building how it was that, in cultures that preceded ours, and on which perhaps ours is built, it was normal for the local church or cathedral spire to dominate the village or town skyline. That is not so in Canberra. This place does, and that flagpole on the top does, and we need to be very careful not to become too presumptuous in believing that we are, if you

like, at the top of the dung hill and I can only think that the work here of this forum is potentially extraordinarily important.[183]

Reason and gut-level instinct told me he was on target.

I left Parliament House with a determination to give those powerful papers substance, animation and colour. It was one thing to get stirred up at a talkfest and another to have the resolve to create a sounding board in the National Capital where that muffled voice could be amplified. It may sound a ridiculous thing to think in that august place, but it seemed to me this was like Bourke revisited. Like that remote town, the Christian community had been gifted an impressive pile of quality research, but it had no permanent home.

At the same time, it seemed an impossible dream.

Philosopher Alain de Botton believes that buildings perform in choirs[184], and if that's true, then there is a rich voice missing from the Canberra chorale. 'Capital cities' are meant to showcase the accumulated capital of the nation – the invisible things that underpin our common wealth.

I walked along the rim of Lake Burley Griffin where our accrued wealth in terms of art, music, science, Aboriginal culture, history, and politics is housed in sanctuaries purpose-built to engage and inform the nation. It's an impressive parade, but at the same time exasperating because I knew that in architect Walter Burley Griffin's original blueprint for Australia's political hub, he had designated a space for a Christian cathedral. His purpose was to recognise the spiritual realm as an essential asset in the nation's store of resources.

In our twenty first century, this national cathedral remains unbuilt.

We were seated in the cafeteria of Old Parliament House as Professor Piggin explained this notorious absence to one of the world's most credentialed architects. Shock registered on his face. Having designed signature buildings for capital cities the world over, Eric Kuhne declared that this was another case of modernity stripping our civic centres bare of the richness of faith. "They prefer spiritual anonymity," he said in a disgusted voice. His passion to restore the storytelling element to architecture poured out of him as he began sketching a building that he visualised could become a symbol of faith, capable of drawing visitors from around the world. His vast experience had evidently cultivated his instinct for a great story, and as his pen flew, our humbler aspirations were launched into the stratosphere. We named it The Southern Cross Sanctuary.

Eric was an American working out of London who had designed and built a complex at Sydney's Darling Harbour. I was impressed when I visited Cockle Bay just how skilful he had been by including Australian distinctives throughout. Soon after his return to England, his team delivered a detailed concept document pro bono. It signalled his strong belief in the project and he introduced his spectacular design in ringing tones.

> A civilisation's ability to build a national sacred space is a test of conviction – it is a huge commitment of emotional, spiritual as well as economic resources. Civilisation denied worship fails. I believe the Southern Cross Sanctuary will become a destination for people… to come and discover the momentous foundations of Australia as a people and as a nation. I believe it will become a symbol of Australia's leadership in restoring a deep and abiding faith as a core of its global prominence.[185]

I couldn't recall ever hearing a summons quite like this. It was visionary in the architectural sense and intelligent about spiritual realities. It was in stark contrast to Australia's National Museum, which at the time, seemed to have consigned most of our Christian history to the waste bin! I had to check myself in drawing the easy conclusion that this was familiarity breeding contempt. Rather, we custodians of the Christian archive were probably more to blame for our neglect. It's our story, after all.

How can we condemn our neighbours' ignorance if we don't value the stories ourselves?

I had returned from Regent College in Canada in 1978 not only with my world-view expanded but also a determination to give my faith hardy Australian muscle. Since then, I've listened to a growing chorus of voices, both inside and outside the Christian world, calling for a new approach to spiritual questions and demanding a workable vision for Australia's future. But, as the volume swelled over the next 40 years, there was a recurring refrain that our existing world views somehow just weren't liveable.

Early on, I heard author Donald Horne lamenting Australia's loss of perspective, lack of community and diminishing sense of wonder at the mysteries around us.[186] Biologist Charles Birch framed four questions that he said needed urgent answers if Australians were to escape the formlessness of modern life – how to resolve the chaos inside ourselves, in our relationships, in our environment, and in finding meaning in the cosmos.[187] Psychologist Ronald Conway called for a melding of the sacred and the scientific as a way of making sense of life.[188] Social researcher Jonathan King warned that what he branded 'Waltzing Materialism' would bring bitter disappointment if we kept hurtling along without a moral compass.[189] Historian Manning Clark painted his graphic picture of Australians as bored survivors in the Kingdom of Nothingness.[190]

His questions remain, 'What is an Australian? By what faith does he live?'[191]

After an extensive study of religious practice, sociologist Hans Mol observed that Australia seemed to be either a Christian nation searching for religion or a heathen nation in flight from one.[192] Theologian Bruce Wilson echoed this, noting that most of our citizens gave a nod to God's existence, but lived as if He didn't.[193] Evangelist John Smith described us as a lost nation, wondering if the vessel we were on was really unsinkable.[194] Psychologist Hugh Mackay traced the epidemic of drug-taking and suicide among young people to them being forced to work out everything for themselves. He pleaded with our leaders to provide a spiritual and cultural scaffolding to make sense of who we are. Later, he expressed the hope that it could also rise from the grassroots.[195] Researcher Richard Eckersley was blunt, 'We see others as crippled by ignorance and cowed by superstition; we don't see the extent to which we are, in our own ways, burdened by our rational knowledge and cowed by our lack of superstition – of spiritual beliefs.'[196]

In recent times, one voice in particular gelled with my thinking about interpreter's houses. Philosopher Wayne Hudson declared that Aussies' spiritual lives are in a mess because the secular worldview had failed them. He envisaged the creation of 'post-secular spaces, which combine… rationality and critical scholarship with the public performance of spiritual concerns.'[197] He pictured accessible places where dialogue allowed for differences of opinion – places where all comers are welcomed.

Of late, Walter Brueggemann's prophetic voice has cut in. 'Nobody can change stories unless an alternative story is made richly available with great artistry, love and boldness.'[198] I began to visualise a beautiful sanctuary that would capture Australian imaginations, appeal to their intelligence, and be attractive enough to consider changing stories. I thought that by turning down the volume of both the sectarian and the secular voices, there might be a chance for the stories to touch the seeker's heart. I dreamed it would be a safe place where those whose worldview was proving not quite liveable, could come seeking a satisfying truth without having to check their doubts in at the door.

As a historian, I knew that Australia's Christians have more than earned the right to recount the efforts of their heroes in a national theatre, just as we've done in graphic ways for the ANZACs. I wanted the Southern Cross Sanctuary to be something strong and winsome that will shout to my fellow Australians that it's time to retrace our steps with honesty and admit that Jesus has walked alongside us, no matter who we are or where we come from. A well-presented gallery of lives inspired by his idealism could be compelling evidence that God has walked among us and fostered justice, education, law, and myriad works of compassion. I'm confident that, religious or not, Australians will be proud of most of the stories they hear.

I want every visitor to walk away from the Southern Cross Sanctuary wiser, encouraged, inspired… different.

And sobered!

It will also mean having the courage to admit to the bitter rivalries, grey joylessness, endemic corruption, proud superiority, entrenched prejudice and sexual abuse that have marred the face of the church. It will demand that all of us, Christian and non-Christian alike, come under the scrutiny of the Jesus who despised all of those things.

Confession will be good for our collective soul. Humility will help us redeem our story. Forgiveness could restore broken relationships. It will be a dangerous place too. The larger destiny to which he summoned the world demanded the utmost of those who dared to place their footsteps in his.

Jesus never left his hearers neutral.

14

BRINGING THE STORIES HOME

Our lifelong nostalgia, our longing to be re-united with something in the universe from which we now feel cut off, to be on the inside of some door which we have always seen from the outside, is no mere neurotic fancy, but the truest index of our situation.[199]

C.S. Lewis

I've recounted my journey with story in the hope of drawing you out on your individual narrative adventure. But what is a quest without a destination? One single idea lingers in my inner library. It sets firelight flickering on the walls and generates warmth and welcome. It's best described by the quaint expression 'hearth and home' that I heard in childhood, with its suggestions of security and shelter. It was the magnetic pull that drew so many of the stories I absorbed, both real and imagined, to a satisfying conclusion.

I've decided it's the most intense force of all because it tugs at every kind of emotion and forces, even the toughest minded to yield to its charm.

I'm fortunate that, for me, homeliness conjures up a scene where memories are passed easily from hand to hand around the meal table, accompanied by banter and laughter. My grandparents' and parents' most enduring bequest to our family has been laughter born from taking one another seriously. Over the years, having a place to narrate stories – even the saddest and most tragic – has provided an opportunity for reflection and deepening of ties. Home accommodated pain – it created the space where lost loved ones can be well remembered and valued.

Shared history has drawn my family into a unit, anecdotes have grown into the legends that knit us together. Singing and shared faith have strengthened communion. It's a place of belonging and identity where it's safe to be yourself, because you're known and accepted. You readily fit in – you have a fixed point around which to centre yourself. It's made me believe that, at day's end, all true storytelling should draw us home.

The sheer ugliness of war sharpened the image for me. History reports that the pervasive feeling that drifted through the World War One trenches in France was the resolve of the soldier on both sides to protect his home – to 'defend his fireside.' In the thick of battle, the vision sown by the high-flown rhetoric of political leaders shrank to the size of a trench. Instead, combatants spoke of the band of brothers they fought alongside becoming their surrogate family on the battlefield, breeding some of the best ideals of mateship.

Many of the movies I grew up on were carried by sentimental songs urging loved ones to 'keep the home-fires burning' or promising them 'I'll be home for Christmas'. Present-day soldiers on active duty overseas still appear on our screens expressing the same sentiments. It's easy to dismiss these emotional surges as tinsel, but I suspect they tap a well of nostalgia sunk deep beneath the whole human drama.

To ignore the intoxicating idea of homecoming is to drain story telling of its power.

When I was a boy, Robert Browning's description of the crippled lad shut out on the mountainside when the Pied Piper led the children of rat-plagued Hamlyn into a land free of corruption left me with a sharp pang of sadness.[200] This same dread of being left out stayed with me from an anonymous black and white movie where the father long-believed lost, returns, looks through the window to see his family celebrating Christmas with a new father, turns, and walks away into the snow. The recollections of real people who had been widowed, orphaned, or left homeless have taught me that these emotions are not always cheap sentiment, but among the most profound feelings possible.

This was reinforced when I heard in 2018 that the British Government had appointed a Minister for Loneliness because this affliction was costing the health sector billions of dollars. Japan has since followed suit, and with the crushing effects of Covid lockdowns there are calls for this initiative to be taken here at home.[201]

Evidence suggests that lostness and social isolation is a global pandemic that is robbing us of enormous human resource. Our personal journals reveal a yearning for an assured point of arrival. Creating hearths or campfires across Australia where our stories are told, and the lonely are welcomed, could be a simple way of generating hopeful communities.

Not everyone has positive memories of home. I've met many people for whom their home is a house of horror – the only fire that burned there came from hell. Safe houses offering alternative narratives present the best chance of healing. I witnessed first-hand my parents welcoming the wounded into our home and the way our fireside warmed them and provided a sanctuary. When people entered that shelter, they experienced love and heard stories that fostered hope.

I've seen that repeated often enough in my experience of bringing young people into an intentional Christian community, to convince me that the longing for 'home and hearth' is more than sentimental emotionalism. Simply inviting a broken man, woman, or child to our table for a family meal has had a powerful redemptive impact. Some of them have gone on to fashion healthy households of their own that minister to other wayfarers. It's not an accident that the word *hospital-ity* contains the suggestion of cure.

The ideal of a permanent refuge is fundamental to the human race, and it penetrates both secular and sacred storytelling. It even reaches into eternity. I've conducted the burial of a friend who always insisted he was an atheist. At his request, the mostly secular folk present sang the well-known words of Psalm 23, with its assurance that the good Shepherd will steer us through the valley of the shadow of death and welcome us into his house with feasting and gladness. I'd sent him a copy of the *Miracle on the River Kwai*,[202] and I wondered as we sang that ancient song of hope there under the coolabah trees, whether the story of the Aussie private kneeling before his Japanese executioner to read from his New Testament, had caught his attention. Before the sword fell he called to the chaplain, "Cheer up padre, I'll be alright!" The words he read assured him, and my friend I hope, that he was going home.

In sporting arenas, I see athletes point skyward and dedicate their successes to departed family and friends and express the firm conviction to waiting cameras that someone is watching them from beyond the grave. The possibility of an afterlife has haunted the human race from the beginning – the litter of simple burial markers and elaborate mausoleums across the globe is a silent witness to that belief.

The lingering idea of a celestial home just won't go away in spite of efforts by our materialist society to delete it.

Without a doubt, the longest and most detailed homecoming epic in history is contained in the Bible. From start to finish, the narrative is driven by the conviction that the rebellious human race has been on the run from their Maker and he has been pursuing them down the ages. The heart of the story is that God point-blank refuses to leave his children orphaned and has been unrelenting in his efforts to bring them home. To my reading of it, this is the only explanation that makes any sense of the whole Judeo-Christian drama and the prodigious expenditure of energy that has brought it to the present.

Over time it has inspired a myriad of gallant lives, which means that the business of gathering and articulating our Australian faith stories is far more than detailing the half-forgotten actions of a bunch of do-gooders. It is bringing to light the fact that these people believed selfless acts of service were laying the foundations of a permanent kingdom located both inside and outside of time.

They were convinced they were creating a home where dreams really do come true.

They caught this conviction from Jesus. Of all the people in history that I have come across, he had the strongest sense that human beings are far too easily satisfied with their small doings here on earth. He urged his followers not to spend their energies in activities that offered only fleeting reward, but as he put it, to 'Lay up treasure in Heaven.' For him, it was a tangible reality. It's significant that these were not the murmurings of a mystic but came from the lips of a very grounded, energetic man – a carpenter with his sleeves rolled up, giving himself to meet the needs of people around him. He was able to look death in the eye in Gethsemane and, alone on the cross, he trusted his spirit into his father's hands. He was so confident he would be raised to life again that he promised a home-coming to the thief dying next to him.

Jesus brought the tragedy of lost humanity to an appealing conclusion with his brilliant short story of the repentant prodigal son limping home to the embrace of his waiting father. This image drove him to the cross on Skull Hill outside Jerusalem. His enemies saw themselves getting rid of a threat – Jesus saw himself constructing a welcoming entrance for his missing brothers and sisters into his Kingdom. His resurrection chocked the front door of eternity open and turned wishful thinking about a heaven into thoughtful wishing, as C.S. Lewis put it.[203]

This triggered the spread of communities carrying his remarkable life-story worldwide. I delight in telling the little-known story of the London-based Clapham group, championed by William Wilberforce, which was just one of these dynamic cells. This 19th century Christian think-tank engineered the abolition of slavery in the British Empire and also worked to end the era of convict transportation to Australia. Their trainees shaped the early colony and helped transform the Pacific

Islands with their conviction of a purposeful human history headed for a culmination in eternity.

The efforts of faith communities like this drove author C.S. Lewis to say that the Christians who did the most for this present world all left their mark because their minds were occupied with heaven. When they cease to do this they become ineffective in facing the challenges of present-day life. I've often repeated his sharp summing up. 'Aim at Heaven and you get earth thrown in; aim at earth and you get neither.'[204]

The search for a defining story drives much human activity. We've all tried to capture beautiful experiences from our journeys on camera but found the images don't quite do them justice when we relay them to friends. We've felt an inconsolable longing beneath the brief moments of exhilaration that come from scenery, discoveries, music, art, poetry, achievements and relationships. Lewis holds that the sweetness that pierces our souls comes from beyond the things themselves. In fact, it sweeps in from another country – a tide of nostalgia for our true home.

This longing pulsed through the hymns and spirituals that spoke to me all my life. I felt the longing of the slave workers when they looked up and sang of a bright world where 'there ain't no sickness, toil and sorrow' and their conviction was that 'this world is not my home, I'm just a' passin' through.'

Haunting melodies stirred my heart with assurances of a welcome at the journey's end, of a mighty chorus of angels filling the skies with music, and of a joyful homecoming to friends and family. I saw anthems like the Hallelujah Chorus lifting weary human spirits with a thrill of hope. More often than not, this music rose out of the darkest times, and the backstories spoke of tested realities. I've sung simple hymns at the bedside of dying family members and friends and sensed the reality of heaven present in the room. Something in me registered that these moments were not just placebos used to ease distress.

It demands explanation as to why confident homecoming music has been the signature of the Christian community the world over for 2000 years.

Repeatedly my faith has been stirred by Jesus' promise to write a personal affirmation for life stories that have been joined to his. When Mother Teresa came to Bourke, she reminded us that he said he would gladly give a 'well done' to the smallest act of kindness performed for the least of his creatures. It elevated even the humblest biography to a permanent hall of fame. Jesus went further. He urged that these stories be set like a beacon against the skyline so that people will see them and lift up thankful hearts to our Father in heaven. These acts of kindness would have a preservative effect in our neighborhoods.[205]

He gave us a charter to traffic in anecdotes that inspire the best in us and raise our people's hopes.

If we accept this as true, then we need to embark on the kind of bold storytelling that will break the modern enchantment that has tried to convince us that we are merely animals born of chance. My observation is that people are not really content with having no particular destiny other than returning to dust. Spellbinding stories of another kind are needed – stories that bring echoes of our true home.

I was encouraged when I heard psychologist Jordan Peterson confirm that refreshing our cultural memory is essential in bringing meaning into life. 'If you can provide people with nobility of purpose then they can tolerate the suffering of existence … Cultures that don't do that are dead – they're done! They don't have a story anymore, they don't have a call to adventure.'[206] He confirmed for me that the effort to promote the finest stories from our past motivates people to excel themselves.

Observers of Western history have noted that this present generation is the first to live without a transcendent storyline. For all practical purposes, the idea of a divine Author has been edited out and each person left to invent their own narrative in a 'choose-your-own-ending' style. I've met plenty of people for whom this constant effort to decide the meaning of life inside the narrow confines of their own imagination, has led to a growing sense of desperation. The secular view of our history has serious questions to answer about integrity, because it so often chooses to ignore the optimistic faith which motivated so many of these men and women who have lived out an alternative story.

The stern rationalism that has dominated Western culture for the last few centuries has expanded our mental horizons but shrunken our souls. Being told that matter is the only real thing that exists flattens the human storyline. It has created a world devoid of divinity and invited us to be content in a space bereft of any sense of cosmic drama. There are many showmen who astonish us by revealing the marvels of life on our planet with a dramatic flourish but then conclude that, in the end, it's all futile.

New generations have been made to tell themselves over and over, there's no homecoming.

I find many Australians have yet to meet a version of God large enough to account for the demands of the scientific age or a character great enough to command their highest respect and loyalty. For me, Jesus offers both. The quest for God isn't always sparked by an intellectual question but from meeting a person of faith or hearing a story of someone whose quality of life demonstrates richer possibilities. This challenges me daily to make sure that I am being authentic. It has also sent me searching for the genuine stories that will prise people's minds open. I once interviewed noted historian Professor Edwin Judge at Macquarie University. He is one who urges the Christian community to realise the potential of recovering its own story. 'People in the churches should not accept our age is post-Christian. It is profoundly Christianised in its basic attitudes. The place of the churches is not to disabuse people of this, but to introduce them to the master they ignorantly worship'.[207]

There's a thought!

Creeping boredom has probably driven more people away from the Christian worldview than outright disbelief. In a culture offering a smorgasbord of attractive alternatives, a common objection to religion is that it spoils our fun. To many, it seems only able to throw a grey blanket of respectability over our happily hedonistic world.

Australian film producer, George Miller, argues that cinemas have transformed themselves into 'covert cathedrals' because sacred storytellers have sterilised their grand narrative and driven many Australians away.

> I believe cinema is now the most powerful secular religion, and people gather in cinemas to experience things collectively the way they once did in church. The cinema storytellers have become the new priests. They are doing a lot of the work of our religious institutions, which have so concretised the metaphors in their stories, taken so much of the poetry, mystery, and mysticism out of religious belief, that people look for other places to question their spirituality.[208]

That sets a challenge for present day 'sacred storytellers'. It's an invitation to embrace the excitement of introducing new generations to the great song-line that arches high over human history. We need to find fresh ways to fire the hearts of new generations with noble deeds that outmatch the fictional super heroes. Movies connecting people to genuine adventures, had by real people, telling redemptive stories, have the most power to grip the soul with a hopeful vision for the future.

Big-picture thinking can diminish the sense of cosmic orphanhood. People's imaginations in NSW were sparked at Christmas 2020 when the Abdullah and Sakr families, whose four children were killed by a drunk driver earlier in the year, called for an annual 'I 4give' Day. They wanted to live out their faith by turning away from anger and bitterness, and they saw this as a way of encouraging others to do the same. The Christian hope of being reunited with their children lifted their spirits above the pain.[209] Testimonies of this calibre become catalysts for real conversations about the conclusion of our earthly journey.

To keep the balance, dreariness isn't exclusive to churches. I used to look at the bored faces of people combing through endless racks of videos at Blockbuster and think, 'Are we amusing ourselves to death?' I suspect that bingeing on Netflix could be having the same effect. The technical efficiency of the modern world can make us all blasé, and predictable routines leave us flat. Pubs and parties, travel and novelty all have a used-by date and there are only so many cooking and DIY shows you can stomach. The affluenza epidemic infecting us with the itch to acquire just a bit more stuff has shown itself to be a very draining and, in the end, disappointing exercise. The promise that increased education will resolve all our problems and medication deliver a stress-free Utopia has yet to materialise.

Rousing faith stories can ignite aspirations that will benefit the world. It was educationalist Dr Miriam-Rose Ungunmerrbauman's lifetime effort to bridge the divide between Aboriginal culture and mainstream Western society that earned her recognition as 2021's Senior Australian of the Year. She was the first qualified indigenous teacher in the Northern Territory. In the foreword to the book *Our Mob, God's Story*, a colourful retelling of Biblical stories through the work of Aboriginal artists, she explained the source of her hopeful outlook. 'I am beginning to hear the gospel at every level of my identity. I am beginning to feel the great need we have of Jesus – to protect and strengthen our identity, and to make us whole and new again.'[210]

How refreshing!

The rapid multi-cultural shift of recent times should add urgency to our storytelling. There are pockets of immigrants who know little or nothing of the hidden spiritual narrative, which underpins Australian culture. On the surface, they see a relaxed, hedonistic lifestyle that seems to pay little or no attention to questions of the spirit. Many assume this materialist paradise is 'Christian' without anyone to lead them into the back-story of Jesus. That this has been one of the main agents making Australia an attractive place to call home has been well argued by historians like Stuart Piggin.

More than I think we realise, many immigrants come with Christian faith stories of their own. Listening to the story of a recent arrival from Kenya convinced me that it is primarily an educational responsibility – he truly wanted to know our story. If newcomers are to fully appreciate the substance of our culture, Christians need to step up and tell it like it is. Together we could redecorate the walls with new images of what home should look like.

Storytelling is a two-way street. When both sides listen and learn, it turns foreigners into friends. I have enjoyed the responses from various visitors to our home when we've swapped yarns over a meal. We're actually writing a fresh story together that creates vibrant new communities if carefully crafted. I see this happening in Bendigo, where our friends through Cornerstone have embraced a whole cross-section of new immigrants at The Old Church on the Hill. What was a 100-year-old building with an honourable, but fading history, is now bursting with life.[211]

The 'White Australia Policy', with its message of racial superiority, was still a fact of life when I graduated from University. As a teenager, I had memorised St Paul's radical claim that Jesus had broken down the walls that divided races to create a new humanity. It took me longer to learn how to make that new household a reality in the space I inhabited. The true test of a story's calibre is its capacity to face its characters' failures and shortcomings. Undeclared, they are toxic. But, frankly admitted, they breathe life back into the narrative. Courageous honesty wins respect, adds authenticity, and swings the door wide to welcome strangers.

Genuine pride in achievement is best accentuated by open admission of times of arrogance and conceit.

This was the fire in Jesus' gut as he called out corruption in the religious practices of his people at the time. His dramatic cleansing of the Temple in Jerusalem with a whip was housekeeping on steroids! His shout can still be heard, 'My house will be called a house of prayer for all nations, but you have made it a den of robbers.' He was declaring he wanted all his children to come home to a welcoming place, cleaned and swept, with a hearty meal on the table.

Ballet is definitely not my storytelling genre. I only ever read one book on dance, but a single piece of advice from the experienced choreographer stayed with me. She said she invested 40 percent of her time planning the finish because the climax was the most significant part of the performance. It made real sense to invest time thinking long and hard about the ending.

The possibility of the whole human story culminating with a bang, not a whimper, is both sobering and elating. If there is a Maker who will weigh up the value of our lives, then that will change the way we live here and now. Jesus' authentic life and the audacity of his promise that our tiny stories can be caught up in a cosmic drama convinces me that this is the true index of our situation and not a neurotic fancy. It makes the most sense of life and breathes anticipation into our fragile narrative. More grave is the possibility of living our story and leaving God out of the script. Should he find a place for us in his? If not, that would turn out to be a tragic finale.

Prophetic voices hold up a mirror for us. Folk singer Eric Bogle challenged my generation with the story of Claire Campbell, a Sydney woman whose body was found in her home after she had been dead for twelve months. I've sung this song many times. She died utterly alone and unmourned. That jolted him to write a song that I think ripped the cover off the longing for immortality that haunts secular Australians living in their materialist world.

The song is both a lament and a debate.

> *Don't talk to me*
> *'Bout life seasons,*
> *Don't ask me for answers,*
> *Don't ask me for reasons:*
> *I don't wanna hear*
> *I don't wanna hear it at all.*
> *From the moment we're born*
> *We start to die*
> *A man can go crazy*

If he keeps asking why
That's just how it is,
Don't look for a reason for it all.
That's just how it is,
Don't look for a reason for it all.

At the same time the other voice argues the counterpoint:

Can't you understand
What I'm trying to say?
There must be an answer
And we've gotta try
To make some sense of it
To try and find a reason for it all
We are not born just so we can die,
There must be an answer,
And we've gotta try
To make some sense of it,
To try to find a reason for it all.
Ah, there must be a way,
There must be a reason for it all.[212]

Our stories can awaken echoes of this argument in every conversation we hold. Thomas Keneally, one of Australia's most accomplished storytellers, says it's the most human of quests. 'We're almost hard-wired to pursue the questions of meaning and significance. We all want to know if our story has any meaning at all. There's no escaping it, wherever you go.'[213]

That says to me there's a longing for home.

Eric Bogle wrote another moving ballad of a black South African prisoner who was being led out to be executed in the days of apartheid. His legs drained of strength as the guards marched him past the cells of the other inmates, and when he staggered, his countrymen began to sing a song that gave him courage and hope. They explained they were 'singing his spirit home.'[214]

To my mind, that brief instant soars above those things that divide us and reminds us of what matters. I visualise our community of Christian faith with a shared conviction about eternity, willing strength into a faltering brother or sister for the homeward leg of the journey with a song of hope.

I think that's the highest calling possible, one we could all embrace.

Storytellers of our Homeland.

15

TELLING ANOTHER STORY

The story I had heard a thousand times turned out to be the story I had never heard at all.[215]

Paul Kingsnorth

I've concluded that, contrary to popular opinion, the radical life and teachings of Jesus have mostly been silenced in Australia, not by contradiction, but by co-option. The stories of those who have followed in his steps have been absorbed into our culture and domesticated. Many of these Christian game-changers have been quietly rebranded as secular humanists – homogenised so as not to offend popular sensibilities. As a volunteer, I guide visitors through the excellent Royal Flying Doctor Service Visitor Experience in Dubbo. John Flynn is the most memorialised Australian and the string of museums from Broken Hill to Darwin testify as to how much his legacy is appreciated. Yet I have searched high and low all along that trail for any serious explanation of the belief which drove his vision. Without the shadow of a doubt, Flynn saw his extended team as living links in a chain of women and men energised by the resurrection of Jesus from the dead.[216]

Warm appreciation has dumbed-down this vital part of the story. Bush people never hesitate to give their hard-earned cash to the RFDS. The popular bush race meeting at the village of Louth on the Darling raises tens of thousands of dollars annually, the Dubbo Outback Trek has generated $30M over thirty years. I've seen the ceiling of tiny Hungerford Hotel on the Queensland border thick with bank notes – stuck there by patrons who would be staggered to learn that the impetus for Flynn's flying ambulance came direct from a preacher who grew up in back-country Galilee 2000 years ago!

No Jesus, No Flying Doctor Service?

From what I've heard, Australia's highly valued *Lifeline* telephone counselling service has likewise been house-trained. It began in 1962 as the brainchild of the Rev Sir Alan Walker – a Methodist preacher once dubbed 'the conscience of the nation' for his spirited confrontation of social issues. I met the feisty old campaigner in the 1970's and he left no doubt that his lifelong calling was as an evangelist. He named *Lifeline* as one of his most satisfying initiatives and was adamant that the Christian purpose of evangelism is its supreme aim and it must never be lost.[217] He would be astonished to hear that today Lifeline's 11,000 counsellors respond to a million calls for help every year and as the COVID crisis peaked in 2020, the 40 centres across the country were handling a call every thirty seconds. I wonder if the fervent preacher who stirred 1950's Australia would get a job there now?

Fewer and fewer Australians realise the social capital this alternative story generates daily in their neighbourhood. I liked journalist Greg Sheridan's tongue-in-cheek chapter heading in his recent book: 'What did we ever get from Christianity – apart from the idea of the individual, human rights, feminism, liberalism, modernity, social justice and secular politics?'[218] Most would be astonished to learn the impetus for this began over 3000 years ago when Moses had a public showdown with the power culture of Egypt and led his people out of slavery. He then set about shaping an alternative social community that was meant to reflect the vision of God's freedom – a place where justice and compassion were to be the hallmarks.

That's a story that most children once heard in Sunday school, but no more.

The well-published obituary notice of the Christian faith is very premature. Our culture is still connected to a dynamo built from biography after biography of people of faith attempting to realise this alternate society. These heroes are flawed human beings like us, yet somehow their collective histories gather momentum to an astonishing climax. You'll find that the story of the Bible doesn't peak in a manifesto, a mandate or a general design for living, but in the compelling personality of Jesus.

His life-story has gripped the imaginations of people across the planet like no other. His resurrection provoked another extraordinary succession of biographies of people who have carried the template of his alternative society to every nation on earth. It's a living drama in which you and I are handed the script and invited to play a part right here in Australia. I look at my crowded bookshelves and think, "these are only a fraction of the mountain of books written about him over the past two millennia!"

How many Australians have even read *one*?

It should be clear by now I'm driven by the disappointment that we Australian Christians undervalue this human chain that has brought us to the present. Memories have faded and dementia has set in. I ask myself "How on earth have we reduced this epic to pale, once-upon-a-time bedtime stories, disconnected from modern life? How can we revive its sparkle and colour?"

Walter Brueggemann, a watcher of our times and a man with a clear prophetic voice, has put it well: '...the church has no business more pressing than the reappropriation of its memory in its full power and authenticity.'[219] He predicts this would empower it to project a strong alternative story over against the dominant materialist narrative being churned out day and night across the Western world.

A popular fable I've heard repeated in this new millennium has been, "All stories are created equal". This spineless post-modern mantra is a cop-out and often translates into, "Don't try to challenge the workability of my story. Leave it alone. Keep yours to yourself." People don't dare have their draft plans scrutinised under arc lights. The tragic failure of inadequate life-stories can be measured in climbing suicide statistics, mounting crime rates, increasing numbers of broken families, widespread alcoholism and hospitals filled by patients with depressive illnesses.

All stories are manifestly not equal – there are bonfires of failed scripts burning day and night all across Australia.

Jesus made the bold declaration that people trying to live a life which edits God out, don't realise they're poor and blind and naked. He began his public teaching career with a ringing call to accept his story of an alternate kingdom. He made the unique call to die to your broken, home-grown stories and to embrace his story – one he promised would be large enough to meet your deepest needs and to bring you to God. Day after day, eyewitnesses watched him paint the picture of a radical realm under the rule of his Father – a kingdom built on uncompromising love. Ordinary folk received it as good news, but it made such a serious challenge to the contemporary religious, economic and political power-brokers, it got him killed.

Many of their kind have come and gone but his commanding figure continues to tower over human history, because the story he lived out had its roots in eternity.

I love telling that story, but there's still a tension between his good news and the culture we live and breathe in. My experience is that people comfortable inside a construct of their own making, resent someone attempting to persuade them to investigate another story. Awkward efforts at 'converting people' can be off-putting and at times I've been guilty of this myself. However, I'm glad to report that I've seen people far more inspired by the genuine efforts of convinced believers to simply share the story that has transformed their own lives.

Mind you, my delivery wasn't always brilliant. As a young teacher in a staff room full of hearty cynics, happy pagans and fuzzily religious types, I wanted to stand my ground as a historian convinced of the strong evidence in the case for Christ. The trendy Drama teacher brought the staffroom to attention one day announcing, "Paul, I met a couple of your blokes on the beach on the weekend who tried to convert me! I gave them a hard time and they gave up and left." In the silence that followed he paused and said, "But I have to admit I was impressed. There was something genuine about them."

Our life-stories were worlds apart. His bohemian lifestyle in the inner city couldn't have been more different to my more conservative suburban world. Another day he strode through the door and declared, "Paul, you and I need to talk about Jesus sometime soon!" A number of very open conversations followed and we became friends. He taught me a lot about honest inquiry and having the courage of your convictions. Together we explored the possibilities of the alternate culture Jesus had announced.

I was born into a tightly-knit, English/Scots church community where evangelism was direct, heartfelt and well-intentioned. Looking back, I recall the genuine warmth of the fellowship they generated and the sincerity of their convictions and that their authenticity enhanced the story they were telling. I've also watched scornful opposition drive Christians into a defensive posture where they use a 'gallop over the drawbridge to lay the message on a few pagans and then retreat behind the safety of the church walls' approach.

This shrunken version of the good-news is too often delivered clumsily and off the back foot.

Our storytelling is best when it's a dynamic partnership where the Spirit of God teaches each individual what it is in their personal narrative they should abandon and what it is they are free to keep. Watching the way Jesus has transformed people I've known, it's clear he isn't interested in churning out photocopies, but in creating originals.

I once interviewed an accomplished storyteller named Tony Morphett, whose fictional characters lived in the imaginations of generations who followed shows like *Certain Women, The Sullivans, Blue Heelers* and *Boney*. These, along with a number of successful film scripts, earned him the highest awards in the media world. He was an absolute gun at creating believable stories about ordinary Aussies. Speaking in the 2WEB studio at Bourke, Tony was adamant that his twenty-year career as an investigative reporter had prepared him to tell the difference when handling factual material and true-to-life fiction writing. He had prided himself on being certain there was no supernatural world and would not accept that Jesus was anything more than a man. In his own words, he was 'a rationalist bigot', 'an egomaniac who was objective on everything except religion.' He never had any desire to have anything to do with church and what really riled him was 'Christian superstition' in his fellow Australians.[220]

Then something rudely punched a hole in the roof of his tightly sealed, secular world view. He was challenged, for the first time in his life, to do what any good reporter should do – check the sources. He told me as he read the four parallel accounts of Jesus' life, 'I was appalled. What I was reading wasn't legend, it wasn't naturalistic fiction…These were first and second-hand accounts of extraordinary events…Reporting has a taste, and that taste is in the gospels. I found myself face to face with the evidence of what happened when God invaded time in the flesh of a man.'[221]

The thing that struck me listening to him was that he really hadn't wanted to believe it. He had a neat turn of phrase for his journey to accept what he had despised. He said he found himself "walking steadily backwards towards the light!"

I have met people from different cultures who made this same paradigm shift. No two stories are the same. All human beings are conditioned by their culture and I understand why they react to what appears a criticism of their inherited outlook. If they are helped past the initial shock, and the alternative story made clear, then the possibility is they will find their deepest hopes and dreams begin to take on solid shapes and richer colours.

Jesus was a master of these kind of transformative meetings. Once, he detoured his students into an area considered a no-go-zone by the Jewish community. They were appalled and cringed behind their prejudices. On return from an excursion for food, they discovered him deep in conversation with a woman living as an outcast on the fringe of her town. She kept him at arms-length by using some well-worn cultural weapons. He vaulted over the ethnic and religious taboos and broke through her defences with a fresh telling of the God-story she thought she knew. A world of new possibilities broke in on her and she bolted to town to announce that she had met someone who had freed her mind and heart with a vista bigger than her traditional outlook.

For his part, Jesus told his disbelieving disciples the dialogue had been better than a hearty meal! He promised this story-realignment would be like a spring of fresh water bubbling up in any soul thirsty for change, any place, any time.

I met someone with an experience like that. My friend Dave had been living by a story that brought him to suicide. Family members and friends had taught him to survive by theft and to use alcohol and drugs to dull the pain of despair. The recording playing on a loop in his mind told him he was useless. He had deflected his grandmother's prayers as nonsense, but somehow, he had survived numerous vehicle accidents and overdoses. Somewhere in his thirties the whole thing collapsed and he was walking to a station to throw himself under a train, when an Alcoholics Anonymous sign on a church challenged him to take his pulse and be grateful he was alive. That simple message jolted him awake to the possibility of an alternate story to the one that had failed him.

Blunt advice from AA friends and a book gifted by a stranger pushed him to open his mind to something else. With a dictionary in one hand, the near-illiterate Dave took a painstaking six months to read the *The Purpose Driven Life*.[222]. Its explanation of the story of Jesus began to show him answers to his deep questions about meaning. One Easter, the sight of a steeple drew him to church to discover more. The friendship of people he met there fleshed the whole thing out for him and, like the Samaritan woman, he experienced a whole new story that penetrated every level of his being. It has transformed him into a bloke who loves to work and a husband who has found fulfilment in a family.

Everywhere I go I hear people rehearsing stories that bolster the framework through which they interpret what's happening around them. That's our coping mechanism. No living culture is static and more skill than ever is required in studying the changes in our world and adjusting our response to them.

There is danger that any of us can too easily declare our viewpoint bullet-proof and ignore the truth present in someone else's. Nevertheless, I believe it is crucial to settle on a story that answers the questions best. History has demonstrated to me the gospel narrative's ability to both stand the truth test and to reach across cultural boundaries over a long period. The culture Jesus generated has arched above the temporary schemes and speculations of tribes and nations. That's its genius. Let me give some examples.

I tutored an intelligent student from West Papua whose people had made a quantum leap from the Stone Age into the 20th century only a few decades before. While discussing the gospels, I placed some rocks from a Galilean beach in his hand. He stared at them in astonishment before explaining, "I thought all the things in the Gospels happened in Heaven! I didn't know you could go there."

He not only absorbed the story of Jesus, but translated it into his own Melanesian outlook. His basic understanding of the gospel widened and deepened and proved supple enough for him to give his own culture fresh strength. He worked as a police liaison officer in Bourke and I was amazed when he reported that he had transferred the story of 19th century Christian social-reformer William Wilberforce's success in ending the English slave trade, to a street gang known as 'The Back-Lane Boys'. He told me that those Aboriginal lads were intrigued hearing of a white man fighting to free black slaves. Coming from a dark-skinned man whose country has been invaded, made this Jesus-story mean something different to what they thought of as a white man's religion.

He hasn't stopped there. He has developed a passion to teach what he has learned to new generations in his own country who are facing the onslaught of Western materialism and imported Islam. Along with other Danis we taught, he is working to deliver a story vigorous enough to harness to West Papuans' struggle for political independence. Their hope is it will lift their people above the violence and chaos they're facing.

Men and women who were serving as missionaries in Irian Jaya in the 1960's, have described to me the astonishing conversion of the whole culture - 250,000 people – in a very short period. The key to opening their understanding was the decision of the Westerners to make every effort not to deliver a European version of the gospel, but to locate concepts already present in the native stories. Anthropologist Don Richardson located these bridges and later traced the same phenomenon in other indigenous cultures in a book titled *Eternity in Their Hearts*.[223] His research showed that across the world, indigenous peoples had been anticipating the coming of an alternative story that would set them free. The Dani tribes – people I met in the Highlands – spoke of coming out of darkness into the light.

I don't know what made me choose Ernest Gordon's World War Two memoir, *The Miracle on the River Kwai* as a school book prize, but it's a story that has shaped my outlook for over half a century. It sits at a special place on my bookshelf as a spiritual milestone. The Chungkai prison-camp in Thailand was a crucible test of world-views – British, Japanese, Australian and Christian.

The author was caught in this vortex after the surrender of Singapore in 1942. Forced into building the Burma Railroad, Allied prisoners were viewed as expendable. The Japanese created a micro-world filled with atrocities driven by an Empire-building mania to win economic resources at all costs. Exploited in the 19th century by Western merchants, they burned to prove themselves the masters of their own destiny. Fuelled by worship of the Emperor as a god and the brutal Bushido warrior code, it was a world view destined to self-destruct.

Sustained cruelty put the blowtorch on the traditions the Allied prisoners had brought with them. Disease, poor rations and inhumane work crushed their spirits to the point where they were reduced to 'every-man for-himself' as the means of survival. Ernest Gordon saw the young men all around him plunge into a pit of fear, selfishness, hate and despair and it set him searching for deeper answers.

One day, the broad figure of an Australian sergeant filled the doorway of his hut. He came straight out with a request from his mates. Like him, their Sunday School knowledge of Christianity had worn thin. They had decided to find out if their inherited religion was 'the real dingo' as he put it. They'd seen men kicking their cobbers in the teeth, stealing from the dying and crawling like rats to the Japanese and figured there had to be something better. Because Ernest was a fighting soldier and he'd been to University they asked him to teach them. He was a reluctant volunteer.

I love the picture of the atheist teacher and his class of hard-nosed Aussies meeting to hammer out their own version of the gospel. Hell is going on all around them, but they discovered a flesh-and-blood Jesus they had never known. He was a working man like them – he'd gone hungry, slept rough, suffered, been shafted by mates and died fearless. He was no kill-joy. He enjoyed parties, mixed with the less respectable and had friends like theirs. He was never intimidated by men or demons who had tried to destroy him.

Together, Ernest and his friends began to recover the belief that this carpenter from Nazareth was God walking with men. His brutal crucifixion assured them God was suffering with them. His resurrection showed his promise of life extending beyond the grave was certain. As they began to follow him, a wave of kindness, faith and hope penetrated the most God-forsaken place on earth.

The inventive Australians created workshops and laundries, made shoes, distilled alcohol and started a brick works. Nursing teams formed, craftsmen made artificial limbs, a library appeared along with a kind of university. Choirs formed, concerts were held, numbers at church services swelled. The decision by a group of Aussie soldiers to check whether the story of Jesus was 'the real dingo', triggered what became known world-wide as 'the miracle on the River Kwai.'[224]

This gritty story has embedded itself in my psyche as a stress-tested proof of the alternative story I live by. It demonstrated that for Japanese, British and Australian soldiers, the second-hand dreams of Empire builders were never going to satisfy the deepest reaches of their souls. Dreams of peaceful existence post-war and providing material security for family were honest enough, but when stripped to the bone, unable to answer questions of life and death.

Ernest found the rational arguments and cynical atheism of his university training rang hollow and empty in the grim confines of a prison camp. Neither could the dogma, abstract theology and formal religion of churches at home sustain the human frame under that duress. Even the cherished Mateship myth of the Aussies had proved a bit thin in the extremities. On the other side, Japanese like Mitsuo Fuchida, found life lived by the Bushido code wanting in the shadow of the atom bomb.

Time for a deeper, higher, richer, more fulfilling story.

There's a current rush to dynamite symbols of our past, jeer at ancient beliefs, blot out our cultural memories and harass people of faith. It would be a mistake to equate this global groundswell as a sincere search for a more satisfactory story. It looks more like vandalism than intelligent inquiry and I've been encouraged that respected journalist Greg Sheridan has spoken a warning with an Australian voice. 'If God is gone, then the basis for our ethics is gone…As we cut ourselves off from the roots of our civilisation, our civilisation will be damaged. At our moment in history there is a perfect storm of factors militating against Christianity in Australia and in the West generally.'[225]

Sheridan forecasts a long series of battles for religious freedom and he's right in calling for Christians to respond cohesively as a bold, situation-aware minority. Israel's prophets were an outstanding example of guerrilla tactics. Though speaking from the margins, they never shirked pointing out failed components, first in their own lives, and then in their people's track record. I've urged younger generations at Cornerstone, to learn from these unique lay warriors, who fought hard in their day against the wholesale dismissal of the legacy passed down from their ancestors.

The ancient Hebrews knew nothing of the distinction between 'subjective' and 'objective' experiences when telling their stories. For them, the material and non-material worlds were a natural blend and so everyday physical events could become vibrant with spiritual significance. This vantage point enabled the prophets to interpret fluctuating national and international events with calm and clarity. Jesus was the greatest of them.

If Australia is to recover its core spiritual narrative, it needs this kind of lucid-thinking prophetic storyteller.

A few months ago, I sat in the hospital ICU with a friend. He was connected by a network of tubes and wires to sophisticated apparatus blinking and beeping out the last vestiges of his life. Attentive nursing staff hovered, doing what they could to help his breathing and ease his pain. The medical bustle was a hymn to human fragility and a ritual admission of technology's limitations when it came to facing death.

The journey into the valley of the shadow of death is one we all must take. What comforting story will walk with us and promise rest for our souls?

It was good to talk together of the mysterious, well-trodden path stretching away from the present into the dawn of history – one beaten by the feet of those whose lives testify to the reality of another story. We had been shown it in the Bible. Those who recorded that journey have been brave enough to give us the unwelcome diagnosis that humanity is in rebellion against its Creator and that physical and spiritual death has been the fallout. They've forged a sturdy chain of testimony that has proved itself strong enough for a multitude of truth-seekers.

The frail figure of my friend lying prone in the bed was gripping that chain as an anchor for his soul.

That ancient story filled the sterile hospital room with life. It became a song with the transcendent note – a sweet promise of amnesty. Geoff confessed his failures and knew he was forgiven by God. We shared the confidence we had in Jesus – the one figure in history who gave everything he had to rescue us by putting his life on the line.

Jesus was the only one who has ever declared he would defeat death and returned to talk about his victory over mankind's last enemy. He rewrote the bottom line of human existence single-handed. Who else in history has had the temerity to stand at a friend's graveside and declare to his grieving family, "I am the Resurrection and the Life. He who believes in me shall not die but have everlasting life?"[226]

And the power to call his dead friend Lazarus back to life!

Geoff requested a hymn and we sang it together – he, muffled by an oxygen mask. It had a refrain, *It is well with my soul!* I explained it had been composed a century and a half ago by Horatio Spafford, a successful Chicago lawyer who in a short space of time, had lost his business and all his children in a series of tragic accidents. The strength of that bereft man's faith in a living Jesus reached across time and space and filled us with comfort.[227] As I left my friend and drove away from the hospital, I asked myself "What other story can transform deathbeds with hope?" I knew in my heart that this was, without doubt, that other story our souls long for.

Jesus' promise is that he wants to one day gather all our stories to compose a mighty, soaring doxology to the Creator of life.

I headed this chapter with a line written by Irish poet and essayist Paul Kingsnorth when explaining his long circular journey away from what he assumed was an irrelevant Christian childhood, only to return. 'The story I had heard a thousand times turned out to be the story I had never heard at all.' I believe there are many

Australians sharing his pilgrimage. Kingsnorth compared his early experience to that of a Muslim friend whose family had a faith integrated into their worldview. He recalled having nothing like that.

> … at least my friend's religion seemed to pulse with some sort of living energy. The same could not be said of the Christianity which, when I was a child, was still at least nominally the national faith. I grew up singing hymns, listening to parables recited by teachers at morning assembly, and performing in Christmas nativity plays with a tea towel tied around my head. I knew the Lord's Prayer by heart. Whether I liked it or not, I was taught as a child the outline of the Christian story—the story that had shaped my nation for more than a thousand years. I didn't realize that my nation was surviving on spiritual credit, and that it was coming close to running out.[228]

Ignorant of the real substance that the Christian faith had gifted Western countries like ours, he set off on a search for meaning that took him through atheism, environmentalism, Zen Buddhism, paganism until finally he became a Wiccan priest, worshipping nature gods in a coven that performed its rituals in the woods under the full moon.

All the time, he knew every culture in history had been built around a spiritual core, but none of the stories he explored had supplied any substantial answers to his deeper questions. One by one, a series of events, natural and supernatural, reintroduced him to the faith he'd despised. He concluded,

> The more I learned, the more Christianity's story about the world and human nature chimed better with my experience than did the increasingly shaky claims of secular materialism. In the end, though, I didn't become a Christian because I could argue myself into it. I became a Christian because I knew, suddenly, that it was true.[229]

A strong attempt is being made to banish God from Australia's public consciousness. But I stand with Greg Sheridan's recent analysis that he may be out of sight, but not quite out of mind. I too persist in hearing rumours that God 'has not left the building'. I've had people report sightings or have heard shy confessions of a fleeting glimpse. I believe the footprints of Jesus are deeply imprinted in our soil. While the public culture may vary from being inattentive through to outright abusive, the aching nostalgia for God remains. [230]

It's time to turn those rumours, sightings and glimpses into concrete evidence. Time to tell another story, an Australian story, in such a way that it grabs wandering attention and deflects uninformed abuse. Australian cultural commentator Mark Sayers has coined a neat phrase for this – 'narrative warfare.'[231] The ancient Greeks gifted us a storytelling template for this task. They said authenticity comes from combining three things – ethos, logos and pathos. Ethos says we must speak with integrity. Logos demands we have rational content that makes our story believable. Pathos urges passionate delivery – singing the music of the Australian heart.

The bards among my canny Scots ancestors said the same thing in their own lyrical way. 'Storytelling is eye to eye, mind to mind and heart to heart.' If that aching nostalgia for God reported lurking beneath the surface of our public culture is to be met, our stories must ring true for our hearers. Jesus would add that, above all, the story must be delivered with a deep love for all our people.

I've retold the story of my own journey with story, in the hope it will inspire others to become raconteurs, engaging Australians old and new in classrooms, pubs, kitchens, street cafes, beach-side caravan parks, migrant hostels, workshops, prisons, churches, offices, hospitals, shops, malls, gyms, art galleries, theatres, sportsgrounds, parliaments, men's sheds, lecture halls, retirement villages, service clubs, golf courses, night clubs, on-line and around campfires – wherever Aussies gather, hungry for real community. Purposeful storytellers, reviving stories of the Jesus whose footprints are all across Australia.

Echoing in our mountains, hills and valleys, drifting on the wind across our deserts, plains and beaches, rising above the noise in the streets and suburbs of our cities, I hear the voice of Jesus, the great storyteller, the Teller of The Great Story, promising those who would have the courage to follow him, 'You will know the truth and the truth will set you free.'[232]

If you'd like to learn more of The Outback Historian, go to
www.theoutbackhistorian.com.au
or email Paul, **theoutbackhistorian@gmail.com**

As a means of adding colour and interest to the book, you'll find photos and information related to each chapter as well as blogs and YouTube clips of Australia's faith stories that you can put to use in your own place. You will also find updates on Storytelling workshops to help you hone your skills.

ENDNOTES

PREFACE

[1] Roe, Paul. *Making the Invisible Visible.* (Macquarie University, PhD Thesis 2016.) Ch. 7. Kuhne, Eric. *The Southern Cross Sanctuary.* Civic Arts.

INTRODUCTION

[2] The Outback Historian Bourke Cemetery Tour Video https://www.theoutbackhistorian.com.au
[3] Gallo, Carmine. Stories literally put our brainwaves into sync, 'Quartz at Work' June 7, 2018 https://qz.com/work/1298571/stories-literally-put-our-brain-waves-in-sync/
[4] Chatwin, Bruce. *Songlines,* (New York: Penguin 1988), p. 13.
[5] Deuteronomy 6:7 *The Message.* (Colorado Springs, Colorado. NavPress Publishing Group. 1995).
[6] Flew, Antony. *There is a God.* (New York: HarperCollins 2007), p. 132. https://www.inspiringquotes.us/author/9860-anthony-flew
[7] Novak, Michael. 'Story' and 'Experience', Wiggin J.B. (ed.) *Religion as Story,* (New York: Harper & Row, 1975), p. 175.
[8] Luke 24:13-33.
[9] Bean, C.E.W. *On the Wool Track,* (Sydney: Angus & Robertson, 1965), p. viii.
[10] Banks, Robert & Stevens R. Paul. *The Complete Book of Christian Experience,* (Downers Grove, Illinois: Intervarsity Press, 1997) p. 967.

CHAPTER 1

[11] Chukovsky, Kornei. *'Storytelling'. World Book Encyclopedia,* (Chicago, USA: World Book Inc., 1986), 18.
[12] White, Paul. *Alias Jungle Doctor,* (Sydney: Attic Press, 1977), p 174.
[13] Voysey, Sheridan. *Open House, Vol.3.* (Sydney: Strand Publishing, 2010), pp.111-120.

[14] Petrovich, Olivera. '*Japanese children's explanations of the origins of natural objects: Some comparisons with UK children.*' https://www.neuroscience.ox.ac.uk/publications/347099
Zwartz, Barney. 'Infants have natural belief in God' *Sydney Morning Herald*. July 26, 2008.
Evans, E. Margret, 'Cognitive Contextual Factors in the Emergence of Diverse Belief
  Systems: Creation versus Evolution', *Cognitive Psychology*, 15(5): May 2004, pp. 295-301.
Evans, *Cognitive Psychology*, 42: pp. 217-266, 2001.
Bloom, Paul. "Religion is natural", *Developmental Science*, 10:1, 2007, pp. 147-151.
Trigg, Roger. *Equality, Freedom and Religion.* (Oxford: Oxford University Press, 2012),
Interview with Roger Trigg; July 2012 www.theosthinktank.co.uk/comment/2012

[15] Costello, Tim. *Hope,* (Melbourne: Hardie Grant Books, 2012), p.131.

[16] Idriess, Ion. *Australian Dictionary of Biography.* https://adb.anu.edu.au/biography/idriess-ion-llewellyn-6786

[17] Palmer, Vance. *The Legend of the Nineties.* (Melbourne: Melbourne University Press, 1966), p. 52.

[18] McPheat, W Scott. *John Flynn Apostle to the Inland.* (Sydney: Hodder & Stoughton, 1963).p. 18.

[19] O'Brien, John. *Around the Boree Log.* (Sydney: Angus & Robertson Publishers), p48.

[20] Pavlovic, Lily. 'Morris Gleitzman on Why Young People Need Stories More than Ever.' https://blog-actf.com.au/morris-gleitzman-2018-australian-childrens-laureate/

[21] Piggin, Stuart. Ed. *Shaping the Good Society in Australia.* (Macquarie Centre NSW: Australia's Christian Heritage National Forum, 2006), p17.

CHAPTER 2

[22] Cahill, Thomas. *The Gifts of the Jews.* (Oxford: Lion Publishing, 1998), pp. 128-129.

[23] Idriess, Ion. *The Desert Column, Ion Idriess's Greatest Stories.* (Sydney: Angus & Robertson Publishers, 1986), p. 578-579.

[24] Lewis, C.S. *The Screwtape Letters.* (London: Geoffrey Bles), pp. 48-49.

[25] Roe, Paul. *Australia and the Solution to the 'Palestine Problem.' 1946-49.* History Honours thesis, UNSW 1972. P. 73.

[26] Dalziel, Alan. *Evatt the Enigma.* (Melbourne: Landsdowne Press, 1967), Cited in Roe, Paul. 'Australia and the Solution to the 'Palestine Problem'.p. 36.

[27] Brasch, Rabbi R. *The Star of David.* (Sydney: Angus & Robertson, 1955), p. 261.

[28] Palmer, Parker. '*To Know as we are Known.*' (New York: HarperCollins 1993), pp xxiii-xxiv.

[29] Clark, Manning. *A Historian's Apprenticeship.* (Melbourne: Melbourne University Press, 1992), p. 9.

[30] Butterfield, Herbert. *Christianity and History.* (London: Fontana Books, 1964), p. 36.

[31] Butterfield, *Christianity and History,*. p. 36

[32] A Prayer of Sir Francis Drake. '*Disturb Us Lord*' https://pilgrimchurchprayers.wordpress.com › disturb-u..

[33] Bright, John. *A History of Israel.* (Philadelphia: Westminster Press, 1975), p. 347.

CHAPTER 3

[34] Smith, Patsy Adam. *Outback Heroes.*(Sydney: Landsdowne Press, 1981), p. 11.

[35] Bean, C.E.W. *On the Wool Track*. (Sydney: Angus & Robertson, 1969), p. 43.

[36] Smith, *Outback Heroes*, 11

[37] Bausch, William. *Storytelling, Imagination and Faith*. (Mystic CT: Twenty-Third Publications/Bayard, 1984), p. 63.

[38] McPheat, *John Flynn, Apostle to the Inland*, p. 54

[39] *Interview with Captain Bill Drage* – Paul Roe. The Outback Historian. CARP VIDEO.

[40] Bird, Nancy. *My God it's a Woman*. (Sydney: Angus &Robertson, 1990), p. 73.

CHAPTER 4

[41] Cameron, William. Ed. *The History of Bourke, Vol. 3*. (Bourke: Bourke Historical Society, 1971), Frontispiece.

[42] Burrows, Robyn & Barton, Alan. *A Stranger on the Darling*. (Sydney: Angus & Robertson, 1996).

[43] Cameron, *The History of Bourke*, Frontispiece.

[44] Note: These two energetic women are specially recognised by the Catholic Church as saints. Mother Mary MacKillop sent teaching nuns to Bourke in the 1880's and Mother Theresa recruited nuns from overseas who served the town for fifty years from 1969.
https://www.abc.net.au/news/2016-09-10/mother-teresa-in-bourke/7822916?nw=
0../../paulroe/Desktop/Ordered Memoir/Fifty years ago, Mother... - The Western Herald - Bourke ...%0dhttps:/www.facebook.com › posts › fifty-years-ago-mo...%0d

[45] Fred Hollows https://monumentaustralia.org.au/themes/people/humanitarian/display/20485-fred-hollows

[46] Sullivan, Phil. *Australian National Geographic*, No.90. April/June, 2008, p81.

[47] Buchanan, Colin. Consultation with Paul Roe, Sydney 2011.

[48] Greentree, Jenny. https://www.backobourkegallery.com.au

[49] Glover. T.R. *The Jesus of History*, (London: SCM. 1923), p 56.

[50] Lewis, C.S. *Mere Christianity*, (London: Fontana Books, 1966).

CHAPTER 5

[51] Winkworth, Kylie. *'Let a thousand flowers bloom; museums in regional Australia.'* National Museum of Australia. The development of regional galleries. http://nma.gov.au/research/understanding-museums/MRich_2011.html

[52] Mc Hugh, Evan. *Outback Heroes*. (Melbourne: Penguin Australia, 2004), p. 261.

[53] Kenyon, Peter. Bank of I.D.E.A.S. http://www.bankofideas.com.au

[54] Roe, *Making the Invisible Story Visible*. Ch. 5.

[55] Duncan, Dayton and Ward, Geoff. Consultation with Paul Roe, Florentine Films, Walpole, New Hampshire, September 2000.

[56] Ward, Geoffrey C. *The West*. (London: George Weidenfeld & Nicholson Ltd., 1996), p xvii.

[57] Burns, Ken. www.theatlantic.com/.../ken-burns...1-1-3/257165/15 May 2012.

[58] Lawson, Henry. 'Freedom on the Wallaby' *A Campfire Yarn*, Henry Lawson Complete Works, 1885-1900, (Sydney: Landsdowne, 1984), p. 146.

[59] Bryan, Gregory. *To Hell and High Water*. (Sydney: Big Sky Publishing, 2012), p. 6.

[60] Burrows, *A Stranger on the Darling*, p 26.

[61] Bryan, *To Hell and High Water*, p. 6.

[62] Ogilvie, W.H. *Saddle for a Throne*. (Netley: Griffin Press,1982), p. 23.

[63] Wright, Judith. *Preoccupations in Australian Poetry.* (Melbourne: Oxford University Press, 1996), pxxii

[64] Prescott, Andrew. 'Avoiding the Rear-View Mirror.' https://medium.com/digital-transformations-talks-and-presentations/avoiding-the-rear-view-mirror-870319290bb2

[65] International Coalition of Sites of Conscience https://www.sitesofconscience.org › ...

CHAPTER 6

[66] Wright, Don. *Alan Walker: Conscience of the Nation*. (Adelaide: Openbook Publishers, 1997), p. 276.

[67] Grenfell, Wilfrid. *What Christ Means to Me*, (London: Hodder & Stoughton, 1926), pp. 30-31.

[68] Pratney, Winkie. *Youth Aflame*, (Bloomington, Minnesota: Bethany House Publishers),1983, p. 14.

[69] Spoerri, Theophil. *Dynamic out of Silence*, (London: Grosvenor Books, 1976), pp. 70, 74.

[70] Howard, Peter. *Frank Buchman's Secret*, (London: William Heinemann Ltd, 1968), p157.

[71] Lunn, Arnold & Lean, Garth. *The Cult of Softness*, (London: Blanford Press, 1965).

[72] https://www.cornerstonecommunity.org.au/

[73] Wright, Don. *Alan Walker: Conscience of the Nation*. (Adelaide: Openbook Publishers, 1997), p. 276.

[74] Garvin, Mal. *Us Aussies*, (Sale: Hayzon Ltd, 1987).

[75] Smith, John. *Advance Australia Where?* (Sydney, Anzea Publishers, 1992).

[76] McIntosh, Elvira. *Cornerstone Community*. (Bendigo: Bart'n' Print, 2016).

[77] Holland, Tom. *Dominion. The Making of the Western Mind*, (London: Little, Brown, 2019).

[78] Sheridan, Greg. *God is Good for You*. (Sydney: Allen & Unwin, 2018), p. 325.

CHAPTER 7

[79] Cordiner, Graeme. *Love Follows Death*. (Sydney: Christian Living Publications, 2018), p. 86.

[80] Mattingley, Christobel. *Our Mob God's Story*, (Sydney:Bible Society, 2017).

[81] Matthews, Janet. (recordist) *The Two Worlds of Jimmy Barker*,(Canberra: Australian Institute of Aboriginal Studies, 1982), p. 67.

[82] Williams, Diana. *Horizon is Where Heaven and Earth Meet*, (Sydney: Bantam Books, 2001), p. 230.

[83] Shanney, Bob. *Three Bush Saints*.

[84] *Lousy Little Sixpence*, https://www.roninfilms.com.au › feature › lousy-little-si...

[85] Peter Gibbs Story. https://www.sbs.com.au/nitv/nitv-news/article/2016/04/04/how-death-custody-became-catalyst-iprowd

[86] Interview with Pat Doolan,.www.theoutbackhistorian.com.au

[87] Horner, Jack. *Bill Ferguson, Fighter for Aboriginal Freedom*. (Sydney: Australia and New Zealand Book Company Ltd), 1974.

88 Horner, p. 55.
89 Micah 6:8
90 Lewis C.S. *The Four Loves*, (New York: Harcourt, Brace & Javanovich, 1960), p. 49.
91 Dixon, John. *Bullies and Saints, (*Grand Rapids, Michigan: Zondervan Reflective, 2021).
92 Williams, p. 15.
93 Williams, p. 434.
94 Naden, Neville. Cited by permission.

CHAPTER 8

95 Bean, Charles. *Sydney Morning Herald*, April 4th 1925.
96 https://www.thebiblemuseum.com.au/about/military-bibles-in-world-war-one.html
97 https://www.thebiblemuseum.com.au/about/military-bibles-in-world-war-one.html
98 https://www.jwire.com.au/the-sea-of-the-galilee-an-aboriginal-soldier-and-his-horse/
99 https://www.thebiblemuseum.com.au/about/military-bibles-in-world-war-one.html
100 Nelson, Brendon. https://livinghistorytv.com/dr-brendan-nelson-director-of-the-australian-war-memorial/
101 Lake, Marilyn. Ed. *Memory, Monuments and Museums*, (Carlton: Melbourne University Press, 2006), p. 73-74.
102 Newsome, Brad. 'Trek to Understanding.' *The Age*, July 5th 2007.
103 Doogue, Geraldine.'Cronulla to Kokoda.' *Compass*, ABC Television, July 8, 2007.
104 Bogle, Eric. https://genius.com/Eric-bogle-and-the-band-played-waltzing-matilda-lyrics
105 Life and death on the Thai-Burma railway. https://www.abc.net.au › news › milton-snow-fairclough.
106 Mitsuo Fuchida, https://www.christiantreasury.org/content/mitsuo-fuchida-forgotten-story-faith
107 Grattan, Michelle. *Back on the Wool Track*, (Sydney: Vintage, 2004), p. 36.
108 Butterfield, Herbert. *Christianity and History,* (London: Fontana Books, 1964), p. 177.
109 Kipling, Rudyard. *Rudyard Kipling's Verse*, (London: Hodder & Stoughton, 1930).
110 Mansfield, Stephen. *'Never Give In. The Extraordinary Character of Winston Churchill.'* (London: Cumberland House, 1996), p. 190.
111 Bean, Charles. Australian War Memorial 3DRL6673/573

CHAPTER 9

112 Horne, Donald. *The Lucky Country*. (Harmondsworth, Middlesex: Penguin, 1971), p. 37.
113 Furphy, Simon. 'A Sporting Nation.' Australian of the Year Awards, 2015. http://www.australianoftheyear.org.au/the-awards/awards-history/
114 Stiles, Jason. *'Melbourne Cup a Winner for National Economy.'* The New Daily, 30th October 2104. http://thenewdaily.com/news/2014/10/30ecomomic-impact-melborne-cup/ Hutak, Michael. 'Melbourne Cup 2015: half full, half empty'. The Drum, ABC. November 4th 2015
115 Horne, *The Lucky Country,* p. 37
116 https://www.goodreads.com/quotes/715176-if-jesus-christ-be-god-and-died-for-me-then
117 MacAloon, John. Ed. *Muscular Christianity in Colonial and Post-Colonial Worlds*, (London: Routledge, 2007)

[118] Hughes Thomas. *Tom Brown's Schooldays*. https://www.gutenberg.org/files/1480/1480-h/1480-h.htm

[119] Kingsley, Charles. Kathryn Hughes, 'Back to school', *The Guardian* 20th September 2008. http://www.theguardian.com/books/2008/sep/20/booksfor childrenandteenagers

[120] Mazurkiewicz, Michał. 'The Manly and the Religious.' https://depot.ceon.pl/bitstream/handle
Mehaffey, John. Rugby School Inspired Founder of Modern Games https://www.reuters.com/article/uk-olympics-london-rugby-idUKLNE83H00O20120418

[121] The Cambridge Seven. https://www.5minutesinchurchhistory.com› the-cambri.

[122] Grenfell. Wilfrid. *What Christ Means to Me*. (London: Hodder & Stoughton, 1927), p. 37.

[123] McPheat, Scott. *John Flynn: Vision of the Inland,* (Melbourne: Oxford University Press, 1964), p. 18.

[124] Grenfell, *What Christ Means to Me,* p. 31

[125] https://www.tradiesinsight.support/

[126] Marks, Kathy. 'Fijians Apologise for Ancestral Cannibalism. Independent, 13 November 2003.

[127] Cuthbert, Betty. *Golden Girl,* (Sydney: Strand Publishing, 2000), p. 132.

[128] Waugh, Steve. *The Meaning of Luck,* (Macquarie Park, Sydney:Sam's Marketing 2013), p. 55.

[129] Waugh, *The Meaning of Luck,* p. 113.

CHAPTER 10

[130] Bausch, William. *Storytelling, Imagination and Faith*, Mystic, (CT: Twenty-Third Publications/Bayard), 1984.

[131] Studdert Kennedy, G.A. *The Unutterable Beauty,* (London: Hodder & Stoughton, 1947), p. 15

[132] Ramsey, Russell W. *God's Joyful Runner,* (New Jersey: Bridge Publishing, 1987).

[133] Smith, John. *Advance Australia Where?* (Melbourne: Collins, 1985).

[134] Conway, Ronald. *The Land of the Long Weekend,* (Melbourne: Sun Books, 1978).

[135] Mackay, Hugh. Interview in *Warcry* magazine 20th January 2001.

[136] Wilson, Bruce. *Can God Survive in Australia?* (Sutherland, NSW: Albatross Books, 1983).

[137] Flew, Anthony. *There is A God.* (London: HarperCollins Publishers, 2007).

[138] Williams, Roy & Myers Elizabeth. *Mr Eternity.* (Sydney: Acorn Press, 2017).

[139] Russell, Bertrand. 'A Free Man's Worship' in *Why I am Not a Christian,* (New York: Simon & Shuster, 1966).

[140] Thomas Hassall, in *The Evangelical Dictionary of Biography.* (Sydney: Evangelical History Association, 1994), p. 159.

[141] https://www.wayfm.org.au/the-atheist-who-wants-more-churches-in-australia/

[142] Gallico, Paul. *The Snow Goose.* (London: Random House Publishing, 2007).

[143] https://winstonchurchill.org/resources/speeches/1940-the-finest-hour/we-shall-fight-on-the-beaches/

CHAPTER 11

[144] Salusinsky, Imre. 'Hitching a ride on Faith', *Weekend Australian*, April 23-24th, 2005.

145 Canberra National Gathering. *Understanding our Christian Heritage Vol 2.* http://www.chr.
org.au › books › page15

146 Salusinsky, *'Hitching a ride on Faith'*

147 Berg, Chris. https://www.abc.net.au/news/2011-03-22/history_and_chrisitanity/45416

148 https://www.abs.gov.au/ausstats/abs@.nsf/lookup/media%20release3

149 Harris, John. *One Blood.* (Sydney: Albatross Books, 1990).

150 Williams, Roy. *Post God Nation.* (Sydney: HarperCollins, 2015).

151 Lake, Meredith. *The Bible in Australia.* (Sydney: New South Books, 2018).

152 Piggin, Stuart. *The Fountain of Public Prosperity.* (Melbourne: Monash University
Publishing, 2018).

153 Sheridan, Greg. *God is Good for You.* (Sydney: Allen & Unwin, 2018).

154 Sheridan, Greg. *Christians.* (Sydney: Allen & Unwin, 2021).

155 Scheu, Anne. '*The Coming of the Light' Celebrating 150 years of Christianity in the Torres
Strait.* State Library of Queensland. Queensland Memory | 28 June 2021

156 https://www.eternitynews.com.au/australia/my-great-grandmother-
fought-spanish-flu-in-newcastle-with-constant-care/

CHAPTER 12

157 Rothkopf, Joanna. Interview with Bruce Filer. *Salon* Jan. 3, 2015. https://www.salon.
com/2015/01/03/you_have_to_go_on_a_journey_how_one_man_traveled_
to_the_end_of_the_earth_in_search_of_spirituality

158 Belt, Don. '*Sacred Journeys'.* (Washington: *National Geographic,* Special Edition, 2010)

159 Smith, James K A. *On the Road with St Augustine.* (Grand Rapids: Brazos Press, 2019), p. 4.

160 *Sermons of Columbanus, Sermon 8, p97.https://celt.ucc.ie/published/T201053/text008.html*

161 Kipling, Rudyard. *The Explorer* http://www.kiplingsociety.co.uk› poems_explorer

162 Cook, Thomas. *Thomas Cook History: The Tale of the Father of Modern Tourism.* March 21,
2021- Jessica Norah https://independenttravelcats.com/travel

163 George Harrison visits Haight Asbury https://www.youtube.com/watch?v=aOAEEiqcbkg

164 https://christianhistoryinstitute.org/incontext/article/augustine

165 McGrath, Alister. *The Journey. A Pilgrim in the Lands of the Spirit.* (London: Hodder &
Stoughton,1999), p. 3.

166 https://sheridanvoysey.com/following-god-into-the-unknown/

167 Remembering World Youth Day 2008 https://www.cathnews.com/
cathnews/32637-remembering-world-youth-day-2008

168 Inteview with Bruce Feiler, https://www.pbs.org/walkingthebible/interview.html

169 Hull, Andrew. *Interview with Paul Roe,* Bourke, NSW, July 2012.

170 Elder, Bruce. https://www.travelagenciesfinder.com/AU/Bourke/2241865077
32589/The-Poets-Trek

171 Chatwin, Bruce. *Songlines,* (New York: Penguin, 1988), p. 13.

172 Rothkopf, Interview with Bruce Filer.

173 Chesterton G. K, https://www.chesterton.org/lecture-18/

CHAPTER 13

[174] Breuggeman, Walter. *Cadences of Home: Preaching Among Exiles,* (Louisville: Westminster, John Knox Press, 1997), p. 35.

[175] McCrindle Research

[176] Ashton, Paul & Hamilton, Paula. *'At Home with the Past.'* Australian Cultural History, no.23, 2003. https://www.academia.edu/6931897/At_home_with_the_past_initial_findings_from_the_survey

[177] Davison, Graeme. 'What should a National Museum do?' *Memory, Monuments and Museums,* ed. Marilyn Lake. (Carlton: Melbourne University Press, 2006), p. 91.

[178] Christian Ashrams. https://www.estanleyjonesfoundation.com/about-esj/history-of-the-christian-ashrams/

[179] The Story of the Krait. https://www.abc.net.au › austory › the-story-of-the-krait

[180] Port Arthur Massacre https://www.youtube.com/watch?v=7FDVFg3w7wI

[181] *Simpson and his Donkey.* Australian War Memorial. //https://www.awm.gov.au Australians

[182] Piggin,Stuart, ed. *Shaping the Good Society.* (Sydney, Macquarie Centre: Australia's Christian Heritage National Forum. 2006), p. 20.

[183] Piggin, (ed.) *Shaping the Good Society.* p. 25.

[184] Alain De Botton, *The Architecture of Happiness.* (New York: Vintage, 2006), p. 217.

[185] Kuhne, Eric., *Southern Cross Sanctuary,* Canberra: Design Presentation, London: CivicArts Production, 2009.

[186] Horne, Donald. *The Lucky Country.* (Harmondsworth:Penguin, 1971), pp. 235 & 247.

[187] Birch, Charles. *Confronting the Future,* (Ringwood: Penguin Books, 1976), p. 306.

[188] Conway, Ronald, *The Great Australian Stupor,* (Melbourne: Sun Books, 1971), p. 14.

[189] King, Jonathan. *Waltzing Materialism,* (Sydney: Harper & Row, 1978), p. 11.

[190] Clark, Manning. quoted by King, *Waltzing Materialism,* p. 11.

[191] Clark, Manning, quoted by King, *Waltzing Materialism,* p. 127-28.

[192] Mol, Hans, *Religion in Australia,* (Sydney: Nelson, 1971), p. 302.

[193] Wilson, Bruce. *Can God Survive in Australia?* (Sutherland NSW: Albatross Books, 1983), p. 8.

[194] Smith, John. *Advance Australia Where?* (Melbourne: Collins, 1985), p. 5.

[195] McKay, Hugh. *Reinventing Australia,* (Sydney: Angus & Robertson, 1993), pp. 6 & 29.

[196] Eckersley, Richard. *Well and Good: Morality, Meaning and Happiness,* 2nd edition. (Melbourne: Text publishing, 2005), p. 43.

[197] Hudson, Wayne. Wayne Hudson, *'Beyond the Pathology',* (Griffith Review, Autumn 2005, 'The Lure of Fundamentalism'), p.195.

[198] Breuggeman, Walter. *Cadences of Home: Preaching Among Exiles,* p. 35.

CHAPTER 14

[199] Lewis. C.S. 'Transposition and Other Addresses.' *The Weight of Glory,* (London: Geoffrey Bles), p. 23.

[200] Browning, Robert. *The Pied Piper of Hamelin.* https://www.britannica.com/topic/The-Pied-Piper-of-Hamelin-poem-by-Browning

[201] Purcell, Charles. *'Why we Need a Minister for Loneliness.'* https://www.smh.com.au/national/why-we-need-a-minister-for-loneliness-20210224-p575ej.html February 25, 2021

202 Gordon, Ernest. *The Miracle on the River Kwai.* (London: Collins Press, 1965).

203 Lewis, C.S. *Mere Christianity*. (New York: Macmillan Publishing Co.1960), p. 118.

204 Lewis. C.S. 'Transposition and Other Addresses.' *The Weight of Glory,* (London: Geoffrey Bles,1949), p. 23.

205 Matthew 5: 1-15.

206 Peterson, Jordan. Conversation with John Anderson https://m.youtube.com/watch?v=U4NijLf3M-A

207 Judge, Edwin. *The Market-place*: A Newspaper for Australian Anglicans, 10 August 2005.

208 George Miller, quoted by Frost, Michael. *Eyes Wide Open.* (Sydney: Albatross Books, 1998), p. 100.

209 New national day to find freedom in forgiveness' https://www.eternity news.com

210 Sherman, Louise & Mattingley, Christobel. *Our Mob, God's Story:* Aboriginal and Torres Strait Islander Artists Share Their Faith, (Sydney: Bible Society, 2017), Introduction.

211 The Old Church on the Hill, https://www.theoldchurchonthehill.com/

212 Bogle, Eric. *A Reason For It All.* https://m.youtube.com/watch?v=jYmZ4EeBmRo

213 Keneally, Thomas. https://www.hopechannel.com/au/read/thomas-keneally-meaning-is-everything

214 Bogle, Eric. https://m.youtube.com/watch?v=QHe7DJjS7KI

CHAPTER 15

215 Kingsnorth, Paul. 'The Cross and the Machine'. *First Things*, June 2021. https://www.firstthings.com/article/2021/06/the-cross-and-the-machine

216 Flynn, John. *The Bushman's Companion.* (Melbourne: Brown, Prior & Co, 1910), pp. 62-65.

217 Wright, Don. *Alan Walker, Conscience of the Nation.* (Adelaide: Open Book Publishers), pp. 160-162.

218 Sheridan, Greg. *God Is Good for You*, (Sydney: Allen & Unwin), p. 96.

219 Brueggemann, Walter. *The Prophetic Imagination.* (Minneapolis: Fortress Press 2111).

220 Morphett, Tony. *A Hole in my Ceiling.* (Sydney: Hodder & Stoughton, 1985), p. 11-12.

221 Morphett, *A Hole in my Ceiling,* pp. 13-14.

222 Warren, Rick. *The Purpose Driven Life.* (Grand Rapids: Zondervan, 2002).

223 Richardson, Don. *Eternity in Their Hearts.* (Ventura: Regal Books, 1984).

224 Gordon, Ernest. *The Miracle on the River Kwai.* (London, Collins, 1963).

225 Sheridan. *God Is Good For You,* pp. 12-13.

226 John 11:25

227 Story Behind *It is Well, with my Soul* https://www.staugustine.com/article/20141016/LIFESTYLE/310169936

228 Kingsnorth, 'The Cross and the Machine'.

229 Kingsnorth, 'The Cross and the Machine'.

230 Sheridan, *God Is Good For You.*

231 Gospelbound 17 March 2020 *A Handbook for Thriving Amid Secularism*. Interview with Mark Sayers.

232 John 8:32